MAROONED WITH VERY LITTLE BEER

GRAHAM MACKINTOSH

Graham Mackintosh

BAJA DETOUR PRESS

SAN DIEGO, CALIFORNIA

Marooned With Very Little Beer   ISBN 978-0-9626109-2-9
Library of Congress Control Number 2008901699

First published in the United States of America by Baja Detour Press

Cover design by Graham Mackintosh
Interior design and layout by Ellen Goodwin: ellengoodwin@cox.net

First Edition

Address all Correspondence to:

Baja Detour Press
P.O. Box 1982
Lemon Grove, CA 91946

E-mail: bajadetour@aol.com

For Bonni
Thanks for your friendship, love, and support

Unattributed quotations in the text of this book were either spoken by the author into a small tape recorder or were extracts from his journal.

Consider the ravens: for they neither sow nor reap...
and God feedeth them

[Luke 12:24]

Satellite View of the Sea of Cortez

CONTENTS

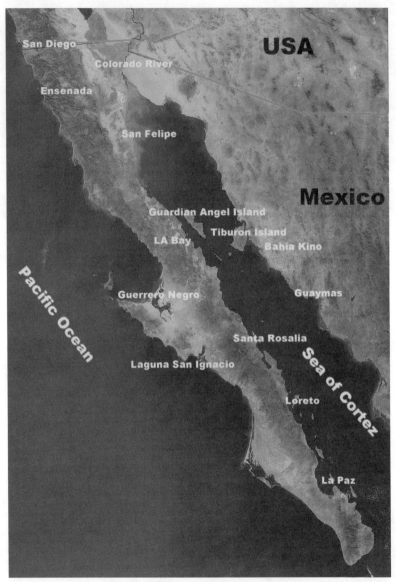

Baja California and the Sea of Cortez

Chapter 1

Baja on My Mind

Come ye yourselves apart into a desert place, and rest awhile.

Jesus [Mark 6:31]

I have always thought of myself as easygoing ; my wife Bonni likes to call me "E-go" for short.

But every few years I revolt against my sedentary, safe and comfortable existence, and when my love handles seem to be on a roll I heed the call to stretch myself mentally and physically and maybe shed a few pounds. It seems I need to be hungry and alone and facing the unpredictable to regain a sense of proportion and recharge my spiritual batteries—a process that has led to the writing of three books.

In the past I've satisfied such yearnings along the shores or in the mountains of the great wilderness of Baja California. And such is my connection to that desert peninsula I just assumed that Baja would once again be my testing ground.

However, having just become a US citizen, and feeling saddened and disturbed by some of the actions of the government, my government, and finding myself alienated by the abysmal level of political discussion on the airwaves, the negativity, the anger, the name calling—scum, vermin, maggots—I got into my head that I was going to hike across America to respectfully listen to and document the views of those with whom I found myself disagreeing.

It had come to me in a blinding flash—I would walk across America with one of my dogs, Penny or Pedro, heroes of my last book on Baja California. I would start out with the endlessly amiable Penny, the best ambassador a man could wish for, and when her unkempt thirty pound terrier frame wore down her stubby legs to less than serviceable length I'd switch her for Pedro, our fast and elegant greyhound mix.

I would walk across America from southwest corner to northeast corner, and choose the route that took me through the most conservative, Republican heartland. I had my views…but essentially I wanted to try to understand an outlook and mentality that largely eluded me. How in God's name could any intelligent person support this Bush Administration? That meant I should only take up invitations to stay with Republicans.

Penny the ambassador   *Pedro would leap in when Penny falters*

By way of getting my prejudices out there and up front, like Martin Luther pinning his theses to the church door, I would post my questions and opinions on my website… and beyond that my desire was to LISTEN. There seemed to be little enough listening going on in America. Vilification and demonization and suggesting your opponents are either evil or mentally sick seems to be the preferred approach. No wonder Americans are so fond of shooting each other!

I intended posting ten theses about my President. I struggled to keep his demonization to a minimum so that if the blinding flash really did lead to my enlightenment I'd have the option to gracefully backtrack and backdown and thank my hosts for explaining it all so clearly. In order not to bore you with politics, let me just offer a sample here.

1. Have President Bush's Mid-East policies led to more terrorism, less stability in the region, less respect for the US around the world? Is he making enemies and fanatics faster than he can kill them?

2. Bush gambles and loses and refuses to take responsibility? He should resign or be impeached. It is not enough to say we must stay the course in Iraq, no matter how painful, without asking if the leader who dragged us into that mess should be removed. That's a separate question.

3. Bush's one undoubted achievement—he has significantly shifted the wealth of this nation from the less well off to the more well off? The promise being that we will all benefit from increased enterprise and trickle down. He didn't tell us that the nation would have such meager and fragile results after six years of increasing debt, a falling dollar, and all the painful cuts we see before us.

FAMILY VALUES

The time came to share my idea with my wife and son. I explained—think of it as a new citizen walking across his America. I'm sure I can do it in six to nine months. It will be a plea for civility, "Why can't we listen to each other?" "Why can't we have genuine debate instead of slogan shouting, mindless labeling, and ridiculous rhetoric?" To that end I'll opt to stay with right wingers—I need to associate with "sinners," like Jesus associated with prostitutes, tax collectors, and publicans. "You see, they even had an earlier version of the GOP back then," I quipped.

My 17-year-old son Andrew was first to respond, "That is the stupidest idea I have ever heard. No one is ever going to read this book anyway."

My wife Bonni was similarly unimpressed. "Same old crap—you will lose half of the few fans you have. And don't think I'm going to be there to support you. You're on your own."

Confronted by such enthusiasm, the notion of returning to Baja gradually reasserted itself. At least the proposed six to nine month "Walk America" idea had the benefit of making a, say, two month trip to Baja much more palatable to my wife.

People come to Baja California for many reasons—to see whales and cave paintings, to fish, to drink, to kayak, to surf, to bask in the sun, to explore the sea and the desert, to own a home on the beach, to enjoy the laid back lifestyle, to off-road, to hide, to transport illegal drugs—and these are all good reasons.

But for me its attraction is the sense of freedom it conveys and the spiritual feelings engendered by its majesty and its vast (if now rapidly) receding emptiness. I keep returning not because I live in San Diego less than ten miles from the border, not because my experiences down there are generally positive, but because Baja keeps calling me; calling me most loudly in the heart-piercing silence of its lonely shores and cactus-studded mountains. Calling me to stand awed, sometimes overawed, alone and fearful… to confront it and to confront myself once again.

"Baja, Baja," I cry sheepishly. "Where? Where this time? I have slowly, tentatively, worked my way around your flowing outline and eased my way down your spine and across your swelling peaks and camped for months in the pine shadows of your tallest mountains. What quiet corner is left?"

Guardian Angel Island in relation to LA Bay

Chapter 2

With Time and Supplies

*I wasn't "an adventurer." I wasn't about to dash off up the Amazon, or trek
the Kalahari, or go searching for something one step ahead. I had found
what I wanted. I belonged to Baja and to those who felt that they belonged.
Again it was the feeling that was the undeniable truth, the absolute
certainty that this land was sacred to me.*
Graham Mackintosh—Into a Desert Place, 1988

In an oft-quoted passage in the *Log from the Sea of Cortez*, John Steinbeck
recounted his 1940 visit to the lonely shores of Isla Angel de la Guarda
(Guardian Angel Island).

The long, snake-like coast of Guardian Angel lay to the east of us; a
desolate and fascinating coast. It is forty-two miles long, ten miles
wide in places, waterless and uninhabited. It is said to be crawling
with rattlesnakes and iguanas, and a persistent rumor of gold comes
from it. Few people have explored it or even gone more than a few
steps from the shore... The difficulties of exploration of the island
might be very great, but there is a drawing power about its very
forbidding aspect—a Golden Fleece, and the inevitable dragon, in
this case rattlesnakes, to guard it. The mountains which are the
backbone of the island rise to more than four thousand feet in some
places, sullen and desolate at the tops... We are so used to finding on
the beaches evidence of man that it is strange and lonely and
frightening to find no single thing that man has touched or used.
Tiny and Sparky made a small excursion inland, not over several
hundred yards from the shore, and they came back subdued and
quiet... Islands have always been fascinating places. The old
storytellers, wishing to recount a prodigy, almost invariably fixed the
scene on an island—Faery and Avalon, Atlantis and Cipango, all
golden islands just over the horizon where anything at all might
happen... Perhaps this quality of potential prodigy still lives in our
attitude towards islands. We want very much to go back to Guardian
Angel with time and supplies. We wish to go over the burned hills
and snake-ridden valleys... and we are willing to believe almost
anything we hear about it. We believe that great gold nuggets are

found there, that unearthly animals make their homes there... It is one of the golden islands which will one day be toppled by a mining company or a prison camp.

Steinbeck never returned, at least not in the prison of time and space that we call reality, but having read those words and having often stared across the deep and treacherous Canal de las Ballenas [Channel of the Whales] I had always known that one day I would visit that beckoning island and be there "with time and supplies," to make my own exploratory excursions inland and along its shores.

A little over sixty years since Steinbeck's visit, three circumstances brought Guardian Angel Island to the forefront of my mind.

The first was an exciting day trip I had made to Guardian Angel Island in February 2003 with an elderly Canadian gentleman in a twelve-foot aluminum boat.

The second was an article about paddling to the island written by famed California-to-Hawaii kayaker Ed Gillet.

The third was getting involved in a film being shot at Bahía de los Angeles (LA Bay) about two young Americans attempting to cross the Sea of Cortez (also known as the Sea of Cortés or Gulf of California) on a Hobie Cat who were caught in a storm, shipwrecked, and nearly died of thirst.

Cal Sherman from Alberta is a quiet spoken, modest man who walks, or rather boats alone. A snowbird, he spends most winters camped simply at LA Bay with his twelve-foot aluminum Valco pulled up on the beach. He said that in 1989 he first began asking locals in the town about the big island and was quickly told, "Forget it. You'll drown trying to get over there in a twelve-foot boat; there are huge cliffs and no beaches to land on."

"Then one day I was camped on the beach by *Villa Vita* in LA Bay and I looked across at the island with binoculars, and about a mile or two south of Humbug Bay I thought I could see a tall smokestack, a big chimney going straight up into the sky. And I talked to the locals again and asked if there was some kind of factory or building over there... and they said no there was nothing, maybe drug runners. There's no water. 'You'd better stay away from there,' they repeated."

"Curiosity got the best of me and I loaded my boat with my camping gear and took off to the island. The mirage turned out to be a twelve-foot elephant tree on top of one of the mountains. Then I thought I've got to see more of this coastline; I went south, right past Este Ton [a small enclosed bay]; didn't even know it was there. I went down about another three miles and there was a gravel beach that looked good to land on so I pulled up on that and pitched my tent and went for a hike up a narrow wash; and you could hardly step without stepping on flowers. Hummingbirds were zipping around, and

Cal Sherman taking me on my first trip to the island

there were butterflies all over and I thought, oh my God this is paradise. I spent three nights there; and that was my first trip."

Cal Sherman is now 72; he's not the biggest guy and he doesn't have the biggest boat, but he has a huge heart and unbounded courage and common sense. Since 1990 he has made 25 trips to the island and completed 7 circumnavigations, most often alone. However, his first circumnavigation was in 1992 with his wife Janice. And he has found, "There is a gravel and more rarely a sand beach within every mile around this whole island where kayakers or cartoppers can pull out and camp."

His enthusiasm for the place was infectious. "This fascinating island has everything that you and I love," he said, "primitive beauty, silence and solitude. One could spend a lifetime on Guardian Angel and you still wouldn't learn all its secrets. When I am alone on La Guarda, or at any isolated spot in Baja, I have such an overwhelming sense of freedom and peace of mind that any risk involved in being there is well worth it. If you die in Baja you are already halfway to heaven."

He attributes his "apparent daring and recklessness" to having "rode bulls on the pro rodeo circuit for 27 years. I didn't get rich or famous. Never really wanted to. I was free and independent. What more can one want?"

We were kindred spirits. In February 2003, I accompanied him on one of his Guardian Angel excursions. It was my first trip out there. We left LA Bay at first light moving out among the islands of the inner bay, watching anxiously for any sign of wind, ready to camp for days on the big island or anywhere else if necessary. There's a point in the middle of the channel where you're truly exposed and, on the wrong day, more than halfway to the Pearly Gates.

Cal and Janice Sherman

Cal's calm, self-effacing Canadian demeanor and dry sense of humor inspired confidence. He brought me up to speed with the nautical numbers:

"It's approximately 130 miles to circle La Guarda from our trailer site [in LA Bay] and back. It's 19 miles straight across to Este Ton. My 15 hp 4-stroke Suzuki uses 8 gallons of gas to make the round trip. It runs my boat 14 mph at half throttle. And my boat is so well designed that my back-up motor [a 3 hp Yamaha] will put this boat right up on plane at 8-10 mph"

The sea remained flat calm. Apart from the odd bird or sea lion on the surface, the approaching mountainous island, strikingly gold and red, was perfectly reflected in the water. Layer upon layer of warm morning colors reached to heaven, and also straight out from the shore to welcome us. Under other circumstances it might have seemed like we were motoring into the jagged jaws of hell.

Approaching Guardian Angel Island

We first visited the beautiful sheltered cove of Este Ton, and ran north along miles of the rugged west coast, into and around Humbug Bay. Looking at the lonely, unsullied black and ashen gray cliffs topped with a reddish-brown layer of cooled lava, I fancied I might have been there not too many million years ago when the mountain range destined to become Guardian Angel Island, was violently ripped from the peninsula at the same time as the peninsula was separating from the mainland.

Apart from a single kayaker [A resident of Northern California who spends much of the winter in the LA Bay area. Most gringos know him as Kayaker John, whereas his Mexican friends call him Juan Coyote] who we knew to be in Este Ton, we didn't see a soul... just birds, whales, seemingly untrodden shores undulating with sea lions, and when we went ashore, great, great beachcombing. The beautiful delicate bleached skeletons of a

© Cal Sherman

Sea horse skeleton   *Paper nautilus*

seahorse and a paper nautilus somehow survived their final journeys onto a stony rocky beach.

Cal called me over to look at what he feared was the mummified remains of a human hand! Closer inspection suggested it might be the flipper of a young sea lion.

I returned to LA Bay with my head full of Guardian Angel. We had been lucky with the winds. Two nights after we got back a furious northerly gale hit the area. I lost camping gear blown off the roof of my pickup; the surf was horrendous, booming and exploding on northern points; the sea a churning mass of white.

Encountering drug runners on one of the islands or even on a remote stretch of the peninsula coastline is always a possibility. Cal related the time that he took his boat up to Asamblea, on the Baja peninsula, forty-five miles north of LA Bay, "because I wanted to pitch a tent and do some hiking. Unfortunately, some Mexicans were sitting there with rifles in pangas; obviously they were drug runners. They were sitting there in their pangas right where I wanted to go ashore. I fiddled around for a while and landed on a small island and pretended to do some fishing because I hoped they'd leave and I could go and pitch my tent; but they didn't, they just sat there watching me. Then I saw them talking on a CB radio; pretty soon another panga came. There's a spot about five miles south of Asamblea called El Muertito, the panga came out of there and came over and passed me real slow, looking me over. And one of them was sitting there with a rifle across his lap, so I thought this is no good, they're doing something that they don't want me to see. So I reeled up, got in the boat and took off, waved to the guys in the panga, and they waved back, and away I went across the channel to the north end of Guardian Angel Island."

He continued: "Almost anywhere around the big island you'll hear boats going by at night; you'll hear them at one or two o'clock in the morning,

THE PROLIFIC PANGA

Over 30 years ago the World Bank commissioned a Yamaha-led consortium of Japanese motor manufacturers to design a boat to help promote fishing in third world countries. They were instructed to design a relatively low cost, rugged, seaworthy vessel that could stand up to the demands of daily use with minimal maintenance—one that would be fuel efficient, easily driven by small engines, and safely carry heavy loads. The Yamaha group warmed to the task, which they saw as helping to utilize the ocean's vast fish stocks while creating an enormous market for their outboards.

The boat they created was the panga, named after the large, heavy machete-type knife ubiquitous in Africa and Central and South America. The blade in profile looks exactly like a panga boat. Pangas are long and narrow, shallow-draft (8-inch) open boats with pointed, flared bows, square sterns, and a wide lip around the gunwales. The outboard acts as the tiller and is attached to a cheap external fuel tank. When the water is calm the panga easily planes, lifting the bow and running with minimal drag at the stern.

Popular for both inshore and offshore use, pangas are the world's most prolific commercial fishing boats; there may be as many as 100,000 in use around the world. There are several manufacturers in Mexico. The Mexican and Central American version is usually 22-24 foot long, and powered by a 40-90 hp outboard.

pangas with no lights on; obviously they aren't fishing when running in the dark like that. But I've never had them bother me. But those guys kind of spooked me sitting there with rifles. And they weren't hiding them; as they went by, one picked up his rifle and held it for me to see. That was meant to discourage me... and it did."

"And another time at the northwest corner of Smith Island, there's a little bay in there, and in 1995 I was with Janice and another lady in my boat, we came into that bay and there was a panga loaded three feet above the gunwales with big bales of probably marijuana and there were several guys there and they immediately picked up their rifles so that we could see them. I told Janice and the lady with us, 'don't even look at them; just pretend we're admiring the fish in the shallow water,' and when we were ready to leave I just started the motor and turned around and waved and away we went. We were camped at La Gringa and that night as soon as it got dark we heard a panga come into the bay on the island; there was a red light showing on shore; I imagine that was a signal to come in."

I asked Cal if he keeps a low profile or if has a campfire when visiting Guardian Angel Island. He replied, "Not a very big one. I don't want to attract any attention. I can't really see that anybody would rob you when you're that isolated because it would almost be a death sentence. But quite often when I leave for a hike I'll let my tent down to the ground and throw a camouflaged netting over my boat; then it's pretty hard to see from out on the water. And I'll feel a lot safer when I hike away from camp and I'm going to be gone for four, five, or six hours."

My interest in the island was boosted by this article which I edited for 2004 publication in the *Discover Baja Travel Club* newsletter.

"The Sinking Panga"
by Ed Gillet

Our group of 14 kayakers was camped on the east side of Isla Coronado [Smith Island], adjacent to the Canal de las Ballenas, preparing for our journey to Isla Angel de la Guarda. Canal de las Ballenas is frequently too rough to paddle safely, so we were anxious to get up early and put the 15-mile crossing behind us.

Waking at 3 A.M., the light from my headlamp reflected off clouds of cotton candy fog blanketing our cove. Strangely, the sky overhead was clear and steady stars shone brightly in the black sky.

We breakfasted on granola bars and coffee, packed our kayaks quickly, and launched in the dark—chemical lightsticks and headlamps marking our individual boats. The fog was only about 30 feet high, but our visibility at the surface was reduced to a few yards. After much shouting, my paddlers materialized one by one and fell into a tight formation. We proceeded slowly on a compass course to the big island. We called to each other every few minutes to keep track of our little pod and help any stragglers catch up to the group.

The fog lifted shortly after sunrise. Red and gold tropical clouds and a brilliant green flash heralded the sun's return. We spotted several fin whale blows silhouetted against the sunrise glow. Guiding a group of untested paddlers across this exposed, swift flowing channel is always a harrowing experience for me. I relaxed a little when I could watch all my ducklings at once.

After the bright cool dawn, however, the day turned oppressively hot, humid, and still. Guardian Angel shimmered and

Paddling into the early morning fog   © Tomás Campbell

danced in the heat haze, the intensely colored ochre layers in her ridges appeared bleached white by the sun. A mirage created the illusion that the island was floating above the horizon.

"Hey, Ed! Wait up. We need to talk", someone yelled from the back of the group.

"What's happening?" I asked.

"My shoulder's frozen and I can't paddle any farther."

I thought Bob was kidding.

"Do you want to take a longer break?" I asked.

"That won't do any good. I have some sort of impingement and when this happens to me, it takes three weeks of chiropractic work to get my range of motion back. Right now my hand is totally numb and I can't move my arm."

Bob had certainly picked an odd moment to mention his shoulder injury. Now 14 kayaks were bobbing in mid channel with someone who couldn't paddle at all. We had too much invested in this trip to easily abandon our itinerary, and since we were more than halfway across the channel, I decided to tow Bob to the island.

Towing dead weight is perhaps four times harder than paddling your own kayak. I sweated and panted. Time stopped. No matter how hard I paddled, the receding island seemed to stay at the same distance.

We reached the closest shore on Guardian Angel during the hottest part of the day, landing our boats at the base of a tall sandy cliff at low tide. The heat reflecting off the cliff turned the beach into an oven. And when the tide came in, the beach would disappear. Clearly, we needed to get Bob back to town. I decided that our best chance lay in hiring a Mexican fishing panga to ferry him back to Bahía de los Angeles. Most local fishermen I know are barely scraping by, so an easy $100 evacuation ride is a welcome windfall. I knew that the closest Mexican fish camp was at *Puerto Refugio* at the north end of the island, 20 miles away.

We camped for the night in the big bay boaters call "Humbug Bay" because the anchorage is so lousy. Conditions on the beach were not much better: our tilted tent sites were buggy and rocky.

The next morning I hooked the towline on Bob's kayak and labored up the coast. After towing Bob against the current for 7 miles, I was exhausted. We landed for a break at what I'll always call "turtle beach." I love visiting this place because I am transported back to the magical night a big green sea turtle emerged from a stormy sea and forced us to move our tents so she could lay her eggs in her birthplace. We happily obliged her. While there, a rare 15-knot southerly breeze sprang up. I jury-rigged a sail from our sun tarp and the wind pushed Bob's kayak the remaining 12 miles to Puerto Refugio faster than many in the group could manage.

We coasted into Puerto Refugio, a gorgeous bay protected by several islands. My heart sank when I scanned the shoreline looking for fishing pangas. The normally active shark fishing camp on *Isla Mejia* was deserted.

We camped. Despite a day without paddling, Bob's shoulder was still unusable. I had to get him back to Bahía de los Angeles before we could continue our circumnavigation. From a vantage point higher up the beach, I searched

Paddling and "sailing" to Puerto Refugio

© Tomás Campbell

the islands again. A small dot on the beach at Isla Granito drew my attention. As its name implies, tiny *Isla Granito* is composed wholly of granite. The island appears unnaturally white against the deep reds and browns of the surrounding extrusive igneous rock. Through my binoculars, the shimmering spot resolved itself into a panga pulled high up on the beach. It seemed to be our only hope, so I paddled over to the island in the late afternoon, hoping to enlist the aid of the panga's owner.

I landed next to the panga, expecting that someone would greet me. Baja fishermen rarely leave their outboard motors unattended. But, save for a sleeping sea lion, the beach was deserted.

I walked toward the only structure on Isla Granito, a hovel made from cardboard, thorny ocotillo arms, and kite string. I stopped short when I crested the beach. Three guys were lying side-by-side, face up in the sun. Flies crawled on their faces. The place looked like Jonesville after the Kool Aid party. At least one of them was alive. The middle guy snorted, waved the flies off his face, and half rolled over. Baja fishermen always let you know they are approaching your camp by whistling. I whistled a phony Mexican tune, smiled, and walked noisily in their direction.

The fishermen were from *Puerto Lobos*, about 80 miles away on the Sonoran side of the Gulf. They told me they were nighttime spear fishermen. They showed me a hooka dive rig

Cruising with jury-rigged sail past Sail Rock—near Puerto Refugio

© Tomás Campbell

powered by the rustiest compressor I'd ever seen. A 12-volt car headlight bulb was wired down the air hose to the regulator. An old car battery powered the light. They proudly pointed to another impossibly rusty contraption: a lawn mower engine attached to a car's alternator that charged the car battery. Normally, they could do pretty well spearfishing at night, paralyzing big grouper and pargo in their spotlight. Everything worked, they said, except the battery would not hold a charge. So they had not fished lately; they were out of commission until they found a fresher battery.

We introduced ourselves. Ramon and Pedro looked to be in their early twenties. Jesus, the obvious group leader, looked about 50. These guys were desperately poor. We discussed the possibility of my hiring their panga to take Bob back to Bahía de los Angeles.

Jesus wanted no part of driving the boat to Bahía de los Angeles, but he was willing to drive a hard bargain on behalf of his companions. We shook hands on our agreement. I would buy all the gas for the trip, and pay the guys $150 - fifty bucks apiece - a week's pay, at least, for a day's work. The young Mexicans seemed eager to do the trip, but I wondered if they really understood they were in for a 100-mile panga ride.

"You guys ready for this?"

"Si."

"Do you have enough gas to get to LA Bay? We can buy more gas when we get to town."

"Si, we have enough gas to get there."

"Well, it's going to be long trip so we should leave early."

"Si, very early is best."

Bob and I were packed and ready at first light. Hours passed. As the day warmed, the bobos buzzing around our faces drove us crazy. By 10 A.M., I couldn't stand waiting any longer. As I was shoving my kayak off the beach to paddle over to Granito to find out what went wrong, I spotted Ramon and Pedro motoring in our direction.

Now, most Baja pangas are eminently seaworthy - fast when empty, stable when loaded with fish. My stomach fluttered when I looked at Pedro's panga in the strong light of day. The plywood and fiberglass motorboat was blunt, awkward, and poorly built. Several mismatched paint colors and layers of old fiberglass patches added to the makeshift, haphazard look of the craft, which was grossly overpowered by a 75 horsepower engine.

We were out of better options so we loaded Bob's kayak and gear and took off. We flew around the north end of the island in calm water. Forty-five miles left. I started to relax. Maybe I misjudged these guys, I thought.

Clearing the northwest corner of Angel de la Guarda, we hit a wall of west wind blowing out of the peninsular canyons. A stiff 30-knot breeze blowing all night across 10 miles of fetch had kicked up a mean, steep sea. Ramon didn't slow down at all in the rough conditions. We were flying off the tops of waves, slamming hard into the troughs. When we bottomed out, the panga's loose plywood sides vibrated and rattled as though the boat was breaking up.

"Jesus," I screamed over the wind, the thumping boat noises and the whine of the engine, "do we have to go so fast? You're going to sink your panga!"

Panga taking kayak and disabled kayaker back to LA Bay

© Tomás Campbell

"We don't have enough gas to go slow." Ramon shouted back. "We'll run out if we slow down."

Conversation stopped while our panga went into freefall off the top of a big steep wave. I straightened my arms, pushing my butt off the hard seat, bracing for impact. Wham! Bang! We belly flopped on the hard water. The crash unsettled us all. Bob ended up on his rear end in the bilge. The cracks between the seats and the boat's sides were wider; more water leaked in from somewhere. Ramon slowed down, clearly rattled.

I suggested, "Let's cut straight across to the coast where the waves are smaller, and stop at the fish camp in *Bahía Guadalupe*. I'll buy more gas there."

Ramon nodded in agreement and slowed to a saner speed. We all took turns bailing. Pedro ducked under the bow and lit a joint. He grinned and blew smoke in my face. He passed the joint to Ramon while he took his turn with the bleach bottle bailer. A deranged look crossed Pedro's face. "Fresh water coming in," he said with a giggle.

Even Bob with his frozen shoulder took his turn bailing. Rounding *Punta Remedios*, eight miles from the fish camp at Guadalupe, the motor coughed. We all looked back at the 20-gallon chemical storage bottle that served for a gas tank. The dark liquid inside looked pretty low, maybe a couple of gallons left. Pedro picked up the reagent bottle and cradled it in his arms like a baby, allowing the intake hose to sip the last of the rotten gas. The motor was coughing again when we hit the sand at the Bahía Guadalupe fish camp. No way would we have made LA Bay. On our old course we would have run out in mid-channel.

There were more guys at Guadalupe than I'd ever seen there. And anchored in front of the fish camp were several loaded pangas with tarps hiding their cargo. I suspected it was harvest time and the dope was moving through the Midriff.

After a long negotiation, a group of fishermen agreed to loan us some fuel. We would buy enough gas in Bahía de los Angeles to replace their fuel plus five gallons in interest. We poured 25 liters into our chemical bottle and we roared off.

The west wind had calmed, as it generally does in the early afternoon, and we were running throttle wide open once again. Something was wrong. All four of us looked at our feet simultaneously. There were six inches of water in the panga, and a thick round geyser shot up in the center of the boat. We were sinking, fast. I yelled at Pedro to turn around and run for the fish camp.

We desperately bailed with our hands while our crippled panga made a screaming beeline back to the fish camp. Our gunnels were nearly awash when we scraped bottom. We hit the beach so hard that a wave of water started at the stern and poured over our bow.

The crowd on the beach thought that was the funniest thing they had ever seen. About 30 joking, smoking, jeering guys helped us take the motor from the transom and flip the sad little panga over. Our boat looked like it had been shot through with an artillery shell. A patch covering a gaping 8-inch diameter hole in the bottom of the panga had peeled off. The hole had obviously been patched many times, judging by the number of paint layers peeling from the area.

Claiming that it was virtually irreplaceable, the Bahía Guadalupe fishermen would not part with their carefully hoarded fiberglass cloth and resin. We would have to travel to town to buy the materials. But that meant that we needed another panga. My offer to pay for a ride to Bahía de los Angeles was turned down by several idle boatmen with flimsy excuses - I guessed the cargo would be heading north later that night.

After an hour-long search, I finally found Juan, a bible-thumping fisherman who claimed to be disgusted by the moral turpitude at Guadalupe. He had a nicely painted wood panga with neatly coiled lines and meticulously stowed fishing gear. He looked and acted more like a seaman than any of the other *pangueros* I had met that day. More money changed hands; the four of us piled in Juan's panga and we were off. Unfortunately, the spark plugs in Juan's engine were bad; we had to stop every 15 minutes to re-gap, sand, and mutter over the worn-out plugs before the engine fired again.

I dropped Bob off at Guillermo's RV Park and restaurant. He would have to spend 9 days there until we returned to take him back to the U.S. Our time in Bahía de los Angeles was productive. Juan found a couple of used spark plugs that looked like they might have a little life left in them. I bought some beer and filled several water bags for my group. Sammy Diaz sold us some fiberglass resin in a plastic soda bottle, and a tiny amount of watery catalyst in a glass 7-Up bottle. No one had fiberglass cloth for sale. Our resin was almost useless without cloth to make a patch, but we took what we could get and headed back to Juan's panga. Pedro and Ramon used most of the money I paid them to buy a new car battery and supplies for their island camp. I hated to see that battery come aboard, since it meant that the destructive and illegal practice of night spearfishing would resume, but these guys were walking ecological disasters whether they had a working battery or not.

"We ate a little sea turtle, last night!" Pedro had proudly announced at our first meeting.

"Turtles are protected, aren't they? Isn't it illegal to kill them?" I posed my assertions as questions so as not to appear too confrontational.

"Oh, it is illegal to sell the meat, but not to eat it." Pedro knew that I knew this bit of sophistry was absurd, but as he obviously hoped I would drop the matter, I did. The turtle was dead. Perhaps the money and supplies would keep them from killing another for a while.

With our new spark plug, we were making pretty good time, until Juan changed course to do several donuts around a humpback whale and her calf. I shouted at Juan to stop harassing the whales. He seemed surprised at my vehemence. I think Juan believed he was giving me a naturalist's tour at no extra charge. We left the terrified animals in our wake and reached Guadalupe as the sun was close to setting over the rugged brown *Sierra La Asamblea*.

After an hour of hemming and hawing, a fisherman coughed up a few feet of fiberglass cloth. We carefully scraped and cleaned the boat hull around the hole and applied our fiberglass patch. We waited for an hour, but the patch stayed wet. It looked as though the patch might not harden at all.

Ramon and Pedro sat smoking on the overturned panga and watching the stars come out. Every few minutes one of us touched the patch. Still tacky. A sober, grizzled fisherman stopped by, tapped the patch and let out a hissing whistle, which, in Baja, means, "You guys are completely screwed."

"What do you think?" I asked. "Will this panga get us to the big island?"

"Hard to say...maybe."

That was good enough for us. The sun had set an hour before and the pink glow behind the Asamblea ridgeline was fading quickly.

There was just enough light to keep from stepping on broken glass, a rusty can, or tripping over some old piece of nylon gill net as 15 guys waddled the patched panga to the water. We gently set our boat down in knee deep water to protect the patch. So far so good. Ramon and Miguel grunted down the beach with the heavy outboard and installed it on the stern.

We motored slowly at first. The night was calm and mild. Our wake glowed with green bioluminescence. The trip back to Angel de la Guarda took two hours. I blocked my mental images of our imminent sinking by calculating our distance from shore and picturing the changing tidal currents so I would know which way to swim when the panga sank.

I had not been as worried on the trip over when there was a kayak aboard to serve as a life raft. I would survive: Mexican fishermen generally do not swim well and I could wrestle the kayak away from one-armed Bob.

As we drew closer to the black hulking island, Pedro and Ramon relaxed. I knew we were home free when Ramon and Pedro lit up a joint and ran full throttle past the uncharted rocks they may or may not have known about.

Our entire kayak group assembled on the beach when they heard the sound of the panga. They had almost given up on my returning that night. I ran up to my tent and grabbed my spare spear gun to give to Pedro and Ramon along with some extra money to let them know I appreciated their good cheer throughout a harrowing day. They might have had one or two failings but they had risked their lives to help me out. We said goodbye, standing ankle deep in the water, embracing each other with the genuine emotion of lucky survivors.

Postscript:

Two years after my insane ride with Pedro and Ramon, I was circumnavigating Isla Angel de la Guarda with another set of clients. On the fourth night of our trip, we camped near Punta Pulpito, on the wilder east side of the island. On an afternoon stroll to a tidal lagoon, I spotted a small boat turned upside down next to a ruined shack. The little panga was obviously beyond repair: someone had scavenged the transom, seats, and gunwales for firewood. I recognized Pedro and Ramon's old panga from the gaping round hole in the bottom, precisely where the water geyser shot skyward in Bahía Guadalupe. On the wall of the shack, directly over the wrecked panga, someone had drawn a disconcertingly realistic picture of an AK 47 assault rifle between two marijuana plants that crossed like swords above the weapon. An emblem of tribute at the final resting place of a Baja working vessel.

In spite of an increasing concern about the drug traffic through the area, the more I read and heard about the island, the more I wanted to be out there. Going back was beginning to take on the character of a simmering obsession. Coincidences multiplied. Every twist and turn of my life seemed to be directing me, daring me, energizing me, to make a leap of faith and just do it.

The final precursor came out of the blue in October 2005. I received a phone call from some representatives of a British film company who wanted to shoot a docudrama about two Hobie Cat sailors who had become marooned on (you guessed it) Isla Angel de la Guarda. [The film was first shown in the US on Discovery Channel in 2006]

In 1995, Southern Californians Mark Sorensen and Robert Rusnak were trying to "island hop" across the narrow "Midriff" of the Sea of Cortez from LA Bay to Kino Bay on the mainland, when they fell foul of a sudden 50-60 mph westerly wind. Their small catamaran began taking on water and breaking up, and was eventually dashed onto the western coast of Guardian Angel. They spent four harrowing days trapped under cliffs on the island with practically no food or water. Blistered by the sun and plagued by tiny biting insects—noseeums—they survived largely on the flesh of Sally lightfoot crabs and the juice of a cardón cactus which they said "tasted like half-baked bile." The alert crabs were almost impossible to catch but were susceptible to thrown stones.

The film company needed a location for the re-enactment and wanted my input about filming close to San Felipe. My attempt to dissuade them against using the relatively low lying northern Sea of Cortez was successful. In spite of the logistical advantages of good hotels and relatively easy access from the border, the scenery was way too different, and the tides were too great, making even getting a boat into the water problematic for much of the day.

I strongly recommended LA Bay as the best location. And so I became the "location scout" for the Darlow Smithson production of "*I Shouldn't Be Alive*," which coincidentally is something many disgruntled readers say after buying my books. A few weeks later I was in LA Bay with an advance party looking for a convincing cliff-backed cove and settling on accommodations for the actors and crew.

We found a suitable location a mile or so north of La Gringa, across from the great volcanic form of Smith Island. And a few miles north of the town, arrangements were made to divide the actors and crew between two new hotels—*Los Vientos* and *Villa Bahía*. The latter was a laid back, intimate, beachside, dog-friendly, bed-and-breakfast establishment where the beer always flows freely from a large barrel. I had got to know its owner, Roger Silliman, about 15 years earlier and we had stayed in touch over the years.

With Guardian Angel Island stretched along the far eastern horizon, and knowing I had over two months free after New Year, I realized the time had come for commitment. As well as visiting the island, I had long wanted to kayak a remote stretch of Baja coastline. I formulated a plan. I would head out to the island with a kayak and my old buddy Pedro.

Confronted by sudden blasting winter winds and swirling currents, boaters regularly get into trouble and occasionally lose their lives in these waters, even inside the relatively sheltered confines of LA Bay, so I had no intention of kayaking fifteen miles out to Angel de la Guarda. I would arrange a ride in a panga and spend that two months exploring from one or more base camps, getting to know the island and its "secrets." I was not looking for trouble or any kind of wild

Villa Bahía–looking east to Smith Island. Guardian Angel on the horizon.

Cobra Tandem sit-on-top kayak

Storage space inside

adventure. But I did have the equipment, know-how, and common sense to survive alone on the island if necessary.

Roger was an enormous encouragement; he offered to help every way he could, and invited me to use Villa Bahía as my base. Everything was falling into place.

I dearly wanted to bring Pedro. It was his turn. Penny had spent that summer with me up in Michigan running and paddling her little legs off. It wouldn't be walking across America, but Pedro would be in his element. Supposedly, there are no coyotes out there. My main concern for him was rattlesnakes. I doubted I'd see any on the island in January and probably not in February, but I thought it would be a sensible precaution to take him on a short snake aversion course.

Back in San Diego I bought a kayak—a stable but slow two-seater "sit-on-top" that had been used as a fishing and duck hunting platform on the

Penny laying claim to be the perfect island dog

They shouldn't be alive—What Guardian Angel Island can do to a man.

Colorado River. It was bright blue with a thin camouflage of streaks of gray paint. Like me it had seen better days, but with a 600-pound carrying capacity it would do for my purposes of coastal exploration. And there was plenty of room for Pedro on the 36-inch-wide deck.

I took Pedro on several paddles in San Diego's Mission Bay. He loved it. I was excited for him. The kayak seemed sound and only let in a few drops of water; it certainly wasn't going to sink under me out in the channel.

Penny, the psychic philosopher dog, knew something was up, and in her simple way was making her demure but almost irresistible siren case for being the perfect island/kayak dog. If she wanted something she would sit on it, or next to it, till her slow and dull-witted master finally got the message.

When filming began in December 2005, I was invited to return to LA Bay and help out with the production. I was happy to volunteer as night custodian on the remote set, watching over the equipment and the trailer that served as changing room, wardrobe, make-up, etc. while everyone else was warm and snug and well-watered back in the bars of their hotels.

That suited me perfectly; most every evening Guardian Angel stretched before me catching the last light of day, glowing warm and fruity, the color of watermelon, while the closer islands were in shadow. It was easy to imagine being marooned out there, with a few comforts and cold beers. I began making notes and detailed plans.

And I had plenty of time to reflect on the

Filming at LA Bay. Guardian Angel Island in deep background.

survival drama that was being portrayed in the film. Having been in a few tight situations myself over the years, I had a number of questions:

Why did they put all their water in one container on the sailboat?

Why were they baking and blistering in the sun and being attacked by noseeums when they could be sitting up to their necks in the cool sea?

Why didn't they swim/wade along the shore to explore?

Why eat anything if you're thirsty? You can go without food for a week or two without serious health concerns, but with temperatures close to 100 °F your life expectancy without water, assuming complete rest, is just one or two days!

Eventually, the hapless pair were rescued by passing *pangueros* who were very reluctant to take them to the town of LA Bay, claiming they did not have the "proper papers" to do so. Instead they were dropped on a remote shore, well south of the bay, miles from town, from where, in their stricken state, they had to be rescued again by an elderly American fisherman who had his wife and daughter in the boat. The film skipped over this final interesting drama. Certainly the "Good Samaritan" *pangueros* were involved in something illegal and might well have been drug runners.

When the film wrapped, I negotiated for a few useful items for my island adventure—including a flare gun kit used by the rescue boats in the water scenes, and a waterproof VHF marine radio.

Before leaving the bay I spoke to the energetic and ever articulate and amiable Antonio Reséndiz, who at the time was running the turtle research station in town, but has since retired. Tony and his wife Bety operate an eco-friendly campground, *Campo Archelón*, on the shore of the bay, and it has long been a center for research, education, and conservation in the area.

He was enthusiastic about my plans and offered to help me arrange permits and permissions, and introduce me to people in town who had some knowledge of Guardian Angel.

Antonio Reséndiz

After reading up on the island and talking with Antonio, one thing quickly became clear; I'd be doing the trip alone. No way on earth would I get permission to take Pedro.

There is a small island, Isla Estanque, at the southeast corner of Guardian Angel, barely separated from it by a shallow reef. Recent research has suggested that a subspecies of the endemic Angel de la Guarda deer mouse, *Peromyscus guardia*, "was probably driven to extinction on Isla Estanque by a single introduced domestic cat." The mouse was fairly abundant on the island in 1995. But three years later, a feral cat was spotted prowling Estanque. It possibly escaped from a sailboat as the island has a fairly decent anchorage, or might have come from a now abandoned fish camp. After observing the cat not a single live *Peromyscus guardia* mouse was seen again on the island. The cat was eradicated in 1999.

Pedro—so contented on that kayak.

Recent studies from Angel de la Guarda itself, where there have been numerous sightings of feral cats, have found no evidence of *Peromyscus guardia* which once was recorded there in great numbers; it was last seen on that big island in 1991. "A comprehensive survey of the island is required, with subsequent action for the species recovery and conservation if it is found to be extant." Antonio intimated that expeditions have been sent to Angel to shoot the cats, "nasty things" he called them, and thought the Angel de la Guarda deer mouse had never been photographed and asked me to keep an eye out for it.

Although Pedro would more likely eradicate a few feral cats than any mice, I gave way to the inevitable. Nevertheless, I was devastated for him. By way of making amends for a loss I hoped he knew nothing about, I kept taking him on my training paddles in Mission Bay.

His enthusiasm was sad to see. He kept rubbing his head on my leg, and looking at me with big brown eyes poking from his happy face; I'm sure he was saying, "O master it will be wonderful—kayaking together, hiking together, exploring for two months, free, fit, happy. Oh please master, please. Remember how I saved you from the cougars and the coyotes in the Sierra San Pedro Mártir?"

Poor Pedro. I was going to miss him. And to double the blow, for our drive from San Diego to LA Bay and Villa Bahía, my wife Bonni and I decided to take little Penny, so Pedro could better watch our house. My guilt intensified.

After Christmas, as Bonni and I started loading the kayak and all my gear and supplies in our ten-year-old Nissan pickup, I sent notice of my island intentions to a friend who asked if he could share the news on *BAJA NOMAD*, a popular Baja discussion board.

I had little experience with these internet forums. But having as many Baja enthusiasts knowing I was out there seemed sensible… maybe it'll lead to a few visitations and maybe a companion or two who might want to hike and paddle with me for a while.

I replied:

"Yes, it's time for me to shed a few holiday pounds and write another book. Assuming I can secure permission I hope to be soon braving wind and current "marooned" on Guardian Angel Island. I'll have a kayak and a couple of pair of boots so I can explore all over the island… Looking forward to seeing you again, maybe in March upon my return."

I caught a few of the follow up posts:

what does his family think about him going off on these solo treks all the time?…his wife has to be very understanding…that guy sure likes loneliness.

One isn't always the loneliest number. If she were like mine she would probably welcome the vacation.

I have to hand it to Graham, coming to the USA from England as he did with nada to his name, getting a couple of sponsors, Sport Chalet, etc., to supply him with a pack and hiking boots, walking the coast of the Peninsula, finding material for 3, now a fourth book…heck, I remember seeing Graham below decks of the Titanic…

Bonni and Graham with Andrew and Elspeth

The last comment, referring to the six months I'd spent with Bonni and our two children as "core group" extras on James Cameron's movie Titanic, gently reminded me that my experiences with boats hasn't always been positive. Fortunately, I had found a superb, almost-new lifejacket at a garage sale for $5.

Chapter 3

Science of Island

If you're not part of the solution, you're part of the precipitate.

Henry J. Tillman

There are many islands and islets in the Sea of Cortez. In 2005 the United Nations officially recognized 244 when it bestowed "World Heritage Site" status on them. The largest is Tiburón, situated at the far eastern end of the Midriff group, close to mainland Mexico. The majority of the islands, however, are closer to the Baja peninsula. Isla Angel de la Guarda, 42-miles long with an area of over 360 square miles, is the second largest. It is mostly mountainous. The highest point, in the north, is 4,300 feet. Occasional lagoons, sand beaches, and cobblestone and shingle alluvial fans break up its rugged, cliff-lined coast.

The Ballenas channel (with a minimum width of 9 miles between Punta Los Machos and Punta Remedios) separates Guardian Angel Island from Baja California. Much of the west coast of the island lies less than 15 miles offshore from the peninsula, and is separated from it by a long, narrow submarine trough averaging 4,000 feet deep. The deepest point is more than 5,000 feet.

Puerto Refugio, at the island's northern end, lies about 40 miles from Bahía de los Angeles, and offers extensive all-weather protection for boaters. The splendidly enclosed cove of Este Ton is the closest secure anchorage from LA Bay.

Biology

The islands in the Sea of Cortez are part of the Sonoran desert, like both coasts of that sea, and have been called "a natural laboratory for the investigation of speciation." As *A New*

Este Ton

Island Biogeography of the Sea of Cortés (the current bible on the subject) puts it, "The area is still incompletely explored biologically… even the basic inventory of the terrestrial life of the islands is incomplete…"

The latest count recognizes about 650 plant species on the islands, 205 have been recorded on Guardian Angel. And most of the islands are nearly pristine; very few non-native plants are found.

"The beaches where the larger arroyos reach the coast are logical landing points, and here the visitor gets the first close look at the vegetation. By and large, its constituents are the same beach shrubs… as on the Baja California peninsula, and the same leguminous trees… and columnar cacti…" *A New Island Biogeography of the Sea of Cortés*

A major arroyo meets the coast

But in some ways the islands are very different. Dr. Gary A. Polis, the author of *The Biology of Scorpions* and *The Ecology of Desert Communities*, spent many years studying Baja island ecology—scorpions and spiders in particular. Laurence Pringle wrote a popular children's book about him titled *Scorpion Man*, which examines his exciting career choice.

Gary Polis has pointed out that in deserts, scorpions "may exhibit more standing biomass per unit area than all vertebrates combined." And if that fact isn't sobering enough, the idea of population densities elevated several fold on the islands could send you staggering to the nearest "rehab" facility.

Polis and his team found that scorpions and spiders were much more prevalent on the islands around LA Bay than on the nearby Baja California peninsula.

Swift churning currents bring vast amounts of nutrients to the surface and into the food chain and deposit much of it on island shorelines. By studying this onshore "flow" of nitrogen and phosphorous in the form of seabird guano and beached plant and animal material, Dr. Polis demonstrated that island spiders and scorpions obtain most of their nutrients from the sea, and are therefore in a sense marine predators; a nutrient rich sea in effect "subsidizing" the island's desert ecosystem. And the smaller the island the greater the effect and the denser the population of these predators—as many as ten to a hundred times more per unit area! But even on large islands such as Guardian Angel, there is a significant increase in the number of such predators active along the shore.

Dr. Polis found an interesting effect on those islands that support bird colonies. Tiny flying insects, bobos, swarm around the birds, infesting their eyes and drinking their tears. Spiders prey on the bobos. Then scorpions and lizards consume the spiders and the bobos. So Polis recorded eight times more spiders and up to 15 times more lizards inside the bird colonies than outside.

Mindful about all these scorpions and spiders, I knew I would need to be disciplined about zipping up my tent at night, and careful about where I put my hands. Even so, I couldn't wait to get my biomass out to the island and set up my tent on the beach. If the experience went wrong, at least I'd have the satisfaction of knowing my tears and finally my rotting flesh would be giving a nice boost to the food chain.

LA Bay scorpion on my shoe

And an increased wariness about rattlesnakes is in order. Most studies suggest there are also elevated population densities of rattlesnakes compared to the peninsula. And in the case of the speckled rattlesnake—*Crotalus mitchellii* or *mitchelli*—specimens are significantly larger than their peninsula cousins.

Whales

Many whale species frequent the deep waters of the Canal de las Ballenas. As well as orcas (killer whales) and finbacks, blues, humpbacks and sperm whales are regularly sighted. The finback whale, common to the area, measures up to 80 feet long—only the blue whale is larger.

There is a fascinating *National Geographic* video documentary on killer whales which shows these remarkable creatures grabbing sea lions right off the beach, thrashing them around, flipping them in the air with their tails, and practically skinning them alive. The video invites the viewer to, "Come face-to-face with one of the most feared ocean predators." Just to make sure I was sufficiently paranoid to boost my chances of coming back alive, I watched the video, *Killer Whales: Wolves of the Sea*, over and over till orcas invaded my dreams, dragging me from my kayak and tossing me around like a rag doll.

While I was working with the film company in Bahía de los Angeles, one of the crew had obtained a home video of an incident at the southern end of the bay. A group of tourists on the beach had spotted a commotion in the water, which initially looked like a pair of orcas mating, so they grabbed a video camera, jumped in a small boat, and motored out hoping to get some interesting footage. Approaching the scene, they were surprised to see that a whale shark was part of the proceedings. As it was suddenly partially lifted from the water they realized that they were in fact witnessing something entirely different—a violent and bloody orca attack on the whale shark. The concerned cameraman can be heard recommending that the boat move back. From a safer distance, the video records the continuing attack. As the shark rolls and splashes, the people in the boat watch in awe and horror as the orcas ram and tear at the defenseless shark till it's finally a bloodied, probably mortally wounded mass drifting in the water.

Swimming with whale sharks and occasionally hitching a ride by grabbing a fin or tail has long been a special treat for adventurous souls in the LA Bay area, but I doubt that anyone who witnessed that scene will be quite so quick to slip over the side.

Both films left me with a great respect for orcas. I would certainly not be seeking any close encounters on my kayak.

And I probably wouldn't be looking to surround myself with Humboldt squid either. These voracious predators, many over five-foot long, have in recent decades been turning up in the Sea of Cortez in ever increasing numbers. In one twenty-five square mile area off Santa Rosalía in southern Baja, researchers have estimated there may be as many as ten million individuals. And each one has a total of ten tentacles covered in hundreds of teeth-filled suckers, and a sharp, powerful parrot-like beak capable of biting out sizeable chunks of flesh from anything that gets in their way, including large sharks. There are numerous records of Baja's panga fishermen stating that they would rather fall overboard into a shark feeding frenzy than a frenzy of hungry Humboldt squid.

Baja author and fishing columnist Gene Kira recalls an LA Bay encounter with these jumbo cephalopods in a 2002 *Western Outdoor* News article:

> Later that morning, we launched into a heavy fog, and just off Horse Head Island we ran into a full-on, daytime feeding frenzy of squid on the surface. They would zoom upwards beneath our boat and open their vividly-colored arms to engulf any lure that was dangled above the water for them. It was like being surrounded by a macabre field of enormous, carnivorous, blooming flowers. Amazing. I don't think I would have wanted to run into that on a kayak.

Geology

Seven million years ago the Sea of Cortez did not exist. There was however, along the west coast of Mexico, a long low-lying valley or depression rather like the current Central Valley of California. For about five or six million years this "rift" valley had been subsiding inexorably until it flooded as it dropped below sea level, forming a shallow tropical sea. There is evidence that the first opening to this proto-Sea of Cortez may have occurred in the region of what is now Laguna San Ignacio, thus creating two peninsulas.

The familiar southern opening came later, probably less than five million years ago, as these peninsula ranges began a more westward swing, hinged in the north and moving most in the south, a rotation that continues today.

From two million years ago, there was a period of extensive uplift of the peninsula which left the San Ignacio seaway high and dry, effectively uniting north and south Baja. At the same time, most of the islands around the coast emerged or expanded as the peninsula and Sea of Cortez gradually acquired their present shape and dimensions.

Just in case all that swinging and up and down motion isn't giddying enough, Baja and a good hunk of prime coastal real estate in Southern California also happens to be sliding to the northwest along the San Andreas Fault complex.

Anyone contemplating buying real estate in Baja should be aware that if the peninsula's northwestward drift continues, worst case scenario, Los Cabos will end up somewhere in the region of Southern Canada while coastal property in Tijuana and Ensenada will command fine views of the Aleutian Islands. No more *fideicomisos* perhaps, but dress appropriately and consider supplementing your Spanish with a little Eskimo. (The USAAF World War II Survival Manual offers a number of useful phrases such as "Look at my frostbite" and *Nah-ne Kah-sah tahng-tah*—"Where is there a white man?")

The once-shallow Sea of Cortez is now, apart from the northern quarter or one-third, an extremely deep body of water, especially in relation to its width. The elevation difference between the sea floor and the adjacent mountains of Baja California to the west and mainland Mexico to the east is in many places greater than 10,000 feet. Indeed, the deepest basin, in the center of the Gulf, between Loreto and La Paz, is over 10,700 feet deep; and within the basin there is a towering underwater precipice over 5000 feet high. The highest peak in Baja California, Picacho del Diablo, overlooking San Felipe and the northern Cortez, stands over 10,000 feet.

There are deep trenches in the upper Sea of Cortez too, but the bedrock there is buried beneath 15,000-20,000 feet of silt and debris that has been swept down by the Colorado River. So the northern quarter of the Cortez is generally less than five hundred feet deep.

And at one time the Sea of Cortez reached much further north, into the Salton basin and up to the Palm Springs area of Southern California, but the sediments from the Colorado cut off that section, which eventually largely drained and dried out.

Today, several of the islands in the Cortez punch straight up from the sea with great depths close to shore. Many, like Guardian Angel, are elongated, running parallel to the axis of the Gulf.

So how do we account for all this incredible geological activity in the last few million years? The answer lies in the **East Pacific Rise**. This band of largely undersea mountains and extruding magma runs north from frigid Antarctic waters, across the Equator, and right up into the Sea of Cortez. As the name implies, most of its course runs beneath the Eastern Pacific Ocean

Another, perhaps more famous example of a belt of volcanically active undersea mountains is the Mid-Atlantic Ridge. In both of these zones, deep below the crust, it is thought convection currents rise through the viscous

mantle slowly bringing hotter material towards the surface. Immediately beneath the crust the convection movement turns horizontal, acting like a pair of cog wheels. This initially thinned and pulled apart the crust, then opened fractures for magma to rise up, pour out, and create new rock. According to the theory, this led to a stage of major elevation as the fractured crust yielded to the convection pressures beneath and formed great blocks which dramatically rose and fell in relation to one other. All the while, the crust on either side of the "rise" is being forced apart.

The Mid-Atlantic Ridge remains largely situated beneath the ocean. However, a section of the East Pacific Rise has, during the last few million years, plunged deep under the western coast of North America, initiating a powerful separating pull on the continental crust above, and leading to the sequence of events that we are still witnessing in California and Baja California today.

It doesn't take much imagination to picture the line of the East Pacific Rise where it runs beneath the Sea of Cortez, up through California, and back under the ocean in intimate association with the San Andreas Fault complex.

Any modern earth science text will tell you that the Earth's crust is made of mobile plates "floating" on a not quite solid mantle, and there are three processes operating at these plate margins:

1. Subduction—where one plate sinks beneath another.
2. Spreading—where plates are moving apart.
3. Lateral movement—where plates are sliding past one another.

The theory of "plate tectonics" has led to the postulation of many explicatory models. Everything from picturing the plates as floating on "a simmering pot of oatmeal" to conceiving them to be like "flagstones riding on hot tar" or "like lily pads in a pond" or "like a huge loaf of underbaked bread covered in flaky brown crust" with the warm dough beneath still soft and plastic. If you push the crust sideways it moves and you can quite vividly see the subduction effect when one section of crust slides and sinks under another. On the other hand, if you push the crusty plates apart and push down a little you can actually see the hot plastic dough bulging out and splitting in a passable representation of the spreading East Pacific Rise. This model is perhaps the most popular with earth scientists south of the border, but some Mexican theorists, led by Professor Hellman, prefer a model with mayonnaise beneath the crust, thinking it more accurately portrays the fluid dynamics of subduction—the celebrated *Cinco de Mayo* model. Many find this approach so persuasive, and the images so tangible, that they can practically taste the mayo and pangea. But no matter how much a *Modelo* makes our mouths water, if we are to avoid faulty conclusions, we must always be mindful that the model never ever is the reality.

The heart of the matter as any good scientist knows is how does the model, inevitably a simplified mental construct, relate to the infinite richness and boundless complexity of the "real." How can we account for the fact that our half-baked theories and models, so often patently deficient as descriptions of reality, can still be admirable, indeed indispensable, for leading our thoughts and investigations in a certain direction? To ask the question, is to know the answer.

Having clarified that, we are able to step back and see the bigger picture. For over a hundred million years the west coast of North America was charac- terized by a subduction zone whereby an eastward moving plate, the Farallon plate, was slowly sinking beneath the westward moving North American plate. And for much of this time

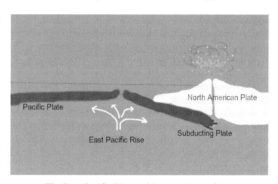

The East Pacific Rise pushing apart two plates

towering Andes-like mountains dominated the west coast as the riding plate was lifted and the subducting plate sank back into the mantle. These high ranges weren't solely due to the physical raising of the North American plate, but also to the spewing out above ground of tremendous amounts of volcanic material—ash, rubble and lava. As it sinks, much of the subducting plate melts, and being lighter than the surrounding mantle material, rises, much of it to the surface, exploiting cracks and weaknesses in the crust caused by the tension of the plate interaction. We can see this process in action in the great volcanoes along the west coast of South America and in the Pacific Northwest (Mount St. Helens, for example)—both zones of subduction.

However, along the coast of California and much of the Pacific coast of Mexico, a few million years ago, the East Pacific Rise, the "motor" that was driving the eastward moving Farallon plate, was itself finally subducted beneath the North American plate.

What happens when such a spreading zone is subducted beneath a continental land mass? We can expect: 1. Stretching and thinning of the crust.

2. Depressing and sinking of the land. 3. The stressed and weakened crust fracturing. 4. Land elevation and deep trench formation with sections of crust rising and sinking in relation to each other.

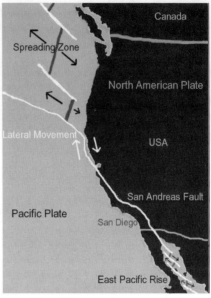

And this is exactly what we believe occurred in recent Baja California geological history.

It would be wrong to see the East Pacific Rise as a continuous straight line of separation. Most of the spreading seems to occur at certain active fronts along these separation zones, with flanks of lateral movement on either side. So looking from above, one gets the impression of more of a ladder or staircase effect, with perhaps the greater

What a little convection current can do

part of this so called separation boundary between plates characterized by lateral faults rather than by active spreading zones. With this in mind, it is possible to think of the San Andreas Fault as just one (albeit a very long one) of many lines of lateral slippage.

Two million years ago, Angel de la Guarda was firmly attached to the Baja California peninsula about 50 miles above its current position. Then an active spreading front opened to the north shearing that block of land away from the peninsula and pushing it south into its present Guardian Angel Island position across the entrance to LA Bay.

In case all this is giving you a headache, there is perhaps another model that might make it abundantly clear. Picture a cross-section of your head, as seen from the front, with the East Pacific Rise represented by the split down the middle of your brain. Imagine hot convection currents rising between the lobes, slowly torquing and pulling them apart; envisage the depressing effect as the top of your skull stretches and thins, and the plates begin to crack apart and grind against each other. Think how your eyes will… Oh, never mind.

Just go on to Chapter 4, and remember that Isla Angel de la Guarda is sitting on top of one of the planet's most stressed and active geological zones, right where the East Pacific Rise is beginning to ratchet up the pressure in the San Andreas Fault.

Chapter 4

Wind, Tide and Current

Moderate northwest gales that last two or three days at a time are frequently experienced in the upper gulf between December and February. These winds are particularly strong in Ballenas channel; they may on occasion raise such a heavy sea that navigation becomes impossible.

A New Island Biogeography of the Sea of Cortés.

Wind

The nearest to a normal wind pattern in the region is to have calm nights and mornings followed by breezy conditions kicking in before noon, with the gradual restoration of calm after the sun has set. However, all conditions are possible from wild blasting night winds to seemingly endless days of flat-calm blue seas.

There is a strong seasonal variation; winter winds tend to be more northerly, while those in the summer are more likely from the south. And all of the Sea of Cortez, especially the Midriff area, is prone to "Northers" or "*nortés*," sudden, violent, cold winter gales from the north or northwest. Blows of 25-35 mph are not uncommon and often last for days.

White caps in the channel between the peninsula and Smith Island

During a typical norté the wind does not relent after sundown, but blows round the clock. A string of these storms and kayakers can be virtually grounded for weeks. Nortés are often associated with cloudless skies. So, even on a calm clear day, the alert boater looks for the telltale signs of an incipient norté—a dark "wind line" or an apparent haze on the northern horizon; surprise larger waves from that direction with surf striking north facing points; or cloud caps suddenly forming on island peaks.

Cloud-capped Smith [Coronado] Island

While nortés can be killers for the unwary, they have the virtue of predictability. If not too far offshore, a watchful boater can find time to run to a beach or to seek safety in the southern lee of an island or headland.

Way more dangerous are the west winds, which usually blow strongest in the spring and the fall. From the peninsula they blow offshore from out of the canyons, taking those on the water away from safety. And well they disguise their killer intent—close in, the Sea of Cortez may appear calm and waveless, but once away from the lee of dunes or cliffs the wind can snatch a victim with a fury that signals that, for a kayaker at least, it is already too late; there may be no way back with paddle power.

Sometimes highly localized and descending in an instant, west winds may come blasting down just one or two canyons, sometimes spinning and eddying to the point of producing water spouts. It becomes almost impossible to hold a paddle in such conditions; and even if one hangs on, a full blown west wind will likely bowl you over. In the worst gusts the only way to avoid spilling into the water is to lie as low as possible and keep your paddle down along the side of your kayak. The moment you lift the blade, you're likely to flip over. You must wait till the gusts diminish. And as you're blown farther from shore, the violent winds will begin to raise awesome waves and surf.

On the peninsula side of the Sea of Cortez, if there's any suggestion of a west wind, stick close to shore, or better still don't launch. If you turn over you will be in serious trouble.

One has to experience such effects to believe they are possible. The inexperienced paddler launching into a calm friendly sea will be stunned by such a turn of events... and it will be largely luck that determines whether he lives or dies.

VHF radio weather reports like those in many parts of the US are not available in Mexico. But in the evening and at night, when AM radio reception is much enhanced, check radio news and weather stations like KNX 1070 AM (Los Angeles), or KOGO 600 AM (San Diego). Warnings for strong "Santa Ana" winds in the mountain passes and canyons of Southern California, often translate into strong north winds in the Sea of Cortez.

If rain and strong west winds are forecast for California, or if there are low clouds pouring over the peninsula mountains, be on your guard for a west wind.

Consult "online" weather sites before you launch. There are several internet cafes in LA Bay. Don't be shy about calling for a weather report at any time on VHF channel 16. Members of the local boating fraternity will likely be monitoring regional "ham" radio nets, and paying close attention to the area weather forecast.

Tide and Current

The far northern Sea of Cortez has spectacular tides with an amplitude of more than 25 feet during full and new moons. That's vertical distance. The actual distance between high and low tides in the gently sloping region can be hundreds of yards, even several miles. Around the Midriff Islands and the Ballenas channel the tidal range can be 12 feet or more. For comparison, the maximum tidal range in Southern California is about 6.6 feet.

For the tides in the Sea of Cortez to rise and fall that much requires an enormous flow of water, and all of it rushes through the island-packed Midriff at speeds up to 6 knots creating hair-raising sounds, whirlpools and spectacular upwellings. When the blasting north and west winds join or thwart these tidal flows the seas can be as confused and dangerous as any on earth.

All that agitation helps lift nutrient-rich cooler water from thousands of feet below, hence the Midriff area consistently has both the lowest surface temperatures in the Sea of Cortez and the richest measured nutrient levels. And, as those nutrients work their way up the food chain they produce a fabulous fecundity and diversity of marine life.

Sea of Cortez Midriff Islands

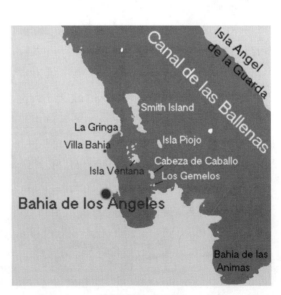

Bahia de los Angeles

Chapter 5

The Blood Red Sea

There must be few experiences in the biologist's world to compare with approaching a "new" island by boat. The ingredients are adventure and suspense, mystery and perhaps even a little danger. There are feelings of discoveries to be made, knowledge to be extended, curiosity to be both piqued and satisfied. Such feelings are shared not only among natural historians but by any adventurous and curious traveler; the more difficult the island is to reach, the keener the excitement of the visit.

A New Island Biogeography of the Sea of Cortés

I tend to be cautious by nature. It was my calculation that I could get out to the island and bring myself safely home. I couldn't eliminate every risk, but I could at least attempt to manage them. And part of the management program for all my trips has been a proto-paranoia, perhaps a full-blown paranoia, to imagine and prepare for the worst, and ironically, to thereby make the experience a little less comfortable.

Before hiking across a desert I'll research all I can about dehydration and beat myself up with stories of those who have died of thirst. Before heading into the drug growing and drug running wilds of Northern Baja I'll dig up all the stories where innocents and unfortunates have been viciously beaten and robbed and even murdered. And before venturing out on a kayak or a boat in the Sea of Cortez I'll want to know about all those who have done the same… and maybe haven't come back.

My wife, who knows me better than anyone, tends to misunderstand this very useful trait, and thinks I'm a hopeless wimp. She can't believe I ever did any of my Baja adventures.

Because of the winds and the currents, boating tragedies occur frequently in the LA Bay area. I nearly became one myself.

In November 1980, on my second trip to Baja, I hitched to LA Bay with my English girlfriend of the time. We camped with some American sport fishermen near the bayside terminus of the old Santa Marta Mine railway two or three kilometers south of town.

We were pleasantly surprised when one of them invited us to take his 14-foot fiberglass boat out to explore and do some fishing. It was a warm, still morning and we were thrilled to run among the islands and peek out from the mouth of the bay. All went well till we were close to *Isla Cabeza de Caballo* (Horse Head Island) on our way to the pair of islands known as *Los Gemelos* (The Twins).

When the wind started picking up from the north, the friendly bay did not look quite so friendly. Time to run for "home." As I was making the turn, the cables connecting the steering wheel to the outboard motor jumped their guides and jammed, sending us running in circles around some increasingly impressive waves.

By the time I figured out and repaired what had happened—a couple of screws had worked loose from a retaining plate—we were out rolling in a wild and dangerous norté, with white caps threatening to crash over the gunnels. My girlfriend and I agreed it would be foolish to try to run in across the open bay, so we chose to head south to the mouth of the bay and then take a miles long detour following the shore back towards town. We wanted to keep within swimming distance from the beach. The downside of that decision was there was no shelter and no place to beach the boat through the churning surf. I went as slow as I could. Even so, it was a wild wet ride; we nearly flipped several times. Fortunately, we made it back and returned the boat to its mightily relieved owner; the experience taught me a huge respect for the Sea of Cortez.

Almost exactly twenty years after my unplanned adventure, another boating mishap off Isla Cabeza de Caballo made headlines around the world.

On March 27th 2000, scorpion expert and island ecologist Gary Polis led his final expedition to the island, just a straight four miles from town. The expedition comprised two boats—a panga and Gary Polis' own 24-foot fiberglass boat, *Los Alacraneros*. They left town at 9 A.M., heading east. On board Polis' boat were Gary Polis 53, Michael Rose 27 (a UC Davis postgraduate researcher), and three of Japan's leading ecologists, Shigeru Nakano, 37, Takuya Abe, 55, and Masahiko Higashi, 45, all from the Center for Ecological Research at Kyoto University, and four other postgraduate researchers and students from UC Davis.

As well as these, the expedition included six "volunteers" who had paid nearly $1000 each to help Polis with his "Baja Island Predators" research. Their participation was organized by Earthwatch Institute, a nonprofit group based in Maynard, Massachusetts.

After a morning counting spiders and scorpions and their prey species, the two boats headed back to town around noon. Shortly after casting off from Cabeza de Caballo they were struck by a fierce westerly wind gusting to around 50 mph.

The panga that contained the Earthwatch group, in spite of all aboard receiving a good drenching, made it safely to town. However, Gary Polis' boat was missing. There was no immediate alarm. Dr. Polis had run to the islands scores of times and was very familiar with the area, so it was assumed that he had taken his boat back to Horse Head Island or into the lee of one of the other islands till conditions improved.

It was a tragic assumption, however. A huge wave had swamped the boat, cutting out the motor. Shortly after, another churning wave capsized the floundering craft, spilling all the occupants into the 65 degree water.

As walls of water surged over the upturned hull, the passengers were desperately trying to keep a hold. Polis and Rose and Shigeru, an experienced diver, battled to the point of exhaustion to keep everyone together. Repeatedly they pulled colleagues back when they were swept away. Nakano strapped his own life jacket onto Takuya Abe who could not swim.

Eventually, Polis and Rose, perhaps feeling the greatest burden of guilt for the tragedy, succumbed. "Their hearts just gave out," said one of the survivors. Not long afterwards the three Japanese scientists began losing their battle with the elements, slipping into unconsciousness and drifting away. After over three hours in the chilling water the four younger UC students and researchers, realizing that no one was coming for them, in a desperate gamble set out to try swimming to the Los Gemelos islands more than a kilometer away. It took them another three hours. They were found wet and cold and exhausted early the next morning.

On April 7th 2000—Chancellor Larry Vanderhoef gave this address to the UC Davis Community:

> The last week of March 2000 will be remembered forever at UC Davis. It was a week of tragedy, of sorrow, of heroism. Loved ones were lost, hearts were broken and lifetime bonds of kinship were forged in the struggle for survival.
>
> It began with all the excitement that a mission of experimentation and data gathering can generate. Research is about ferreting out new knowledge in new ways, in new places, a pursuit that is utterly natural to the human character. The required long hours of work can be tedious, to be sure, but research offers, as well, in those golden moments when confusing bits and parts of information come together into concordance and revelation, the most exhilarating and gratifying moments of one's life. At some level, especially for those visiting the Sea of Cortez research site for the first time, surely there was a sense of great anticipation.
>
> But scientific research has an inescapable element of danger, as well. After all, it is the exploration of new territory, whether in the laboratory or the field. The source of its excitement, exposure to the unknown, is also the source of its risk. That danger came to those nine members of our extended UC Davis family in rapid, unpredictable fashion on Monday, March 27. After they were well out to sea, Dr. Gary Polis and his core group of eight students, postgraduate researchers and visiting scholars saw sudden, strong winds generate unusually high waves that, in turn, capsized their

boat. They all had flotation devices, but those life jackets and strap-on seat cushions did little to protect them from greater perils. Large, intermittent waves continuously battered them away from the still floating upside-down boat. Worse, hypothermia, with the various problems it can cause, was a looming threat.

Rescue retrievals of those washed from the boat were performed many times by several people. Some who finally survived were themselves rescued earlier in the ordeal by ones who eventually perished. There are many stories of heroism to be told.

Our hearts go out to the families of those who died. Perhaps the most poignant moment, for me, came on Thursday. We had met, at the San Diego airport, with the arriving family members of the Japanese visiting scholars who perished. They were headed to Mexico to identify and claim their loved ones' bodies. After describing to them what we knew of the events of the previous days, we asked if they would like to wait for the survivors, who would be arriving soon by ground transportation from Mexico. After one hour together, survivor Becca Lewison said to those Japanese family members, through sobs and tears, "I wish more than anything that we could have brought (your loved ones) and everyone else back with us. They saved our lives."

The light of UC Davis is diminished by our loss. Gary Polis and Michael Rose were everything we hope for in scholarship and character. Our hearts go out to Sharon, Evan and Maia, and to Susan [Gary Polis' three children and his wife]. An exciting, novel experience turned tragic for Drs. Abe, Higashi and Nakano. The loss felt by their families is felt by us.

We are, as well, so very grateful that Gary Huxel, Becca Lewison, Sarah Ratay and Ralph Haygood are still with us. This is for them a significant life-changing experience. We can only hope that with time the memories of March 2000 will be increasingly dominated by their recollections of all that we cherish about Gary Polis, Michael Rose, Takuya Abe, Masahiko Higashi and Shigeru Nakano.

As the tragedy that befell the Polis party was taking place, Kayaker John, (he was the kayaker in Este Ton when Cal took me out there) was on Guardian Angel. I asked him about it:
[JOHN] I was at the southern tip and I was returning to Este Ton where I had a friend in a sailboat that I crossed out with. That was about 18 miles away. It was a dead calm, flat, gorgeous morning. There was a father and son team in a panga close to shore; the father was diving, getting lobster. I bought some lobster from them... and the son threw in two big fat scallops afterwards.

Then all of a sudden he straightens up and looks right past me out in the distance and pulls his diving dad up… and he looks out there. I couldn't really tell what they were looking at, but boy he got in the boat and as he was getting in waves started coming and then a little bit of chop and then I see this like wall of mist coming at us, where the wind is hitting so hard it's just lifting the water up into spray… I actually have a series of pictures I took when I realized what I was seeing. It went from dead calm to black skies and rain in about two hours. It was incredible how fast it switched from gorgeous warm weather to just looking like hell is here. One picture I took in the dead calm and you can see that wall coming. At this point it had already flipped the boat in the bay because of the time it took the wind to get to me.

[GRAHAM] What was the first thing you experienced?

[JOHN] First it was waves that were getting pushed ahead of the wind. Small waves. Very quickly after, a kind of puff of warm air… which I have since learned sends up the antennas, when you feel a puff of warm wind, because that means it's a westy. Then just seeing this spray coming… I took about three shots as it started building. When it got to us, I didn't want to touch my camera, I just wanted to hold my paddle, and paddle. The winds were not incredibly strong because they'd had time to fan out; they were probably maybe forty, forty-five miles an hour.

[GRAHAM] They would have been stronger closer to the peninsula?

[JOHN] I think so. I think they're strongest when they come over Mike's Peak and get driven down. But then they'll fan out. So the winds would be less on the island, but the waves would have had a nice twenty-mile-plus fetch to build… so I was getting all of a sudden six to eight foot faces— breaking, raggedy, windblown waves. My first reflex is to stay near shore, so if the shit hits the fan you get blown up on shore, but it's pretty cliffy along that area and I was getting wind deflecting off the cliffs, coming back at me and lifting my paddle. Coming at me from the west I can see the wind and brace for the big gusts, but when it's coming from the other side, it was surprising me and giving me some problems. So I finally moved out away from the island and I got about a half mile out and it was easier to paddle out there, but I knew if I went over I probably wouldn't make it to shore because of the cold. I didn't think I'd be able to swim that far. So I was in "don't screw up" kind of mode, just hunker down, head down and paddle. I didn't want to camp on any of the beaches and set up in that wind anyway so I just determined I'm making it back to Este Ton. And as the sun dropped the wind dropped too.

[GRAHAM] The whole day the wind was blowing?

[JOHN] It started about eleven or twelve and then went down about six o'clock. And dropped right off to dead calm again. So I got to Este Ton and spent the night on the sailboat with my friend.

[GRAHAM] Did you know anything of what was happening in town?

[JOHN] No, but when I was on the sailboat, his radio clicks in… it was probably about 7:30 or 8:00 at night… "We have a panga with nine people on it, it hasn't come in yet, anybody spots it, give us a call." A short time after that… radio clicks on again, this is so and so at Camp Roman, I think it was, we've got two people that rented kayaks out of here, haven't shown up yet. Anybody sees them, this is where they go. It's not uncommon for kayakers to end up someplace else, or just to paddle out and not look back and not be able to find where they started from once they get out there a ways.

And that same day Cal Sherman was out alone, among the islands, somewhere in his little boat. His wife Janice recalls:

[JANICE] I heard that a boat had overturned. But nobody would tell me who it was. Antonio [Reséndiz] wouldn't come and talk to me because he for a while thought it was probably Cal… and finally I spoke to someone who told me it was the scientists… And then we saw planes flying… the US Coast Guard they allowed to fly down here for search and rescue. Unfortunately there was no rescue for some of them.

[CAL] I was over on the northwest corner of La Guarda, there's a little protected area, maybe thirty feet in diameter, and I pulled in there among these rocks, set up my tent and hiked for a couple of days, and the third day I got up and there was a heavy wind coming from the west, right across from Bahía Guadalupe, crashing five and six foot waves onto the shore; but I'd already hiked for two days and seen everything I wanted to, so I packed my boat with my tent and all my gear and took off and ran twenty miles south to Humbug Bay and set up camp near an abandoned panga. I had trouble landing because the waves were refracting around the point and going up an old boat launch. I took one wave into the back end before I could pull it up above the surf coming in. That evening when the wind had gone down I called in for a radio check and got hold of a person in LA Bay. He came in loud and clear; he said they had some pretty rough water and wanted to know what it was like on the island. I said it was bad but it's quieting down now and I was going to stay there and do some hiking. I was comfortable; had a nice tent setup. And we signed off. This guy turned it into a big fairy tale that there was a fellow in a little boat stranded on La Guarda and he can't come back and he has no food and water and maybe he's dying. [LAUGHS] I'll quit making radio checks if people are going to distort it like that. They might start a search that I have to pay for…

I didn't know anything about an accident. I could hear planes, sounded like they were circling, but it was too far to see them; I'm way up almost thirty miles away. I didn't think too much of it, just it was kind of strange to hear planes circling all the time. I wondered what they were doing. That's why I was so surprised when I got back, Janice came running down the beach crying and threw her arms around me and said she was so glad to see me… I thought what the heck is this, what's the matter with you? [LAUGHS]

Most tragedies in the region excite limited media comment. Another that reached a wider audience occurred in the fall of 2000. Two men "lost at sea" for 13 days were found weak but alive by local panga fishermen on Guardian Angel Island; a third man was found dead.

The three had set off October 4th in a panga from a "mother ship," the 90-foot *Celia Angelina*, anchored in the protected waters of Puerto Refugio, at the north end of Guardian Angel; up to six pangas would depart from her every fishing day.

Both Joseph Rangel, 50, of Riverside and Lorenzo Madrid, also 50, from Malibu, embarked at San Felipe expecting a great adventure fishing the bountiful Midriff region of the Sea of Cortez. Their panga skipper and guide was Jose Luis Ramos Garcia, who was also the ship's cook.

The day started like so many others, with everyone in T-shirts enjoying the calm conditions. Garcia took the 22-foot panga down the west coast of Guardian Angel Island. Madrid caught pargo and dorado and a 25-pound yellowtail; his companion and longtime fishing buddy Rangel caught snapper and yellowtail.

With the sun sinking about 6 P.M., it was time to head back to the mother ship. However, a strong westerly wind kicked up and caught the fishermen by surprise.

The winds drove them against the shore of the island. As darkness fell, they were in danger of running out of gas, and were compelled to risk a hazardous landing and spend the night ashore.

They lost all their fish when the panga swamped in the surf, but they were able to rescue four 15-ounce bottles of water, three cans of beer and a can of Dr. Pepper. The trio built a small shelter, lit a fire with their lone cigarette lighter and spent an anxious night hoping for an easy morning run towards the mother ship which they assumed was still stationed at Puerto Refugio.

Next day, however, the outboard wouldn't start and they found themselves stuck on the island. Garcia told them help may not be arriving as they were supposed to be fishing on the island's eastern shore. And that is where search efforts would be concentrating.

Hoping to be more visible to passing boats, they tried to launch the panga and head out to sea using improvised oars that Garcia knocked together, but the winds drove them back to shore where the boat was battered on the rocks and they were "all scraped up in the process." They were now in even worse shape, losing most everything and with no means to start a fire, the lighter washing away in the rough landing.

The three men spent several days working their way north along the west coast towards Puerto Refugio, walking and wading, pushing and pulling a small raft they used to get around the many steep cliff-lined sections of the island. Garcia was mostly leading the way, pulling the two fishermen on the raft as he waded through the rocky tide pools. Like many Mexican fishing guides, he was not wearing shoes, so Rangel, who did not swim well, eventually loaned the guide his. "I did find a size-11 shoe and… a size-12 thong on the island, but I wasn't comfortable in those so I went shoeless after a while," Rangel said.

Garcia was the main provider, locating a cave each night and gathering capped soda bottles that had washed ashore with a few mouthfuls of life-giving liquid inside.

"We made slow progress and being in the water during the day kept us cool," Rangel said. "We caught some live crabs and some sea snails and sea cucumbers—I've had better."

Madrid, was a close friend and fishing buddy of Rangel, and had been enjoying "the best fishing trip of his life" in the days before their ordeal. He was considerably overweight and started to weaken after three days on the island. The last moments for Madrid came after another session wading through the shallows and clinging to the raft.

"For some reason, that day he said he wanted to be in the back of the raft so we let him, and when I turned around his face was in the water," Rangel said. "He was breathing water."

Rangel and Garcia helped Madrid out of the water, where he collapsed. Madrid drifted in and out of delirium, Rangel holding his hand and comforting him.

"I knew what was happening," Rangel said, "I looked at the palm of his hands and they were blue. So were his feet, and his eyes were…all glazed… We watched the life just go out of his body." Rangel and Garcia carried on heading north with Madrid's body, trying to keep it on the raft.

Being in a survival situation was not totally unfamiliar to Rangel. He had served with the 101st Airborne in Vietnam as a gunner on a helicopter gunship. He was shot down, and for 11 days was listed as missing in action.

In spite of his survival training and experience, Rangel felt his strength waning too. Fortunately, less than two days later, Rangel and Garcia were discovered by sea cucumber fishermen and brought aboard their panga. The *Celia Angelina* was not far away.

Madrid's body was retrieved and the *Celia Angelina* eventually began the trip back towards San Felipe.

"On that boat ride home," Rangel said, "I didn't want to sleep or even nap because I didn't want to wake up and be in a cave again—and have it all be just a dream."

Garcia, who ran a taco stand in San Felipe, was questioned about his qualifications to be a guide; and claimed to have acted as one on 10 previous occasions. While an investigation into his decisions and his suitability to be a guide was underway, Rangel credited his fellow survivor for his tireless efforts during the ordeal.

Rangel's wife, Margaret, believed she would never see her husband again. "I had already signed up for grief-counseling courses... I had pretty well accepted that he was dead. This is just so unbelievable. I'm just ecstatic." She said.

Asked if he'll ever make another fishing trip out on the Sea of Cortez, Rangel thought about it and said, "Probably not... but don't hold me to that."

The April 2004 issue of *Sea Kayaker* tells of another LA Bay tragedy. As the sun was setting, a couple of experienced kayakers were heading into the cove of Puerto Don Juan just south of Bahía de Los Angeles; they were glad to reach a camping place before dark. On the way in, they ran into a group of five college-age paddlers heading out and back to their campground near the town. When asked why they were leaving so late, they said they wanted to get back for tacos and tequila. The night was moonless, and they had a four or five mile crossing before them.

Not long after they left, the wind picked up and was soon blasting from the west. The young paddlers were heading right into it. The two experienced kayakers knew the group had no chance of making it against such a headwind, and half-expected they would soon return. They didn't.

And next morning, the concerned campground owner came into Puerto Don Juan on a panga reporting that none of the group had made it back. The older experienced kayakers joined in the search. Later the campground owner, searching through binoculars, saw a red kayak overturned in the middle of the bay. Eventually the missing kayaker's body was found floating some distance away, near the south end.

After a harrowing night battling wind and waves, four of the group had struggled ashore in various places around the bay, but the fifth had not been so fortunate. The coroner recorded hypothermia as the cause of death. And that was in the spring, when air temperatures in LA Bay can send you scurrying to the nearest shade. Few in such circumstances can imagine the effects of prolonged exposure to the water at that time of year.

[KAYAKER JOHN] I was back in my camp spot at Daggett's Campground having returned from a lap around La Guarda Island, just resting up, when I saw these guys with rental kayaks from the campground. They were very close to my campsite, loading up their boats a hundred yards from the water, which kind of made me pay attention because I've only done that one time, and I think most people who camp out and kayak maybe make that mistake one time... and realizing that now maybe it's too heavy to carry to the water, you've got to unload it to get it down. Then I watched one guy with a five-gallon jug of water trying to wedge it in the rear hatch of the kayak, and typically you want to split your load to keep your boat balanced, and not put that much weight in either end. So I kind of sauntered over and said, "Looks like you guys are heading out?"

"Yeah, we're heading out for five days."

"Where are you going?"

"We're not sure. We're thinking of heading out to the island over there." He pointed to Coronado [Smith]. I said, "You guys kayak here before?"

"No."

I said, "Do you have maps?"

"No, we're just going to these islands we can see."

I said, "OK. Do you have tide charts?"

"No. Do you think we'll need them?"

Someone asking if they need a tide chart really clued me in because there in the Sea of Cortez, where it's like a friggin river running north and south, and it had been a full moon two nights before, so the tides were really ripping. Although in the winter, they're a little more extreme on new moons. But it's still pretty extreme stuff. At different points it will go faster than they can paddle their kayaks. And it can be a real help or a real hindrance just knowing what it's doing. So I said, "Yes, you should have a tide chart," and I explained that to them. Then I asked them if they were familiar with the winds in the area… as it was a dead calm, gorgeous spell the days that they had been there. I said, "Look, I've just got back from a trip and I'm not going anywhere for at least another week or two. I've got maps. I've got tide charts. I've got photos of the islands. I'll be happy to give them to you guys to go out there with." It was kind of late-ish in the morning already at that point; and as I'm talking they just kind of one by one went back to their loading the kayaks, saying we just want to go do this, it's dead calm, and the islands are right there, we can see them. To one of the guys I pointed to two islands Ventana and Cabeza de Caballo and said, "You see these two islands. How far away do they look?"

"Oh I don't know… a mile or two."

"Yes, this one right here—Ventana—is about two miles; but that one over there is four miles."

"You don't have stuff on the islands, trees and things, for size perspective, so distances can be a lot different than it seems. Relating what you're looking at to a map would really help you guys to know what these distances are. I've got them. I'm happy for you to take them with you." But by that point there was only one guy still packing, and he was still trying to get his five-gallon jug in his boat; the others had sort of wandered off.

Another experienced kayaker standing close by could tell that they weren't taking me seriously so he kind of sauntered over and said, "Guys, you really should pay attention to this stuff because this is dangerous water." And I said, "It's been averaging about one death a year of kayakers out here since I have been coming here."

But they never came over for maps or anything, and next thing I know they're struggling with their loaded kayaks and pushing off shore… and there were actually three of us on the beach, shoulder to shoulder with binoculars watching as they're heading out to the islands; and by the time they left, the north winds were starting to kick up a little bit and they were looking kind of iffy out there in their boats. We watched them all the way out to Ventana Island, till it looked like they were OK.

But the one thing they should have paid attention to was when I tried to tell them about those west winds. And I explained that Mike's Mountain behind the town, which you can see from any place they were going, watch it and if you see the clouds building up and not coming out away from the mountain then you need to pay real close attention, because you may be getting a westy come ripping in from 40 to 90 mph. That's the fastest I've heard, anyways, 90 mph. And if they come ripping down you can be in trouble real fast.

Anyway, on the fourth or fifth day a couple of them suddenly showed up back in camp, kind of laughing and excited about their adventure. And I found out from other people that they had gotten separated, and one by one had made their way back to the camp. They were up at Larry and Raquel's Restaurant at the time waiting for their boats to be brought back... but Reuben [Daggett] radioed in to say he'd picked up a body. The friends were devastated

The owner of the camp had gone looking for the fifth person that hadn't shown up yet; they all figured that he was the strongest paddler and was carrying their wallets and all the important stuff; so Reuben went looking for him and found the kayak floating out in the bay, and then eventually found the guy floating face down in his lifejacket. He had ended up in the water and hypothermia did the rest.

They left just as it was getting dark from a protected bay they were in, which they'd been warned by at least two of us... you really shouldn't paddle after dark, because you can't see the signs of the wind coming; very often they come at night, very suddenly. They were not dressed appropriately, and were wearing T-shirts and jeans, which are not easy to swim in; and once you get out of the water, they had about 45-50 mph winds in their faces, it's just going to chill you even more.

The story I heard was as soon as they got out of the protected area one of them flipped and in the process of getting him back in his boat and pumping the water out, another one flipped and then they got him back in but instead of returning to Puerto Don Juan they kept on paddling. And from where they were, it looks like it's only a couple of miles to town, but it's actually much more. And they were going straight into a wind that's kicking up waves and splashing them at 3 second intervals with cold water... so you add the wind and the chill factor from wearing cotton, and on top of however long it took them to get back in the boat after being in the water... and eventually it's too late, your body can't deal with it any more. It stops working.

Chapter 6

Victoria Seay

What a lonely place to die.

Edward Abbey

Complacency was not going to be my downfall. Already I had a head filled with cautionary, tragic tales, with all their attendant lessons. Then the most poignant story of all came to me just two weeks before beginning my trip to Guardian Angel Island. A friend, Klaus Kommos, emailed me this sobering account of the November 27th death of a Canadian kayaker in the Sea of Cortez near the town of Loreto.

> Three young women kayakers got caught in the first wind storm of this season on a crossing from Carmen to Coronado, near our beach. We all know these ferocious northerlies here that turn the Sea of Cortez into a gigantic wild beast and can come any time in winter. All three flipped and one got immediately separated from the others. The waves were so huge and wild that even the best kayaker wouldn't have had a chance to reenter the boat. The one who got separated had a radio and called for help while floating next to her capsized boat.

> This is a pretty remote area; a functioning, official Mexican rescue system doesn't exist out here. Still, her calls were heard, and, in spite of the horrible conditions, several sail boats and private power boats went out, risking their own lives, to search for them. The wind force was estimated to be at least 40 knots. A big yacht almost rolled, struggling around Punta Cojote. The sea is a white chaos of foam and constantly breaking water masses in such conditions, you couldn't see a kayak 100 yards away. Even with the best intentions, the whole rescue operation was pretty hopeless, it was simply too rough to do much anyway.

> Nevertheless, the two others were found and rescued. After 8 hours, a boat, coming from the east side of Carmen, with no clear knowledge of their location, almost accidentally spotted them.

> The third woman lived for at least 12 hours, floating with her kayak. To get some protection from the waves, continuously breaking over

her, she kept her head inside the upside-down cockpit. It was absolutely heart wrenching to hear her plead for help on the radio all day long, getting weaker and weaker.

The few brave souls did what they could, but a search under such conditions needs planning and skillful coordination. She was in the water by 8 in the morning, her last barely understandable message came past 8 p.m. when it was completely dark. It was a heart breaking moaning and a few delirious words—no one, who heard it here, will ever forget it. It is extraordinary that she lasted that long. They found her the next morning, washed ashore at the south end of Carmen.

We arrived a week after this happened and still felt the powerful vibrations on the beach, not knowing what it was at first.

As more of the story filtered out, I learned that the victim was Victoria Seay, 35, an elite Canadian athlete. Seay was from Ottawa but had relocated to Victoria BC to train with Canada's national triathlon and duathlon teams. She worked as an information technology specialist for IBM Canada.

Her companions Christine Richardson and Pamela Fennell were her lifelong friends. Richardson was an emergency room doctor in a hospital in London, Ontario.

It was a clear, reasonably calm morning as they left Carmen Island and set out on what was expected to be no more than a three hour paddle to Coronado Island, close to the Baja peninsula. Richardson said, "By the time we got partway across and the wind started picking up fast, we couldn't turn back."

Fennell's kayak was bowled over. "We managed to get her up," said Richardson. "We tried to hold on to each other. There wasn't time to tie the kayaks together, we were just holding on with our arms." However, they were unable to stay linked and Seay drifted away.

"When we last saw her, she was still paddling strong," said Richardson. They then lost sight of her in the breaking waves and steep eight-to-ten foot seas.

As the two of them struggled in the water they were unaware that at approximately 8:30 A.M., Seay had sent out a Mayday on channel-16 on her handheld VHF radio.

"I wouldn't be talking to you right now were it not for her," Richardson said.

Cold and exhausted, Richardson and Fennell were rescued about 3:30 or 4 P.M. by the sailboat *Ozark Lady*. Only when they were on board, did they learn that Seay had kept radio contact with searchers throughout the day. After warming up, Christine Richardson and Pamela Fennell came on the radio, and were able to speak to her and give encouragement.

"She was frustrated, trying to give the searchers her location, but she couldn't get any sightings. The waves were so high," Richardson recalled.

As darkness approached, the rescue effort intensified. Lights from houses and cars were switched on to provide points of reference. No one left their radios, many adding their words of encouragement

At 8:15 P.M., when it was completely dark, Seay made her last contact with her friends. She said she was cold. She had been struggling in the water almost 12 hours. By that time some of the searching boats, dangerously low on fuel, were forced to return to Loreto and Puerto Escondido.

The following morning, the sailboat *Sea Venture* found Seay's kayak near the southern point of Isla Carmen.

Then *Ozark Lady* with her two friends still aboard found her body floating in her lifejacket. "I can't speak about when we found her," said Richardson.

The official report recorded drowning as the cause of death, but more accurately she died of hypothermia.

Several of the frustrated rescuers encouraged kayakers and kayak manufacturers to put reflective striping on their kayaks so they can be better seen. In water already white with foam, and with spray flying from 30-40 mph winds, the underside, especially the white underside, of a capsized sea kayak is virtually impossible to spot.

Chapter 7

Equipment

We worked hard, but not beyond reason… We had time
to play and to talk, and even to drink a little beer.
(We took 2160 individuals of two species of beer.)

John Steinbeck—The Log from the Sea of Cortez

Used sit-on-top Cobra Tandem Kayak. Length 12 feet 6 inches. Width 36 inches. Weight 60 pounds. Capacity 600 pounds. Made of superlinear polyethylene. Two hatches—a 10-inch round deck hatch and a large 23 inches by 13 inches rectangular hatch. The two-seater version of the Cobra Fish N' Dive, a popular fishing and snorkeling kayak. Stable but slow. I bought it thinking I'd need room for Pedro. The deck design allows both a forward and a rear seating position, and a more elevated mid-position, sitting on the larger hatch cover.

My kayak

Two large dry bags.
Two paddles.
Two life jackets.
One kayak seat.

Orion flare gun and cartridges; and orange and red burning handheld flares, and smoke flares.

Signaling mirror.

Two-way VHF Marine radio—Uniden Atlantis equipped with a rechargeable NiMH battery, but six Alkaline AA batteries can be used. "Waterproof." Maybe 10-15 miles range. Line of Sight.

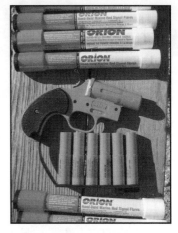

Two kettle stills—comprising two used kettles, two sets of tubes and corks.

Inflatable solar still.

"First Need" water filter and purifier. Would filter out just about any kind of impurities, but not salt.

Digital Camera. Canon A-95, 5MP. Two 1MB memory cards, which hold about 600 high-resolution pictures each.

Magellan GPS unit.

Two small compasses.

Three solar chargers for AA and AAA batteries.

Flare gun and flares

Packs of spare alkaline batteries.

Solar shower bag to heat water.

Solar mosquito repeller.

Insect repellent (Various concentrations of DEET to 100%).

First aid kit with antibiotics and other medications.

Sunscreen (mostly 30, 45 and 50 SPF).

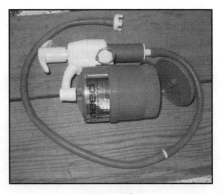

Sunglasses and eyeglasses.

Machete, assorted knives, rock hammer, small shovel.

Three fishing poles, three reels, and a large shoebox of gear and tackle. Small landing net.

Water purifier

Snorkeling gear.

Wetsuit.

Two pair of boots. Two pair tennis shoes. Flip-flops. Water shoes.

Leather leggings (knee to ankle) for snakebite protection.

Two snakebite kits.

Several five and seven gallon water containers—filled.

Walkman FM/AM radio.

Cassette recorder and blank tapes.

Nails, rope, screws, bungees, duct tape, tarps, etc. (To build a shelter)

Large and small backpacks.

Three large zip-up, "virtually indestructible" Eagle Creek bags. Can also function as backpacks.

Lidded plastic storage bins (30 gallons); lidded laundry detergent buckets; assorted lidded plastic bowls. For use as waterproof, and critter proof containers.

Three plastic coolers (two large, one small). Also for use as critter proof containers.

Assorted flashlights. LED headlamp (white/red lights).

Tent, sleeping bag (suitable for temperatures into the thirties), blankets, foam pads, mats, etc.

Lawn chair.

Kitchen gear: saucepans, plates, cutlery, cups and mugs.

Matches and lighters.

Single burner propane stove and six gas bottles.

Bathroom tissue and paper towels.

Library of field guides. Steinbeck's Log from the Sea of Cortez. A few novels.

Binoculars 10x35.

Journal and note paper, pens and pencils, etc.

Roll of large trash bags.

Two months supply of food. Mostly dried and fresh, but several cans for security.

Thirty cans of beer. A 750 ml bottle of vodka. About twelve cans of juice and several liters of diet cola and other soda.

A proponent of the simple life, I guessed that was all I would need to be as happy as a clam for two months.

Chapter 8

Gather Seashells While Ye May

Give me my scallop-shell of quiet,
My staff of faith to walk upon,
My scrip of joy, immortal diet,
My bottle of salvation,
My gown of glory, hope's true gage
And thus I'll take my pilgrimage.

Sir Walter Raleigh c1603 (Written while
awaiting execution for treason against King James I)

It had been a beautiful late December. Any day for a week would have been perfect for the run to the island, but after celebrating New Year 2006 at Villa Bahía, and seeing Bonni and Penny off, I had to wait another week for a day calm enough to attempt the crossing

I put the time to good use downloading satellite images of the island from Google Earth, and garnering information online and from locals familiar with Guardian Angel. They further warned me about the winds, drug runners, rattlesnakes, the tiny biting gnats, and feral cats.

A friend told me of the time he was fishing near the southern end of Guardian Angel when a loaded panga approached and one of the pangueros asked for water. He was given some; the grateful Mexican ripped open a packet of marijuana from his cargo and pressed a generous amount into his surprised hands.

The islands of the Sea of Cortez are protected reserves and one needs a permit to be there. I visited the "Islas del Golfo de California" office in LA Bay, and paid my fees, which at the time were 20 pesos (almost $2) a day. While I was on the island the rate increased to 40 pesos a day.

Antonio Reséndiz helped me with that, then introduced me to Basilio (a much respected panga owner who agreed to take me to the island) and arranged for me to see some people who had lived and worked on Guardian Angel.

I was surprised to discover that in the early 1970s there had been a sizeable scallop fishing camp at the southeast corner of the island, not far from Isla Estanque. The camp was called La Víbora (The Rattlesnake), and at the time there were more people living out there than there were living at LA Bay.

In Spanish, scallops are referred to as *almejas voladoras* (flying clams) after their habit of flapping the two halves of their shell and propelling themselves through the water. Ricketts and Calvin wrote in *Between Pacific Tides:*

> Next to the octopus, the scallop is the "cleverest" of all the mollusks. It is quick to take alarm, being warned of impending danger by a row of shining functional eyes along the mantle fringe, and darts away by clapping the two valves of its shell together.

The targeted species was *Pecten vogdesi*. Even without ever having seen or tasted one, just about everyone on the planet is familiar with scallops of the genus Pecten. The simple outline of the giant scallop, *Pecten maximus*, rendered in eye-catching red and yellow, is one of the greatest brand symbols of the last hundred years—the perhaps supremely appropriate logo of the giant "Shell" corporation.

The corporation grew from The Shell Transport and Trading Company, originally a London based business importing seashells and curios from the Far East. By 1907 the company had drifted into the oil business and had a fleet of tankers, each of them named after a different seashell. The first company logo (1901) was actually a mussel shell, but visually it was about as nondescript as a beach pebble or a pile of bear poo. By 1904 the scallop or "pecten" emblem was adopted.

Most likely the scallop was chosen because a major business partner and later director of The Shell Transport and Trading Company, a man who bore the surname Graham, had a scallop in his family coat of arms, the "St James's (San Diego) Shell." It had been incorporated by the Graham family after one of their ancestors had undertaken the pilgrimage to Santiago de Compostella in Northern Spain.

The origin of the "Shell" red and yellow also has a Spanish connection. In 1915, when Shell was installing gas stations in California, they needed a strong visual symbol to stand out along the highways against the symbols of other oil companies. Because of the state's strong Spanish connections, the red and yellow colors of Spain were chosen and eventually found favor throughout the Shell corporate world.

With Antonio's help, I managed to record the stories of two LA Bay residents who had worked in the scallop camp:

Octaviano Olachea Manrique (Chato) was a young diver then, but he now works as a fishing and hunting guide at Casa Diaz in town. I interviewed him there beneath a pair of borrego horns inside the old dining hall.

Chato was born in La Paz, but grew up in LA Bay. He spent much of, he thinks it was 1972, diving for scallops at La Víbora. Typically he'd work on the island for two months and then have a week back home in Bahía. He estimated that there were about 600 people living in the camp when he was there. They came from Bahía de los Angeles, Santa Rosalía, Mulegé, Guyamas, and from all over the Sea of Cortez for work. A company from Guyamas obtained the permits and bought the scallops from the divers. They paid well. A large boat from Guyamas brought in water, meat, and fresh fruit and vegetables on a regular basis.

Most of his dives lasted about an hour-and-a-half; and normally he'd work about 8-10 fathoms, but sometimes he thought even as deep as 18 fathoms at a particularly productive virgin bank. Chato did one dive a day, and would gather about 100 kilos of scallops, placing them in a net to be hauled periodically to the surface. To protect himself from the cold water he wore a thick wet suit. His air was passed down to him in a tube via a compressor on the boat. He

Octaviano Olachea Manrique (Chato)   *Guadalupe Romero Aguilar*

mentioned that if that pumped air was contaminated with carbon monoxide or even water there could be serious consequences… if the air was too humid the divers were prone to pneumonia. It was dangerous work. One day, Chato remembers, about 17 divers got the bends; they were brought to Casa Diaz conscious, several in severe pain, and were laid out helpless on the floor. Some of them died. After that, he recalls, the company installed a decompression chamber. It was set up on the island and could hold as many as eight people.

I asked him if he ever got sick and if he used any natural remedies. "A bottle of good brandy," he replied.

After work, he would check and service his equipment, shower, play baseball, and socialize. Other people, mostly women and children shucked and packed the scallops. Most everyone got on well he said. There was plenty of everything. Occasionally after rain, there would be water trapped in natural cisterns (*tinajas*) in the canyons above the beach. To supplement their supply they would siphon the water into 55-gallon drums and roll and manhandle them back to camp.

He recalled there seemed to be many rattlesnakes in that part of the island, hence the name of the community.

The villagers had many cats and some dogs… the cats were breeding and began to run wild. Many were left behind when the camp closed for good. The scallops became harder to find and seemed to disappear altogether after some fishermen tried to "trawl" with nets to drag them from the bottom.

He stopped work there when he had his own brush with decompression sickness. After that he moved to fishing and diving at the north end of Guardian Angel Island at El Refugio for grouper, shark, and turtles. Occasionally, he would motor over to La Asamblea on the peninsula, stake out the water hole there and shoot a big horn sheep for himself and his companions.

I also interviewed Guadalupe Romero Aguilar in town near the LA Bay Museum. She was born in San Borja. Her husband—Carmelo Murillo Urbano died three or four years before I spoke to her, and was a native of Loreto.

Guadalupe spent about a year on the island with two young children, in that time returning about three times to LA Bay. She said she worked shucking scallops, placing them in bags, and putting them on ice. Every so often they'd be taken out to a large shrimp boat which anchored offshore, and which offloaded water, ice, bread, fresh fruit, vegetables, meat, and milk—all from Guyamas. The pay was good; the company looked after them. For the people from Bahía, there with their families, it was heavenly. In Bahía, Antero Diaz was the sole supplier of everything at that time, and without a good supply route overland, nothing was very fresh or abundant. And there were so many things they just couldn't get.

Guadalupe thought there were more than 30 or 40 families in the camp on Angel de la Guarda and numerous unattached persons, mostly divers, drawn from all around the region—LA Bay, Santa Rosalía, Guyamas, and Sinaloa.

She confirmed there were more people on the island than at LA Bay at the time.

The community had several small stores, a clinic, and later the hyperbaric chamber. Her recollection was many divers got the bends—on one occasion seven of them were brought to Casa Diaz where maybe three or four died; the others were taken to Santa Rosalía where they recovered.

The people from different towns generally lived in different camps; they kept dogs, cats, even pigs. She also believed that many cats were left behind when the camp was abandoned.

Francisco Uribe Osorio probably knows more about the scallop camp and fishery on the island than any man living. He has worked as a diver for the National Institute of Fisheries (*Instituto Nacional de la Pesca*), commonly known as "PESCA," since 1969, and has traveled all of Baja California in that capacity. He has been involved in investigations of many marine species on both coasts including abalone, octopus, urchin, and scallops.

I spoke to him in Ensenada in the summer of 2007. Francisco recalled that in 1972, he was sent to Guardian Angel Island along with two biologists because a Sonoran seafood company, *Productos Pescero Mexicanos*, wanted a permit to harvest scallops from around the island. The company's request was forwarded from Sonora to the PESCA office in Ensenada, which holds jurisdiction over the island. Before any permits are issued, PESCA is obliged to estimate the size of the population of the target species, and then to stipulate a percentage to be harvested based on what is thought sustainable.

It took Francisco and his companions two days to drive from Ensenada to Bahía de los Angeles on what was at the time mostly dirt road south of San Quintín. (It would be almost two more years before Highway 1 was officially opened.) They brought their own 20 foot panga and spent three weeks on Guardian Angel Island.

Their first camp was near La Víbora. They moved north to sample the scallop beds up the "Sonora side" of the island to El Refugio, and then back down the west coast to Este Ton. They determined that the best prospective gathering sites were on the sandier eastern shores of Guardian Angel Island where there were in places as many as 60 to 80 scallops per square meter. Francisco recalls that the scallops could be readily detected by the horseshoe-like impressions they made in the sand, as if a herd of horses had galloped along the sea bottom. The rounded side of the shell was situated down and the flat "door" was on top.

PESCA granted a permit for the company to take about 25% of the *Pecten vogdesi* population. There was to be a maximum of forty pangas holding 3 people (only one was to be a diver). Each panga could collect no more than 50 kilos of scallop meat per day. The shucked scallops would be sent to Sonora, to a processing plant in Guaymas, and the profits were to be split 50:50 between *Productos Pescero Mexicanos*, a private company, and the Mexican government. Another private company, *Conheladoras de Guaymas*, was involved in the exportation and distribution of the product, selling it mostly to businesses in the United States for shipping worldwide.

And so the operation began. A single large camp was established on a relatively low lying, long stretch of beach in the southeast corner of the island. Divers and would-be divers came from all over, drawn by high wages and relatively good conditions.

However, in April 1973, the *Centro Regional de Investigaciones Pesqueras* (CRIP), the branch of PESCA where Francisco worked, began to receive reports of a disturbing number of diving accidents and decompression injuries on Guardian Angel Island. Francisco Uribe was asked to return to LA Bay to evaluate the situation and suggest a remedy. When he arrived at Bahía de los Angeles the seriousness of the situation was brought home to him when he saw six to eight divers lined up dead on the porch of Papa Diaz's.

Francisco discovered that as more people had arrived, the divers who had initially been working at about 30 feet were trying their luck at 40-50 feet, and in some cases 90 to 100 feet to exploit the richer scallop beds. But at whatever depth, they were typically staying down too long.

Francisco was trained in Fort Lauderdale, Florida as a commercial deep sea diver. He has salvaged ships, done underwater construction, and worked under oil rigs. By comparison, Francisco said most Baja divers at the time had little or no training and an extremely limited understanding of problems like the bends (*ruemas*).

During a dive, pressure increases linearly at a rate of 1 atmosphere for every 33 feet of descent in sea water (34 feet in fresh water). So, thirty three feet down, the pressure is twice that at the surface; at 100 feet it is roughly four times as much. The increased pressure causes more gases to dissolve in the blood stream and tissues, and more so the longer the diver stays at that depth. Upon ascent, the decreased pressure allows the dissolved gases, especially nitrogen which is inert and can't be metabolized, to bubble out in the body. If the diver returns to the surface slowly, any bubbles that form are generally small enough to be easily transported through the bloodstream and out through the lungs. However, if the diver makes too rapid an ascent, bubbles form (like the sudden decrease in pressure when a soda bottle is opened) that are large enough to block blood vessels and cause tissue damage from oxygen starvation. If restricted to muscles, joints and limbs, the damage may result in just the experiencing of tingling and perhaps severe pain. But if the heart, lungs and central nervous system are impacted, confusion, paralysis, coma and death can result.

Treatment involves either taking the diver back down to a depth where the nitrogen bubbles can shrink and dissolve, or recompression inside a hyperbaric chamber followed by a more controlled "ascent" to normal pressures. Simultaneous administration of oxygen helps eliminate the nitrogen and provides a more immediate benefit to oxygen-deprived tissues.

Tables calculate how much decompression is necessary, if any, depending on the depth and duration of a dive. At 30 feet, for example, decompression measures are essential after 5 hours; at 60 feet 1 hour; at 130 feet 13 minutes. In other words exceeding those times at those depths requires the ascending diver to return to normal pressures slowly through carefully calculated staged ascents.

The high wages meant hundreds of people were being recruited, some from as far away as Ensenada and La Paz—and according to Francisco, "a lot of people without knowledge got in the water." The hired divers themselves were "training" the others. Those with some experience and equipment, as they earned more money, bought more equipment and got friends and family working. To compound the problem, as well as the scant training, there were no depth gauges, no dive masters, and hardly even any reliable watches. After the deaths that Francisco witnessed, "about 100 divers quit and an equal number of support personnel quit and went back to their homes." But always more came. Francisco did not believe there was ever any

The dive chamber arrives at LA Bay.   © *Francisco Uribe*

government compensation for the deaths or disabilities. "Maybe the company paid for the burials."

On the island there had been no other choice for dive accident victims except to decompress themselves underwater. And obviously that was out of the question if the diver was unconscious or seriously disoriented. "They would 'hang' the diver at 60 feet depth, maybe overnight." That prospect was made even less attractive because the camp was producing piles of shells and fish guts, which were at the time being dumped into the sea close by. Sharks were being attracted to the area, so divers facing hard hours underwater could really fear a shark attack, especially at night.

Given the situation, Francisco realized that if the scallop harvest was to continue the divers needed trained medical personnel on the island, someone with some diving knowledge, and above all access to a decompression chamber. The first chamber in Baja had been installed in 1963 in El Rosario. It was working until a few years ago.

Back in Ensenada, Francisco contacted "Diving Unlimited" in San Diego. He was given an estimate for purchasing a two-place, double lock (i.e. with an air lock compartment) chamber. The scallop company accepted the price and made the purchase.

Arrangements were made for importing the chamber and a compressor motor into Mexico and transporting them via flatbed truck to Bahía de los Angeles. Francisco took care of all that. The trip was accomplished in two days.

Diving Unlimited also flew an ex-Navy officer from San Diego to LA Bay to assist with the chamber set-up, initial operation, and also to issue a report, which is partially reprinted below:

31 July 1973

Flew out of Montgomery Field San Diego at 10.00 A.M.

1020   Landed in Tijuana for customs immigration inspection.

1348   Landed in Bahía de los Angeles.

The chamber had not yet arrived. No one seemed to know of it. The diving accidents were common knowledge, but the exact number of deaths was not known.

2015   The chamber arrived, appeared to be in good condition, but was very dusty. Francisco Uribe had escorted the chamber from Ensenada.

1 August 1973

1015   A fishing boat (100 tons) arrived with a 40 ton capacity barge in tow. Had to wait until about 1500 for high tide to offload the chamber and compressor from the truck to the barge. A very interesting operation—was done with human power and one block and tackle.

Learned of the diving operation…and a total of 32 diving accidents (including the deaths). Discussed diving in general until about 10 PM, at which time the electricity is secured.

2 August

The barge had grounded during the night and ripped a hole in the bow. I was told that this did not effect [sic] the sea worthiness of the barge, but that the reason we had not departed for the island was because they were waiting for a generating unit that would supply electricity on the island.

The island [has] about 1500 persons who all worked for the scallop company (including the children)… Spent the entire day with Uribe… reviewing diving tables, treatment tables, and general operation of the chamber.

3 August

1500   Left Bay of Los Angeles on the fishing boat with the barge in tow.

2300   Arrived on the island. Talked with some divers, the nurse and the construction men about where the chamber was to be located.

Slept on a fold out cot in the fish factory.

4 August

Discussed decompression treatment with the nurse. Met the two most serious cases of bends, whom they…wanted me to treat in the chamber. Due to the length of time that had passed and the seriousness of the cases I refused to treat them recommending that they obtain the advice of a qualified diving medical for treatment.

1600   Offloaded chamber and compressor (again by human power). 1900 set up and had the chamber in commission.

Francisco remembers that the boat was a shrimp boat sent over by the scallop company. The chamber was loaded in front of Antero Diaz's place.

The barge was little more than a wooden raft that had been partially constructed right there in LA Bay. And they chose a good day to make the potentially treacherous crossing. It had taken just a few months from initial reports of decompression sickness to carriage of the chamber to the island. On the island the chamber was set up on a cement pad beneath the shade of a corrugated roof.

Even though Francisco had gone over there with a broken ankle, his leg in a plaster cast, the ex-Naval officer soon left the island, telling Francisco that he could see he had nothing more to teach him. It was up to Francisco and the nurse to begin using the chamber in earnest.

Francisco needed to paint the interior of the chamber with special low toxicity paint, but before he could do that, two divers were brought in who needed emergency treatment; the next day there were four more. Then ten divers, in groups, were decompressed in one day!

Upon his arrival, Francisco had found more than 200 pangas were operating, rather than the forty maximum agreed with the company, as the fishermen were getting "good prices on the scallops."

They had begun their collecting in front of the camp, and then fanned out to cover all of the eastern side of Guardian Angel Island from La Víbora to Refugio. Some boats, caught in the surf, fierce currents and confused seas at the southern tip of the island, had overturned spilling the divers and all their equipment into the sea.

When Francisco reported the permit violations there was, as so often is the case in remote parts of Mexico, no provision for enforcement. Besides, no one was willing to intervene, perhaps because the government was working too closely with the private company and had a half-stake in the profits.

After about ten days a Mexican Navy vessel came over with some doctors to check out the divers, but they have a policy of not getting involved in such permit or environmental issues. They regarded it as their duty to concern themselves only if the government or the nation was in danger. One good thing—the ship's company put on a huge barbecue and fiesta that stopped all diving for a day, so Francisco could finally get the inside of the chamber painted.

Aside from the emergency cases brought to the chamber, there was at first a lot of apprehension and suspicion in the community about the strange object that looked a bit like a large propane tank on skis. Francisco urged one diver who felt dizzy and was in pain to get in the chamber, but he refused to enter and insisted on seeing a doctor in Guaymas. He was taken aboard the supply boat heading to the mainland. A couple of hours later the ship came back; the patient was now unconscious. He was placed in the chamber and recompressed to the equivalent of 165 feet, and stayed inside for 72 hours; he eventually recovered.

A more routine hyperbaric treatment compressed afflicted divers to typically 100 feet depth and then decompressed them for 6, 10, or 12 hours. There was no means to administer oxygen beyond normal air concentration.

Inside the chamber, one diver wanted to play his violin and another one his guitar to help while away the hours, so these instruments were passed in. As the people in the camp familiarized themselves with the new chamber, they got to trust it more because they could see obviously sick divers recovering. On one occasion it was used to treat six occupants at once despite being only a two-person chamber. It was saving lives for sure, though Francisco worried that less care may have been taken by some divers on account of the chamber's presence.

There was a Red Cross nurse at the fish camp who was the only medically oriented person stationed there when Francisco arrived. She had some pharmacy supplies, and Francisco further trained her on the chamber operation knowing that he would soon have to leave and return to his work and family in Ensenada. Francisco also asked Productos Pescero Mexicanos for a doctor to be on hand when he departed, but they sent only an intern from Guaymas—a barely qualified MD who still needed practical training. It turned out the intern had "no interest in the chamber" and did not want to learn how to operate it. He did not even seem to want to treat sick children or deal with injuries, such as cuts and bruises. Apparently, he was obligated to be there as pay back for his training, but resented every minute of it.

The head of the Guaymas company came over to Guardian Angel Island and said they'd send another doctor. However, a week later, he returned and told Francisco, "You can resign the government and we'll pay you!" Francisco told him,"No, it doesn't work like that." But his time was extended on Guardian Angel.

Francisco had felt like he was being looked to as the doctor, even over the nurse. So drawing on his dive training, Boy Scout background, and brief experience at age 17 in Mexico City working on Red Cross ambulances, he did what he could. Francisco recalls that 3 children were born on the island while he was there, and he even delivered one.

Francisco turned 24 on the island and ended up staying in the camp two to three months, not just a few weeks as originally planned. The plaster cast on his foot was getting rather "ripe" given the heat and humidity. He ended up having to cut it off himself, and that left him with a problem—he'd only brought one shoe. The nurse helped him out by giving him her slippers, which he wore despite them being pink and provoking a lot of teasing. He was also given an old pair of fisherman's boots that were cut off to serve as shoes.

Footwear could be pretty important in La Víbora. There was a 1950's Chevy pickup truck in the camp that was being used to transport the clam shells to inland dumps since "sharks changed the politics of waste management." Francisco went along one day and the driver warned Francisco not to step down from the vehicle when they arrived. As they were shoveling out the clams they counted 5 rattlesnakes around the 20-meter high mountain of shells. No doubt the snakes, which were already numerous in that area, were finding rich rodent and reptile pickings around the dump.

Of course the rotting heap created a huge fly problem, and lack of decent outhouses compounded the issue.

Francisco recalled a period of several days that the island's population was out of good drinking water—the supply ship's water tanks had been corrupted with salt water. They could use melted ice or the brackish water, but he only drank from cans of fruit juice. The flies were so thick Francisco recalls having to stuff a piece of tissue into the can's opening between sips.

When the operation began, the scallop beds seemed inexhaustible, but within five years the scallops had virtually disappeared from the area. The entire dive operation eventually halted at about 25 fathoms; very few divers were willing to work in those depths. Francisco confirmed that the company made a final effort to claim scallops by sending shrimp boats to drag the bottom with modified nets. It did not work and only hastened the destruction of the beds.

Productos Pescero Mexicanos itself "disappeared about fifteen years ago." The Guardian Angel Island chamber was taken away on a boat to Guaymas where it spent 12 or 18 years in storage. Then commercial abalone divers with the *Cooperativa La Purisima* on Baja's Pacific coast at Punta Eugenia went to Guaymas to buy a shrimp boat. They saw the chamber in storage and decided to buy it. Although there was already a decompression chamber at Bahía Tortuga less than 20 miles away, the rough dirt road made it a long trip for an injured diver. As the abalone fishery diminished and the road improved to Bahía Tortuga, the chamber fell out of use and was eventually sold. Francisco has no knowledge of what happened to it after that.

I was grateful for Roger and Jean's warmth and hospitality, yet in spite of their kind reassurance I was worried about imposing on them as day after day I was forced to wait. I was anxious to get on with it and be on the island dealing with the challenges of being alone. Sometimes the tensions before a battle are worse than those of the battle itself; and sometimes, of course, they are laughably insignificant compared to the horrible reality.

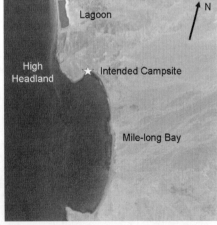

First Campsite   (Image by Google Earth)

Downloading satellite images, e-mailing friends and setting up a story on my website, I had time to do it all, so maybe the delay was for the best.

I decided to camp in a bay south of Punta Los Machos, the closest point to the peninsula, because at that point the island was lower and narrower and easier to cross than at Este Ton. And at the sheltered north end of that mile-long bay there was supposedly the remains of a beach "shack" to offer ready shade if I were lucky, building materials if not.

I found time to type out the following update for my website and also for the Baja Nomad message board:

> January 4th 2006: I am waiting to begin my next adventure—spending maybe two months exploring Isla Angel de la Guarda. I am at Villa Bahía just north of Bahía de los Angeles, on the road to La Gringa. I can see the big island beckoning twenty miles across the channel. A panga will be coming to ferry me out there tomorrow or whenever the wind permits. I have decided to set up a base camp in a cove at Humbug Bay (locally Los Machos) in the middle of the island, along the west coast. After three or four weeks exploring from there I will probably move to different locations around the island either in my blue Cobra Tandem kayak or more likely by panga….Say hi if you motor by. I have a marine VHF handheld radio. If I'm not up in the mountains and anyone is close by I'll monitor channels 16, 68 and 72. Graham

As time permitted, I checked the feedback on the Nomad message board. I had practically no experience of posting anything on line. I usually preferred to venture off into the wilds, do my own thing, isolate myself from what others might think, and concentrate on the pure experience. However, a friend made it easy for me and offered to post any updates that I could get to him. That would still involve first getting a note to Bonni, and then she would type it and email it to him. It seemed sensible to put as many folks in the picture as possible, and I confess to hoping that someone might read about me and want to come out to visit. Besides, it was always nice to hear a few words of encouragement from those "few fans" Bonni mentioned.

Graham is biting off a big task——that island is HUGE, and complicated. As long as his food and water holds out, he should have a fantastic time, but not sure how much of the island he can cover in 2 months—it sure will make for some interesting reading. Hope he takes 3 pair of boots. What a guy!!!!! Part of me is jealous—another part of me is apprehensive for his safety—!!

WOW!!! This is GREAT news!… This should make for a great book. I have always looked at that island and wanted to explore it… I once talked to a guy in [LA Bay] who had seen some extraordinary tracks on the island. They were very BIG and apparently unidentifiable.
GOOD LUCK GRAHAM!

I talked with Graham New Years Eve at Villa Bahía... He has done so many adventures, yet he was still totally excited about his new one. The bay on the island is well protected, stark, but beautiful.

I'm sure he'll have boats bringing him supplies as needed. I look forward to a good read of the essence of the island and some of its secrets revealed.

Oh man, I just got back from a week of kayaking in Bahía de LA and points north. I've always wanted to visit Isla de la Guarda, what a great treat this must be! I'm jealous!

Ran into Graham having some fish tacos at Chinas on the 2nd of Jan. He was getting ready for the trip to La Guardia... Seemed primed for the adventure. Good luck.

I thanked everyone for their interest and positive comments, then added another update:

Friday January 6, 2006. A couple of days of north wind have prevented me from going out to Guardian Angel Island. Today is much calmer inside the bay; but out beyond the near islands there are some good waves running. I have total confidence in [Basilio] my panguero; he predicted as much yesterday, but thinks Saturday will be the day for the crossing. He came to that conclusion by taking into account the moon and the clouds, and studying the bay from an elevated point on the road to town. I reached the same verdict by looking at the weather forecast on the internet.

I have an abundance of time, and Baja has taught me patience. I am putting the days to good use talking to some of the knowledgeable folks here at the bay and doing a little research on line. I also took a couple of long hikes, including out to the rugged shore north of La Gringa, to break in my boots and recover a little lost fitness.

As a reminder about the power of the wind, I watched an inflatable left on the beach suddenly tumble down to the water and go somersaulting out towards the islands! My campsite on the island will need to be sheltered from the north and west winds; and I'll need shade. Even with hat and sunscreen, being fair of face my skin will not appreciate being exposed to two months of wind and sun.

Unless there are compelling reasons to locate elsewhere (such as finding a camp with loaded pangas) I'll be at the narrowest part of the island, I guess about 15 miles or so north of Este Ton, a wonderful little sheltered cove on the west side. Este Ton was my initial first choice location but a glance at a satellite map suggests it is so rugged there that getting along the coast on foot or into the mountains will be a challenge. Humbug Bay is the best place to hike right across the island; I shouldn't have to climb much over 1000 feet.

Luckily at this time of year I shouldn't see too many rattlesnakes, but all accounts suggests that they are there in numbers and one species is huge compared to its peninsula cousin, probably because of the absence of predators and its proclivity for dining on large endemic chuckwallas.

I'm taking 45 or 50 gallons of fluids, mostly water! And I'll have enough food for two months, especially as I'll be fishing most every day...Well, will send next report as I'm able.   Graham.

Chapter 9

Out There

While I nodded, nearly napping, suddenly there came a tapping,
As of someone gently rapping, rapping at my chamber door.

Edgar Allan Poe—The Raven

Saturday, January 7th 2006—I woke at 5:20 A.M. and pulled the covers from my cozy bed knowing that I may not be slipping back into one for two months. Indeed, I may not be seeing the inside of a building for that long.

It was still dark in the room, so before stepping onto the cold tile floor I shone my flashlight to check for scorpions. January was about the last month I'd expect to see one, but it was something I did instinctively in scorpion-infested areas. Just one of my many desert routines, and one of the many reasons why Bonni has me down as a wimp.

I moved the curtain aside. By the first hint of light it looked mostly cloudy, at least in the direction of Guardian Angel Island. Roosters were crowing and I thought I heard the distant hum of a panga. Basilio, already? A wave of adrenalin shocked me into wakefulness. I hadn't even taken a shower or moved all my gear to the beach. I listened carefully. The panga didn't seem to be coming closer or heading away. I concluded the engine noise was only my imagination, but the little burst of anxiety gave me energy and focus.

Every day for a week I had gone through the motions of showering, packing away my personal effects and getting ready, but not really believing I'd be going anywhere. This morning I had no doubt—the panga would be coming for me.

Warmly dressed in sweat pants, hooded sweat shirt, and floppy hat, I stepped outside, quietly closed the door, and walked lightly across the gravel to get a better view of the bay and the sky. I didn't want to wake anybody, but I suspected Roger and Jean would soon be up offering coffee and saying goodbye.

There was little wind and the water was still. If the internet forecast proved accurate the sea would drop to flat calm and stay that way right into the evening. There wouldn't be the usual windless dawn followed by an increasingly blustery day kicking up uncomfortable waves. I would have time to select a campsite. As I moved my bags and gear out of my room and down towards the beach I heard the roosters crowing again, then the far off droning of real pangas ripping out of the bay. There they were, boats and wakes inseparable—black silhouettes against the first rich golden light of day.

A panga was heading north, right along the shore towards Villa Bahía. I hurried back to my room and grabbed the two heaviest bags.

Sure enough it was Basilio and his affable-looking assistant Mango, eager and on time. After a few morning pleasantries, I handed the boxes and bags already on the beach for them to load, then I led them to my room to pick up the rest. Most of it was wrapped in large black trash bags to keep it clean and dry on the boat. Roger and Jean were over to lend a hand, and offer coffee and encouragement.

While Basilio and Mango carried the kayak to the boat, I grabbed all my perishables from the fridge and packed them into my three coolers.

The no-nonsense fishermen looked amused and shocked at how much I was bringing. Being a "fast and light" man myself I knew how it looked to them—the crazy gringo taking everything but the kitchen sink. And I had several large plastic bowls that could serve in that capacity. Unsure I'd see anyone out there, I preferred to have more rather than less.

Anyway, most of the stuff was used, bought cheap at garage sales and swap meets. I had three fishing reels; they might have cost about $2 each. I don't think I had an item of clothing that cost more than a dollar. I did have

Kayak and gear all aboard

an old sleeping bag, bought new for maybe $25, and I'd splashed out $40 on a new, on-sale, Coleman tent. Two or three of my five or seven gallon water containers were new—about $7 each. I had two used kettles, two experienced backpacks, two pair of inexpensive lightly used boots, two paddles, two lifejackets… at least two of everything important. I'd probably give much of it away before the end of the trip, or maybe trade it on the island. Expense never kept me from a Baja expedition.

I helped stow it all aboard. Knowing how fast the panga could fly "throttle wide open," I fussed and secured important bags and items. I was surprised Basilio thought there was no need to tie down the 60-pound kayak. He seemed confident that as the boat rose on plane, the flared bow would push the air aside creating a largely still zone low to the panga. I politely deferred to his judgment… intending to keep a hand on it anyway.

The sun was rising—the golden silhouettes were giving way to the peaches and cream, rosés, and darker wine colors of the later dawn. After hugs and

Adios Villa Bahía

saying a jolly goodbye to Roger and Jean and all their wonderful, hopelessly pampered Villa Bahía dogs, I stepped into the boat as Basilio and Mango pushed the bow off the beach and jumped aboard to push us further out with oars. Looking at the big, happy water-loving dogs retreating to the dunes, I thought about Pedro and was sad to think that he wouldn't be there with me. Times had changed.

The outboard came to life and roared us on our way. I looked back at the spreading wake that showed so well from where we had come. And I hoped, that in a couple of months, I'd be admiring a similar wake with the rugged cliffs and mountains of the island as the final backdrop.

I was sitting just forward of the middle of the boat, closer to Mango standing at the bow than Basilio at the back. Basilio, cigarette dangling from his lips, seemed lost in his own thoughts… perhaps still a little amused by all the gear I was bringing. I tended to limit my conversations to Mango; and tiring of shouting above the outboard, I soon gave up on that. We rounded La Gringa, and headed towards the north end of Isla Coronado, or Smith Island as most American residents prefer to call it; then we powered confidently through a narrow channel between Coronado and a small island at the tip— Coronadito. We woke up a sleeping sea lion. It was hard to see any submerged rocks looking into the morning sun; I trusted Basilio knew the passage well.

Then beyond the steep, almost unscaleable volcanic slopes of Smith Island, all that stood before us across the wide and treacherous Canal de las Ballenas [appropriately pronounced Bye-Anus] was the 42-mile length of Guardian Angel. The water was blue and already nearly flat calm. If it remained so we should be across in an easy forty minutes.

My handheld marine VHF radio was readily accessible, but Basilio's boat had a larger mounted version connected to a tall, sturdy white antenna.

Other pangas were out and more would dare these waters on such a day. If our single Evinrude 60 hp motor failed us we'd soon be rescued.

It was all very different in the spring of 1765. In one of the final acts of Jesuit exploration in the Sea of Cortez, missionary Wenceslaus Linck, the founder of the San Borja mission, visited Angel de la Guarda after some Indians who lived along the peninsula shore reported seeing large fires on the island. Linck boldly sailed out from LA Bay in a small launch with a party of soldiers and Indians to investigate and perhaps make contact with any inhabitants. An account of that expedition was shortly afterwards described by fellow Jesuit, Miguel del Barco.

> On reaching the island they went ashore and reconnoitered a considerable part of it. They not only did not come across any natives, but did not detect as much as a footprint of man or animal; no, they did not find even a water hole. And from what they could see of the rest of the island, they logically concluded that it was all uninhabited. This reasonable deduction they could not prove to the point of evidence through personal exploration of the entire island for lack of water; and consequently, they were forced to take to their boat and return to the bay from which they had set out.

Archaeological evidence suggests that the island had been occasionally visited if never "permanently" inhabited, perhaps by Seri tribesmen from Tiburón and San Esteban. Linck's return was not easy.

> …as they neared [LA Bay] they encountered such a violent wind that they could make no headway, but were forced to return to the island they had just left… On later attempting to reach the bay… the land wind had become so fierce that… the launch was hurled on its side to the consternation of all, as they realized how close they were to being drowned…

After much tacking in mid-channel they were once more driven back to Guardian Angel Island:

> Inasmuch as they were close to the southern tip of the island they had no difficulty in rounding it and finding shelter; but because fierce thirst gave them no respite, they were forced to put all their trust in divine providence and try their fortune by embarking again. They decided not to attempt to make for the bay itself, but rather to reach a point somewhat to the south of it, in the hope that the wind would prove favorable for their landing there.

When, at last, they reached the peninsula they were able to get water from the Indians, and eventually find suitable winds to take them back to LA Bay.

Out in mid-channel with thousands of feet of cold water beneath us, and beneath that, thousands of feet of sediments, and beneath that, the great magma-spewing plate boundary of the East Pacific Rise, our panga suddenly, shockingly, made a fast, banking U-turn. I could only imagine that we were about to collide with a whale. A true Ballenas moment! Thinking the panga was sure to be "hurled on its side" I instinctively grabbed the kayak and held on tight—both to secure it, and use it to steady myself… and maybe to climb aboard if we foundered and sunk. Swiveling around as we regained an even keel, I watched a hatless Basilio reaching over the side for his baseball cap which had blown off. He threw the soggy thing into the well of the boat.

With the sun rising warmly on our faces we zoomed towards the looming

shoreline of Guardian Angel, towards the relatively low point of the island just north of center, towards the supposed remains of the old dilapidated shack. Even a few sticks could offer a basis for shade and shelter; I hoped the reports were true.

Basilio throws his sodden cap into the center of the panga.

As we approached, I scanned the coast and took several digital pictures so I could refer to them later to aid with my coastal explorations. Most of it looked steep and rocky, with awesome cliffs. I studied the few broad washes and narrow openings where cactus-filled valleys ran through the cliffs to the shore. There was no sign of habitation; no boats in the area. It was an intimidating coast even on a flat calm day; I could hardly imagine how wild and hostile it must look in a norther. Or worse still, in a full onshore blasting westy.

I pointed out what I thought was the headland that I had chosen as my shelter, the place where the shack was supposed to be… the headland marking the north end of the bay I knew so well from the satellite images, the mile-long bay within a bay, with the lagoon just to the north of that.

It was 8 A.M. as we pulled into its protection. From that distance, the exposed head was various shades of tan with a few gray/white outcroppings, and towards the sea it fell almost sheer into the water. The lighter rock was most likely volcanic ash—hundreds, thousands of feet of it. Did it all fall in a day, a week, a month through some great Mount St. Helens or Pompeii-like catastrophic eruption, or was it the accumulation of eons… a protracted white-out world of choking ash? Was the Sea of Cortez already there to receive these outpourings?

On the curving tops and sides of the headland, the lighter rock was almost entirely covered by reddish-brown basalt or rhyolite—a vast flow of lava which capped and sealed and stained the ash and debris layers beneath.

Much of the cooled lava had weathered into large roundish boulders. Many hung precariously at the top of the cliffs, looking ready to shatter the skulls of anyone foolish enough to walk or wade beneath. One more act of violence attributable to the subducted East Pacific Rise, and the time when magma poured through the thinning crust to break out onto the surface.

Sheltering headland—north end of the bay.

I looked in vain for the "casa." But there seemed to be something white at the most sheltered spot in the northeast corner. Drawing closer, I could see it was an abandoned panga. [I guessed that this must have been where Cal camped at the time of the Gary Polis accident] It looked to have been run aground then pulled up onto a flat sandy shelf above the rocky intertidal zone.

The shore around the bay seemed to be comprised largely of rounded pebbles and rocks, interspersed with an amazing amount of trash, mostly the bright yellows and reds and blues and greens of various plastic containers. It was stacked above the high tide lines and over the stony palisades into the desert and across the barren salt flats. The scene was very different from that described by Steinbeck in 1940. "We are so used to finding on the beaches evidence of man that it is strange and lonely and frightening to find no single thing that man has touched or used."

The steep red rocky slope immediately above the derelict panga sported a number of large multi-armed cardóns—the great green-columned symbol of the Baja desert, the biggest cactus in the world. The tallest specimen on the headland was the closest to the old panga, a ten or twelve-armed monster, which had a wooden pole dangling high up, like a thrown spear, from one of its foot thick columns. Why, I wondered, would someone be throwing a spear at the top of the cactus?

Some of the steeper slopes of the headland revealed the same grayish bedrock so dramatically revealed in the cliffs. There I guessed the rounded volcanic boulders had already tumbled down.

Basilio eased his panga towards the abandoned boat, towards a partly cleared channel on the shore where the larger rocks had been thrown aside to make a crude slipway.

The sea was so calm, the tide was so high, and the shore sufficiently steep we nosed the panga to the rocks and I was easily able to step out and keep

Decision Time

First Campsite

my shoes dry. Mango and Basilio invited me to look around and decide if this is where I wanted to be. There was considerable trash all about the panga—old cans and bottles, batteries, broken glass, rope and fishing gear—and more inside. The typical refuse of a remote fishing camp. It would take hours to clean it up.

Thirty yards away there was more or less unsullied desert, and clear blue sea. The shore was rocky, but much of the area out to the headland was a flat shelf with soft sandy places for the tent. And there was an abundance of rounded rocks and stones to weigh things down and for other uses. And above the highest high tide line the entire shore was marked by a narrow zone of "drift pumice," a volcanic rock so light it had at one time floated ashore. A hunk the size of a cantaloupe weighed little more than a tennis ball. At the highest tides or with the wildest surf it easily washes off the beach and floats away.

Not finding the remains of the shack was a disappointment. The panga had limited possibilities for shade; but I could maybe rig up a tarp shelter beside it; and it could also serve as a seat and a table. And there was the framework for an old doorless kitchen cabinet with the "table" top intact. There were also two wooden, cable drums and a rusting but potentially useful 55-galloon metal barrel filled with rocks and ashes and burned cans—it had clearly served as a stove and fireplace.

I walked out to the point on the flat sandy shelf. On my right, rhyolite slopes rose to the top of the headland. And at the base of the rocky rise, I took note of some rock walls… definitely manmade. Not ancient, I thought; they probably sheltered fishermen in more recent years.

After a quick peek around the sheer cliffs, several miles north to the dark, brooding headland of Punta Los Machos, I walked back to the patient pangueros, then round into the bay, to a cleaner sandier area that might be better for kayak launching, at least at high tide. On such a breathless, flat calm day, it looked idyllic.

With all my water and supplies I had to get it right. Moving, even just a quarter mile, would turn into a very time consuming chore.

I returned to question Basilio. He said if I camped too far around the bay I'd lose the protection of the headland. I knew he was right. The blasting wind, blowing sand, and the surf and agitation would soon get old.

Mango pointed out if I camped next to the old panga I could anchor and float my kayak off the rocks, where the bottom was sandy. With my mind distracted by the decision before me, I blurted out, "*Si, tengo mucho ropa.*" Yes, I have a lot of clothes! Conversation ended at that point. However, I had severe doubts about hazarding the 60-pound kayak to the sudden squalls and fierce currents of the Canal de las Ballenas. I would need wooden "rollers"—logs and planks—to launch and pull it up from the sea. Fortunately, there was tons of driftwood on the beaches.

I stood, surveyed and thought for a few minutes. The location wasn't perfect. Smith Island dominated to the southwest, and looked like it might block line of sight radio reception to LA Bay.

I could head south to Este Ton or north towards Los Machos or look for something less "obvious," a place where no one would spot my camp when I was away. Time for decision. My entire island experience, the amount of pain, possibly even my life, would be largely determined by the words I was about to speak… Mango and Basilio were waiting, probably eager to go fishing now I'd led them to such largely unspoiled waters.

No more than two miles inland, a long sloping plane and a series of cactus studded washes led to some low mountains. I picked out a couple of potential routes over. The relative ease with which I could cross the island swayed my decision.

The three of us unloaded the kayak, the water, and all my gear and piled it on the stones next to the old panga. I gave Basilio the $100 due and $20 "for some beer." I added, "I'm not sure when I'll want to leave, probably in 2 months. I'll get a message out if I need a ride."

Pumping them for any final tips or information, they believed like many others that there were no coyotes on the island, and I would probably not see any rattlesnakes till the nights warmed a little. But they warned me to watch my food with the cuervos, which I understood to mean crows, but as I found out later, I was being warned about ravens. We shook hands. They said they'd be fishing three or four kilometers offshore for a while. I told them I'd try to raise them on the radio later that morning.

No man could have wished for a more gentle transition to maroonment. They were still in sight, silently drifting, yet I was delighted to be alone. It was so quiet, and the sounds I heard were evocative, calming, and peaceful. The wind was southerly and light. The day was perfect. Smith Island and Punta Remedios looked deceptively close.

The channel between Los Machos and Punta Remedios was the shortest distance between island and peninsula—just nine miles across. On such a day, I was tempted to believe it would be an easy paddle back to the peninsula. All thoughts of the great chasm beneath the waters, of sudden nortés and hypothermia, of orcas, whales, squid, and sharks were forgotten. Anyway, I had no need to paddle back. I knew enough about the murderous channel to be grateful not to have to go anywhere.

With my foot, I scraped clean a sandy area on the seaward side of the panga, positioned a small tarp, then erected my new tent on top of it, door facing the peninsula and the open bay. After placing a heavy bag of clothes,

a box of books, and other weighty items inside the tent, I placed the rest of my equipment and supplies either on top of the kayak, the old panga, or in the shade of its bow.

Barring some unforeseen disaster, I had everything I could think of to be safe and comfortable for weeks. I was congratulating myself about what a great idea this was, what an absolute privilege to be on my own desert island. And looking back at Plan A, what a joy not to be dealing with traffic and rudeness and endless days pounding the pavement. Though I did have a twinge of regret about not having Penny or Pedro with me.

Ravens on a cardón checking out my camp.

While tidying up some of the trash, I saw what looked like a mouse dropping inside the boat. Just one. One single solitary tiny shriveled mouse turd, perhaps the final statement of the Guardian Angel Island deer mouse, but in my mind it quickly took on the dimensions of a panga load of steaming elephant crap. Flayed into action, I started to put all my food away either in the tent or more securely in the lidded plastic containers.

Hearing a sudden loud whooshing above me, I looked up to see two "cuervos" settling on the branches of the large "speared" cardón and, like vultures waiting out a dying man, looking down at me and my gaping boxes of food from 100 feet away. Loud, surreal, rattling caws echoed off the headland. If they had lips, I'm sure they would have been licking them.

A buzzing bee brought my attention back down from the cactus to the panga. The bee seemed particularly interested in one of my five-gallon plastic water containers. Hmmmm. I was watchful and wary. I'd had issues with thirsty Baja bees in the canyons above Santa Rosalía, in the dunes near Guerrero Negro, and up in the high San Pedro Mártir mountains. The persistent bee droned around like a B-24 and in my mind rapidly assumed the proportions of a hornet, a hummingbird, a pterodactyl! When it disappeared, I half expected it to return with the whole hive; my trip coming to a sorry end beneath a buzzing, stinging cloud of killer bees.

With the ravens still watching my every move, I threw tarps over most of my water containers, coolers, and plastic bins of food, then weighed them down with rocks. I was appreciative that it was calm and mostly cloudy.

Basilio and Mango were still there drifting and fishing about two miles offshore. On my first attempt to raise them there was no reply, but ten minutes later I called again—"Basilio, Basilio, this is Graham, do you copy? Hola! Hola! Basilio Basilio."

Basilio answered loud and clear. I assured him all was well. After successfully making radio contact I started on a little exploratory hike around the bay.

Before I'd gone 150 yards the ravens descended to my campsite, and one landed on the only five-gallon plastic water container I'd left uncovered and started tapping it with his beak. I hurried back shouting and gesticulating. They rose noisily and flew over me and landed down the beach. As I walked towards them, they kept moving ahead around the bay. Finally, they flew into a valley and were gone.

Moments later a trio of gulls dropped into my camp. I started to return, then reasoned that I can't be a prisoner. Sure they'll poke around. But I have to leave. I have plenty of stuff. I have gear and supplies in duplicate, in triplicate. Any losses will be tolerable, part of being in action. I could have stayed at home and lost nothing.

The fascinating driftwood, shells, bones, containers and other artifacts washed up on shore helped put the birds and the bees from my mind. I started to imagine all kinds of uses for it. Apart from a few small black

High tide beneath the headland   *Low tide*

beetles, the ground was largely bug sterile, not even an ant. I brought back some fishing floats and a couple of six-foot long sticks to help me erect a clothes line and a shade tarp.

About 1:30 P.M. while I was setting up my fishing poles and enjoying a snacky lunch, I heard Basilio start his motor and head full speed back to town. I was able to talk to him again half way across the channel, and finally near Smith Island. When he was out of sight I could still hear his motor in the afternoon stillness, maybe as far as ten miles away. Then, gulls and normal seashore sounds apart, all was delicious silence.

It was past 3 P.M. The sea was barely troubled by wave or ripple. The sun was poking through the thinning clouds. Its rays fell warm and rich on the hills and ridges where scattered forests of sturdy cardón cacti seemed to have suddenly appeared tall, green, and glorious in the late afternoon light. I opened the first of my 30 cans of beer and sank in a large foldup canvas chair. Two black and white American oystercatchers were contentedly poking beneath the rocks with their long orange bills. It was so relaxing listening to their jolly squeaking, the distant squawking of the California gulls, the sound of birds running on the water taking off, and the occasional shrill haunting cry of an osprey. I could hardly stop myself from dozing off.

The day had been a real gift. And I'd have a fair size moon at night, another gift, to help me get my bearings and get organized.

About 4 P.M. I walked to the base of the headland and made my way under the cliffs. Thanks to an extraordinary fiery sky, the rounded surf-kissed stones were a thousand shades of shiny red, interspersed of course with all the salady greens of the seashore. As well as the precarious volcanic boulders on the cliff tops, car and house-sized slabs of the lighter underlying rock had sheared off and crashed down like huge chunks from a spawning glacier. At high tide the water looked like it would be waist deep, but now there was a walkable path between (and occasionally on top of) some of the rocks.

The first sunset in camp

Keeping one eye on the state of the cliffs above me, I playfully stalked and took pictures of several colorful Sally lightfoot crabs backed into rock crevices. Working my way a hundred yards around the cliffs, I flushed out a bird of prey, which flew out above me with the bloodied carcass of what looked like a duck or a grebe. A pair of limp webbed feet dangled beneath. My best guess—the raptor was a peregrine falcon.

Hundreds of black and white duck-like birds rafted a mile out to sea; too far off to identify with my 10x35 binoculars. But I suspected they were grebes or mergansers.

I returned to my campsite for a simple dinner of peanut butter sandwiches and fruit, followed by another beer and a shot of vodka. I was in a celebratory mood. The evening was special, and there'd be no accounting—that could wait till mañana.

The evening was warm, bug free, and peaceful. The hills in mid-island glowed redder by the minute. Every direction held the promise for exciting exploration and discovery. Almost involuntarily, and with a great sense of satisfaction, I found myself loudly saying, "I'm here." And in the stunning silence, that proclamation seemed to carry to the south end of the bay, and up to the backbone of the island, and half way across to the peninsula. It was a strange sensation, like a a whisper magnified and booming through a sacred cathedral.

By 5:30 the sun was down and apart from a blood red line over the sierra of the peninsula, the scene was more illuminated by a waxing half moon. The tide was rising. I began preparing for the night, pulling the kayak above an obvious last high tide line, up amongst the pumice and dried seaweed.

Then it was easy to sink into my chair again and just listen and meditate: the gentle rush of the surf, the odd glug from the rocks, the fluttering of a bat, the moon struggling to break through clouds that glowed silvery and clean… there was no light from the peninsula, no artificial citrus shades of city shine. Apart from satellites and very occasional planes, there was no light from anything human; just solitude, peace… and maybe the promise of a little light from above.

By 8 P.M. the night sky began clearing, and a breeze kicked in, but it wasn't as yet cool enough to drive me into the tent. I picked out the odd star and then Orion and the other constellations poking through the parting clouds. I could walk around and see fairly well by moonlight. For the sake of my anonymity, I was glad I didn't need a flashlight or a fire. I moved the chair to the tent door area where I could better see or hear anything entering the bay.

By 9:30 P.M. I was ready to retire. I looked at all the lidded plastic containers and coolers and water jugs left beside or on top of the panga, and satisfied myself that everything was secure and sufficiently weighed down for the conditions. I unzipped the tent, slid fully dressed into my sleeping bag and allowed my walkman radio to drag me back to the "real" world for an hour or so. The frantic pace of the presenter's delivery, packing in news, weather, traffic, sports scores and all the messages from their sponsors with all the even more rushed "fine print" suddenly sounded grotesque and insane. Bit by bit I removed my clothes as I warmed, then finally naked and cozy and deep down contented, I drifted into easy slumber.

"It's about quarter to one in the morning," I recorded. "I just woke up. There's a pretty stiff breeze blowing from more of a southerly direction… and, of course, that's the direction that I'm most exposed to. If it blows any harder I'll have to start putting stuff away."

As I listened to the sounds of the wind and the surf I started to hear something emerging vague and uncertain, on the edge of reality; tantalizingly poking through, like the moon through the clouds or the back of a dolphin through the waves.

What is it? Voices? Whales blowing? Distant memories? Imagination?

It sounded like a panga motor "out there," coming and going, but it never came any closer; it was just there, impinging on my consciousness, like the panga I heard that morning in the hotel room.

It's definitely an illusion, I thought, a "ghost panga." "Ha, ha, ha. Ghost Panga!" Just the ringing in my old ears. My friends were right when they told me I was sitting too near the speakers at that "Who, Live at Leeds" concert back in 1970. Just another issue for this aging gracefully—in other words falling apart—fifty-five year old.

After a few more minutes of listening, I sank deeper into my sleeping bag and fell instantly asleep.

I was soon awake again.

Chapter 10

Martial Plan

…and from the tents
The armourers, accomplishing the knights,
With busy hammers closing rivets up,
Give dreadful note of preparation.

William Shakespeare — Henry V

There was a real panga, real close, motoring towards my campsite.

I sat up in shock and fumbled for my tape recorder, managing to whisper a few dry words before a powerful light struck the tent and then swept over my kayak, my coolers and all my supplies. Shit! Drug runners. Who else is out here at one-thirty in the morning? I was frantically getting dressed.

It was hard to tell how many were in the boat. All I could see as I furtively peeked through a corner of the tent bug screen was the blinding light. Snatches of subdued Spanish rising above the deep throbbing idle of the motor confirmed that I was outnumbered. My heart was pounding along with the pistons.

They hovered just off the ramp. In between pulling my socks on, I feebly waved my little flashlight to let them know someone was in the tent. I had no intention of stepping out till I had to.

It could be a panga loaded with drugs, an armed or paranoid crew ready to kill to protect it. This might have been the rendezvous point. Witnesses would not be welcome, and could be easily disposed of, weighted body sinking thousands of feet to the frigid depths... twenty-eight cans of beer and most of a bottle of vodka to ease their night's work.

There was no attempt to hail me, no words spoken, at least none intended for my ears. After a minute that seemed like an hour, they switched off their light, opened up the throttle and crept forward like they were about to gun the motor and run the boat up beside my tent. I momentarily recalled the image of a huge, charging killer whale seizing its unsuspecting sea lion prey from right off the beach and dragging it back to shake it into oblivion.

Then I realized they were turning and heading out of the bay; they weren't coming ashore. I poked my head through the tent door and watched the unlit boat disappear around the point to the north. I thought I could make out three figures. Soon there was only silence and the hissing, buzzing ambiguity of the night.

Maybe they were checking there was no one else camped nearby? Maybe they were going to find their companions? Maybe they'll be back? I laced up my tennis shoes and scurried along the sandy shelf to the point to make sure no one had landed. A hundred scenarios raced through my brain.

Back at the tent I recorded:

> That's done a lot for my paranoia… it might have been the army checking for drug runners… but they didn't check me out, they just left… Now, somebody knows I'm here… I was thinking this morning how the guys fishing are probably not making as much money as they could, and what a great thing tourism is; ecotourism can bring more money and opportunities to these pangueros, but I can see that even beyond tourism there's another way to make a quick buck.

> Well it's 2 o'clock. I was sitting outside my sleeping bag, sitting up watching, but I'm now back inside, it's turned pretty cool… with the sky clearing. I'm going to try to get some sleep. Well, this has certainly changed the character of this trip.

I was glad to wake up and see the early light through the tent. I listened to the sound of the gentle surf and the near continuous white noise of the gulls. Even though I was fully dressed with a wooly watch cap on my head, I felt chilled and in no great hurry to emerge from my sleeping bag.

Outside, on a calm and still Sunday morning, the first thing to greet me was an inquisitive young sea lion swimming right off the rocks. Then I saw a group of mergansers flying by with a gull following. The kayak was only a yard above the latest high tide line! That was a surprise because the tides were not yet close to the extremes. I realized that I'd have to pull it much higher, and eventually I might have to move the tent too.

By 7:30 A.M. it felt hot. I exchanged my jacket, sweater and sweatpants for shorts, T-shirt and sunscreen. There was so much to do, but first I wanted to get the kayak into the water and take a quick look up and down the coast. The tide had fallen sufficiently for me to see the entirety of the partially cleared boat channel, which ran right down to sand.

Someone had thrown the rocks aside leaving a smoother, more stony and gravelly path to the sea, but the waves had rolled a few of them back. I heaved them out to the echoing of rounded basalt, rhyolite, and andesite boulders thudding against other rocks.

I quickly warmed to the task. If I hadn't been so keen on taking advantage of such a fine kayaking morning I might have been pleasantly distracted by seeing all the crabs, shells, sea stars, sponges, anemones, flat worms and sea cucumbers under the rocks. Life was teeming in that intertidal zone. I was looking forward to returning to it when I had accomplished the more urgent tasks.

Driftwood boat ramp   *Challenging coastline*

I began laying some wooden planks and logs I'd collected from the driftwood; placing them like crude railroad ties into the cleared channel. Voila! A boat ramp.

Wearing water shoes and life jacket, carrying paddle in hand, I guided the kayak down the "ladder," and watched with satisfaction as it floated easily in foot-deep water. Even there in the shallows, the water felt too cool for my feet. I threw the lower five or six rungs up above where I thought the tide might reach in my absence, then swung my butt onto the kayak.

I had a choice of three seat positions. I started on the slightly elevated large hatch-cover in the center, but soon moved the clip-on seat to the rear position, which gave me extra room to arrange all my gear in front of me, but raised the front end a bit.

The wide kayak moved effortlessly through the calm water. It never ceases to amaze me how easy it is to kayak. Like walking, it's something you do at your own pace—a good workout or almost effortless. Assuming you don't get into trouble, it's your choice. And at its best, kayaking is an activity that glides you easily into a world of contemplation.

The water was amazingly clear, probably more so than along the peninsula shore. Fifteen or twenty feet below, a plate-sized stingray shuffled before me as if raising the alarm or clearing a path. I paddled inside the bay three-quarters of a mile or more down towards the southern point.

Any initial doubt about being in drowningly deep water or in the domain of the denizens of the deep was allayed by a wonderful sensation of freedom. With the kayak I could go almost anywhere around the island. Even if I couldn't land, I could enter any cave or approach any wall of rock.

The wind and waves were just beginning to stir as I found the courage to move out from the bay and peer beyond the bird-covered southern headland—and what a dramatic coastline stretched before me, seemingly all deeply creased valleys and steeply slanting cliffs. I wondered how much of it was walkable in case I had to ditch the kayak and make my way back to camp on foot. It looked challenging, to say the least. Several times I thought I heard a panga, but none appeared.

As I dropped off the waves, cold water slapped the raised bow of the kayak and shot up through the drain holes in the front, like little whale spouts. Seeing larger waves in the channel, I decided not to risk going too far beyond the point as I had no survival "gear" stowed aboard.

Back inside "my" bay, I headed north towards camp, then paddled far enough around the sheltering headland to see what was on the other side. There was a steep pebble beach that looked to have lots of driftwood on top. And the cliffs seemed generally lower in that direction. There was no one in sight; and as far as I could tell, there was no person, camp, or boat all the way around Humbug Bay to Punta Los Machos. For now, at least, I seemed to be alone.

Thinking about the consequences of being overtaken by a norté and unable to get back to camp, I realized that it would generally be safer heading north to kayak along that apparently more walkable coast where I could enjoy having the winter's prevailing winds at my back as I tired after a hard paddle.

Back in camp, looking at the launch ramp, I confided to my tape recorder:

> This is a very good spot for a panga launch, but maybe if I did this again I'd look for somewhere pangas are not going to pull in… for a better kayak spot where I'm not likely to have a visitor in the night.

Three young sea lions were cavorting in the bay. One was nudging a slowly retreating cormorant. I couldn't understand the bird's lack of urgency; its blindness to the obvious. Concerned that plaything was about to become preything, I willed the cormorant to "wise up." After directing a few ineffective pecks at the nose of the too solicitous sea lion, the lazy or foolish bird eventually winged it out of there before encountering the sharp crushing teeth beneath that soft, whiskered snout.

As the day wore on, my paranoia rose up like a threatened snake. I wondered if the rendezvous was set for tonight. Were the pangueros just an advance party? Supposing they planned to return and earn a little bonus with all my gear and whatever was in those coolers? If I'm robbed and attacked, all my gear, food, drink taken, and if I'm fortunately left alive, what can I do?

One reason I was so disturbed by the panga visit was my lack of preparedness. I was flat out defenseless, caught with my pants down, all my eggs in one basket.

All my money, even though less than $300, was in one spot, my wallet—so I put some with my passport and hid the rest in a glasses case and my daypack. I planned taking nearly all of it and everything light of value and importance with me when away from camp.

Not wanting to end up like the guys missing from the *Celia Angelina*, or the two men in the "I Shouldn't be Alive" film, who were stranded on the island with no water, I placed a gallon of drinking water and a two-liter bottle of diet cola in the shade under the large speared cardón—enough to keep me alive for a couple of days in an emergency. Worried that might be a bit too close to camp, I walked a third-of-a-mile around the bay and hid another gallon in a bush.

Then I carefully filled a large "virtually bombproof" Eagle Creek bag with some essentials: shoes, knife, jacket, hat, socks, sweats, sunscreen, compass, spare radio/tape recorder, bug repellent, snakebite kit, matches, flashlight, batteries, flares, a kettle still, and a few cans of food and drink. It weighed about 50 pounds. I recalled that was almost as much as I had with me when I walked around the coast of Baja for two years between 1983 and 1985. It seemed plenty heavy at the time, and it seemed even heavier now as I struggled with it 400 yards up a canyon, walking on rocks and boulders to leave no footprints. After wrapping it in a tarp, I eased the bag into a little rocky gully, buried it under some rocks, then piled on whatever brush I could find. You'd have to be standing right next to it to see it. I never mentioned the location on tape or in my journal.

On the way down, I found what I thought was a conquistador's helmet. It was the curled, much-weathered shell of a small sea turtle. A distant line of pelicans working their way north looked like a squadron of fighters ready to drop to the attack. In my mind everything now had martial connotations. Every action I took was by way of preparation. Every move and thought subsumed under the headings of—Diligence, Escape, Attack, Defense. The acronym—D.E.A.D.—seemed very appropriate. No longer Mr. feet-up, laid-back, love your neighbor liberal, I whipped myself into a dizzying new whirled view. Evil doers abounded. I was ready to engage in any preemptive strike, endorse any extraordinary rendition, back any enhanced interrogation techniques, to take out any potential aggressor before they could even think of attacking me.

I tried several times to make radio contact with LA Bay, but either I couldn't be heard or I couldn't hear them trying to respond. That was a little sobering, imagining myself in desperate need calling for help and hearing only silence. Possibly I was out of range, but I suspected it confirmed what I initially feared—the rising volcanic peak of Smith Island was blocking the signal. Perhaps if I climbed I'd get better reception?

Exhausted after such a day, I was hoping for a calm, peaceful night. With no time or energy to prepare a meal from my abundance of fresh meat and vegetables, I opened one of my "emergency" cans of chili and cut up an apple with my sharpest sheath knife—and how I relished the feel of the knife in my hand.

I was about to sit down and dine by 95% moonlight and 5% fading light of day when I heard a motor. That elicited a nervous laugh. I didn't know if it was a plane or a panga… but it was real and it was close. I was relieved to hear the sound fading fast, too fast to be a boat.

I went down to the sea to clean my plate and wash out the can, scrubbing it with gravel to remove as much of the oily aroma as I could. Then I put the can in the rusty 55-gallon barrel for disposal later.

As night fell, the temperature dropped sharply, and by 7 P.M. I was anxious to get inside the tent and my sleeping bag. Before doing so, I pulled the kayak up another yard and tied it to the panga. Then I pulled my three-foot-long machete from its sheath and felt its balance and studied its blade. Yep, the blade in profile looked exactly like a panga. I slipped it unsheathed under the tent with just a couple of inches of the handle showing. It would be so easy to whip it out of "nowhere" as I was leaving the tent or being forced to get inside.

Hoping that it wasn't a really bad idea, I slipped a shotgun-like cartridge into the orange plastic flare gun and left it in a corner of the tent. I then carefully placed the rest of my arsenal—knife, and rock hammer—on each side of my pillow.

I think my tactic will be to repeat what happened before. I won't show myself, and won't turn on a light till they're practically here. And then I'll let them know I'm around. I won't actually come out unless they come ashore so they won't know how many people are in the tent.

I mentally pre-ran a worst case scenario—murderous drug runners land and wish to take my beer and torture me to death. Using the element of surprise, I'll run screaming from the tent, shoot a flare into the first assailant's face and follow that up with the rock hammer to split his or her smoking skull. And then after stripping the villain of his gun, I'd deal with his hopefully dumbfounded *compañeros* by shooting them all. Failing that I'd run after them shouting and screaming, and raining down blows, smashing skulls, blood spouting, brains turning to mushy strawberry margaritas.

Finally, knowing this would not look good in a Mexican Court of Law, where the judge and the chief of police might possibly be card carrying cartel members, I ran through some options for getting rid of the bodies and the evidence, and promptly disappearing myself.

I wouldn't be sleeping naked for a while. Indeed, I feared I may not be sleeping at all if I kept dreaming up such graphic scenarios.

Inside the warmth of my sleeping bag I listened to my Walkman radio, to political talk shows from north of the border, where most everyone in George W. Bush's America seemed to be just as unhappy and paranoid as I was. I kept one side of the headphones on and the other off so I could hear what was going on in the bay.

About 8 o'clock, I sat up sharply and pressed the record button: "Well, there's another panga. I can hear it out there." I stepped outside and strained to hear above my pounding heart. I guessed it was way out in the channel. It didn't come any closer and just faded into the night.

I reassured myself that if I were awake I would absolutely know if a power boat came anywhere near my bay. It would be unmistakable. I could hear it half way to the Bay of LA, like I heard Basilio's panga almost to Smith Island.

I'd have time to prepare my defenses, or grab the daypack with all my valuables and hoof it up onto the headland or under the cliffs to hide.

Twenty minutes later I was back inside my sleeping bag to warm up. Then after dozing off for an hour or so, I woke to hear that the surf had picked up but the tent wasn't moving; there was no wind. That bothered me, so I went out again. The thermometer was showing just 50 °F. My end of the bay was flat calm in the moonlight; all the action was at the south end. It was amazingly loud, and was probably just the remnant of the day's wind-whipped waves crashing into the descending silence. Just to be safe, I checked the securing rope and raised the kayak another few inches, pulling it on to my thickest planks.

I woke again after midnight and recorded:

> A sea lion is thrashing around outside. I can hear it breathing; I can obviously hear myself breathing; and it's almost like the Sea of Cortez is breathing too… you can hear this whistling inhalation and exhalation like it's alive!

After a while, I stepped outside to pee and watch the moon setting to the north of Smith Island, close to Punta Remedios, much further north than I would have thought. It suggested that my mental picture of the north-south axis was a little off. That bothered me too. I looked for the North Star to confirm my directions, and figured that Smith Island and LA Bay were almost due south from my camp. I expected them to be more south-west.

I then slept till about three in the morning, when I woke warm and sweaty in my sleeping bag. It's not unusual for me to wake with a dry mouth, especially after a beer or two, but this time it felt doubly dry. I could hear a panga… at least I could hear it until the sound of my pounding heart got in on the act. Napoleon was right when he observed that "three in the morning" courage was a rare thing.

Without the moon it was dark. Maybe the druggies are active after moonset? Maybe they are coming for me? I was fumbling around trying to find my flashlight. I couldn't see anything in the tent. This must be it in this corner. Oh crap, that's the plastic flare gun. I nearly had a 1,100 °F magnesium fireball wedged in an eye socket to help me see better.

Settling for just finding my eyeglasses and my binoculars I scrambled outside and searched the channel and around the bay. Oh shit! The panga! It's out there. The whine of the motor. The rapid thump of the hull crashing off the waves. Or is that just the wind and the ringing in my ears, and the audible booming of my heart? I was desperately trying to convince myself there was nothing there except a billion stars and a sea lion or two. God it was dark. How I missed that moon. I wished my heart wouldn't race so.

Real panga! Ghost panga! I didn't like the choice. Whatever it was, I couldn't escape its adrenaline pumping hold. It gave me an insight into conscience and insanity. It was easy to understand how people go crazy if haunted by a disturbing voice or a sound. What you fear you'll hear.

Chapter 11

The Depths

Sometimes I envy the Mexicans their laid-back happy-go-lucky approach to life. I am inclined to deal with danger head on, to perhaps exaggerate it, but always to be mindful and energized sufficiently by my anxiety to take preventative steps... Such focus and preparedness has served me well most of the time, but it comes at a cost. Focused fears can readily rise way out of proportion to any objective calculation of risk. And one can foolishly burden oneself with so much anxiety it's hardly worth the bother of living.

Graham Mackintosh—Nearer My Dog to Thee

Alone in the Baja wilderness dealing with the stresses and fears of my situation, I have a tendency to temporarily sink into a dark pit of depression. So I wasn't altogether surprised when that happened to me soon after I arrived on Isla Angel de la Guarda.

I tried to turn it around by recalling all my riches. Unfortunately, I couldn't deny I was rich in reasons to be depressed. I was surrounded by rattlesnakes, scorpions, orcas, squid, crazy tides, killer currents, vandalizing crows; and at any moment I could be blown away by a norté or a westy... I was getting old and my brain was getting spongy and full of holes, and probably weighed less than an equivalent sized piece of pumice. The ringing in my ears was louder than a Beethoven symphony. I felt like a total failure as a writer—I'd never really made any money with my books. I was missing Penny and Pedro, my dogs, and my wife of course. George W. Bush was our president. And these were all reasons enough to throw oneself into the deepest darkest depths of the Canal de las Ballenas.

But what was really pushing my buttons was pangxiety, the relentless haunting drone of the ghost pangas.

I thought some kayak fishing would cheer me up. One advantage of fishing from a kayak was... every time I hooked the bottom, which I did often, I managed to paddle around and extricate the lure. Sadly, the bottom was the only thing I hooked.

I've never had the least problem catching fish in the Sea of Cortez. But dragging a lure, drifting with the current for more than two hours, I was skunked. Even in the shallows when the fish seemed to be wriggling by in maggot numbers, I couldn't catch a thing... perhaps because, after a while, I

barely had the strength to raise and lower my lure from the bottom and make it the least bit exciting. I darn nearly dropped the rod and fell off the kayak in my lethargy. I reeled in the line. I'm sure the fish were laughing at me.

I carried on kayaking—slowly paddling, looking down in the water,

Dolphins didn't think much of my bow wave

feeling like I was going nowhere. Actually, because of the current, I was going backwards, so I stuck one end of the paddle in the sea and gradually turned the kayak around. Now with the current behind me, I was perhaps going about three knots; there was a hint of a bow wave and looking back I could almost make out a wake.

But then I got a shock… two fins, two rather large fins were fast approaching from behind. I somehow found the energy to quicken my pace slightly. My head was locked to the front; my eyes cast down; I didn't want to look back again. However, I couldn't miss those fins slowly pulling alongside me. It was a pair of spouting, depressingly jolly dolphins attempting to ride the bow wave. Both dolphins looked at me accusingly. "Pathetic," they seemed to be saying as they pulled ahead and went in search of something more lively.

I headed back thinking I need a beer to cheer me up. Then I got really depressed recalling that I'd only brought 30 cans to the island; 30 cans for sixty days! That's half a can a day. What the hell was I thinking? Half a can a day was barely enough to fill one of the holes in my head.

As I stepped ashore in the shallows and dragged the kayak towards the ramp, two dozen noisy, hungry gulls, landed in the sea and lined up on the boulders. In their eyes returning fishermen meant food. When they realized there were no heads, tails, or stinky entrails, the gulls were aghast, hurling abuse, mocking laughter, and a few white bombs in my direction. One splattered, smack on top of the blue deck.

Standing beside the panga, I was too weary to walk up to the cactus and sit in its shade. I just did the minimum to lather myself in sunscreen, reach into my cooler, grab a cold beer and sink into my chair. My back was stiff, my knees hurt after sitting so long on the kayak… my soul ached. Things did not

Waiting for joy and ecstasies

look good as I disposed of four times my daily beer allowance in one session.

Slowly filling all the spongy parts of my brain with beer bubbles, I just sat there and mouthed the Beach Boys song, Sloop John B; I kept repeating the line, "this is the worst trip I've ever been on."

But I wondered if it truly was. Didn't all my solo journeys have these initial moments of depression and doubt? Didn't I just have to get through them, like passing through a deep dark narrow canyon, to the sunny uplands beyond?

The thought brought a ray of sunshine, a hint of comforts to come. Tomorrow if I wasn't at the bottom of the Canal de las Ballenas with a rock tied to my neck, I might be feeling better. I might even be feeling better if I were down in the deepest, darkest trench, thousands of feet below where the faintest glimmer of light reached.

I told myself with conviction that I would get through it. Yes, my sadness was the necessary gateway to joy and ecstasies to come. Yes, yes, yes, surely I had turned the corner.

I went for a hike. The sunny uplands spread before me. Punching the air in triumph, I shouted, "I'm the king of the island... the king of the world!"

Heading for sunny uplands.

Chapter 12

A New Dawn

I destroy my enemy by making him my friend.

Abraham Lincoln

I knew that the night would be the real challenge, the real test of whether I would still feel like punching the air in triumph or punching myself on the nose for not seeing how black things really were.

Around 2 A.M. the moon was sinking. The wind was dying. I stepped outside the tent. As I listened to the now familiar sound of a bird running on still water and slowly getting airborne, I thought how beautiful can be the voices of nature, the gentle rush of the sea, the whistle of the wind through the cactus, the sweetness of the desert's dawn chorus, and above all, the surprising almost tangible silence. What delicious ambiguity, what channels we open.

Not so with the roar of an outboard motor, the buzz of a chainsaw, the cacophony of much modern music, the strident certainties of so many fanatics for so many contradictory causes, and the depressing level of discord that passes for debate these days. How sad for those forced to live and love such lives... separated from the humbling and healing whispers of the wilderness.

Never more awake and focused, I stood awhile and gazed at the explosion of stars cast across the taut black sheet of night; there were almost too many to pick out the constellations. I mused how during the bright day we rarely think of those countless glorious suns and galaxies stretched out "above." As far as heaven goes, the darker it is, the better we see.

And I knew so well from my previous "forty days and nights" alone in the desert, it was precisely in that dark, solitary state of tension and fear that spirituality resides... at least for me. For there I seem to shed a few layers of my thick-skinned soul and open a more sensitive heart to other sounds, other voices in the wind and the surf. Seek and you shall find. I waited patiently. I sought diligently... even in my dreams.

> It's 3 o'clock. I just woke up and...it's funny I was dreaming I was back in Paddington where I was born; I left there at five, and I was kind of getting a guided tour around the building and I was asking my parents, "Was this where I slept? Was this where the kitchen

window was?" It was too vague for me to remember properly... I was saying to my parents that we all could have led richer lives and I just felt so close to my parents, and I was saying I wish I could have been a better son... I remember when I mailed all my father and mother's Second World War letters playing postman in London. Oh man, what a disaster that was; they never recovered most of them. I thought about all the ways I could have made their lives better and I was asking how could they ever forgive me... and I know that they can. It was really beautiful, like a certainty we will all be together in love and forgiveness... and that was really a wonderful dream.

I woke at six, glad to see the dawn. I could have done with more sleep, but I felt uplifted by the dream, and happy to have gotten that night behind me. Two nights in a row without visitors; a tremendous burden had fallen from my shoulders.

Frolicking sea lions

While walking out to the point, mug of coffee in hand, I heard a loud splash. A pair of sea lions were frolicking just off the rocks. They both stuck their head out and looked at me. I politely waved back. Then the pair got real boisterous and eventually headed out of the bay, leaping from the sea like they were chasing something, or being chased, or maybe just having fun.

While preparing breakfast, I opened a large red plastic container. It was full of fruit and vegetables. I noticed the bags on top were wet and the underside of the lid was half covered with streaking water droplets.

I noticed the same thing when I lifted the lid of my smaller cooler which also contained fruit and vegetables. I assumed at first that sea water had got inside. But I ran my tongue through the streaks of water; it was fresh. The sealed containers were acting like stills—the elevated humidity within was condensing on the lid and the other surfaces. My mind began exploring the

Fresh water droplets condense on underside of plastic lid

possibilities. In a crisis, I could lick or sponge up the water. I could even put a little seawater inside the containers and "harvest" the condensation.

I set out a pair of small solar chargers to trickle charge my AA and AAA batteries. I had chosen my camera, GPS, cassette recorder, radios, and flashlights, because they used AA batteries. And I had a small headlight and pen light that used AAAs. I was hoping I would be almost self-sufficient in rechargeable batteries, but I did have a good supply of alkaline batteries just in case.

It was time to place some "survival" gear inside the kayak. I stowed a two-piece extra paddle then filled a waterproof "dry bag" with shoes and socks, flashlight, flares, Swiss army knife, sunscreen, bug repellent, first aid items, scissors, duct tape, batteries, clothes, waterproof leggings, and a little dried food, and pushed it forward inside the kayak. Apart from the paddle, most of the items were there in case I had to beach in a storm and wasn't able to get back to camp, and also to add a little weight at the front to balance my weight in the back. Immediately-needed items like marine radio, GPS, knife, and other flares, I could slot into one of the pockets of my lifejacket or in the large pouch behind my seat, or in a "daypack" under the large hatch which I could open in seconds from the rear sitting position. Not wanting to overload the kayak and risk damaging it while manhandling it up and down the shore, I decided to add water and extra items like fishing gear on a trip by trip basis prior to launching.

I kayaked north around the headland, again seeing scores of fish in the clear deep water under the cliffs, and then paddled thirty yards from shore beside the steep pebble bank separating the sea from the lagoon. I beached several times and brought back many useful items including a green plastic crate which I loaded with some driftwood, mainly to hold it down on the kayak as there was plenty of wood closer to my campsite.

Contemplation has its place, but keeping active and focused on the tasks at hand, and taking control of, or at least making the best of my world has always been a big part of how I manage my fears and bring about any necessary attitude adjustments.

My next project was to build a shade structure, somewhere to sit, eat and read on a sunny day. I'd brought over several tarps and a "utility" box with duct tape, bungees, rope, string, plastic ties, nails, and screws. Everything else I needed was lying around the fishcamp and on the nearby beaches—mainly wooden poles and fish netting.

Camp taking shape

I selected the biggest of my three or four large tarps and nailed one edge of it to the inland side of the panga so I could roll it out and reef it up as needed.

> I've spent the last couple of hours just rigging up something and it's basically a tarp held up with sticks. I'm inside it now sitting on my chair… The wind is picking up. We've actually got a fairly brisk northerly and I can see surf running in the bay, so I'll have to eventually take this down. I tried to rig up something that I could take down fairly quickly.

When the wind became too much, I furled up and secured the tarp with small bungees, then took my chair up to sit in the shade of the large cardón forty yards above my campsite, where I'd secreted the gallon of water and the two liters of soda. There was a little leveled clearing surrounded by a protective ring of rocks; it would make a good sleeping area if one didn't have a tent. The view over to LA Bay was magnificent. I felt like Neptune on his throne.

However, the neatly rolled tarp did nothing to help keep my coolers, water, and food containers out of the sun. The high north-facing bow of the panga offered an all day, if narrow, zone of shade, but what shade there was along the sides would come and go and largely disappear at midday.

So I lined up most of my water containers and storage bins along the inland side of the panga, simply double folded the silvery tarp over them, and weighed it down with rocks, rope and netting. After a few minor adjustments, it worked a treat to keep everything cool and cuervo-proofed.

With the sound of hammering echoing around the bay, I fixed the rickety but much appreciated cabinet with a few nails and supporting slats then placed it along the side of the panga. The cabinet provided a little more shade, and served as table and wind break for my propane stove. I set up a clothes line next, hoping anything fluttering on it might deter the ravens and the gulls.

I didn't know whether to laugh or curse when I heard another panga. This crazy pangxiety! Why was I letting it disturb me so? I knew it stemmed from the suspense of not having met these nocturnal pangueros, these major actors in my world that I knew nothing about, but about whom I was primed to imagine the worst. I got it into my head that I should have left the tent to greet them the other night… should have offered them a coffee, maybe a sandwich, even a few precious cold beers (or at least as cold as they could get outside the cooler at night).

If that moment came again, I vowed to welcome them as courageous respected island brothers, and extend to them the same hand of friendship and hospitality that Baja California fishermen had so generously offered me over the years.

I looked up, and about three miles out in the channel where the chop rose into a wilder sea, I was surprised to see a very real panga beating north into the wind, towards Los Machos. It was a rough ride; the front was continually crashing down sending up plumes of spray. Occasionally it would stop and the two occupants would lower something into the sea—maybe a net? Yesterday I would have said they were dumping bodies. Whatever it was, the battered occupants eventually turned around and ran back towards the peninsula.

Chapter 13

Explorations

Behold the fowls of the air…

Jesus [Matthew 6:26]

For three blustery days my explorations were largely on shore. The first was brief. I laced up my boots, secured all my gear and supplies in the tent or in the plastic containers beneath the weighed-down tarp, checked the tent pegs were secure, the kayak was high enough, and then climbed the headland above my campsite.

Even though it was a windy day and I doubted that I'd see a panga, I still wanted to keep my camp in sight, so I ended up attacking the headland too directly, taking the short route straight up a 40-degree incline. Concerned about rattlesnakes, I tried to walk on top of the larger rocks. But it didn't take much imagination to see that the real danger was the rocks rolling beneath me with bone-shattering consequences. I went back to stepping over and around most of the boulders and trying to keep my hands and feet away from any snaky shadows.

Out in the channel I watched the waves moving across the water, running straight north to south. But gazing down to my camp hundreds of feet below, the waves were curving around the headland, and the wind gusts were visibly sweeping into the bay and bouncing back from the shore, rattling and shaking my tent from every direction.

Looking through my binoculars, I could see that the ravens were back, casing out the joint! I watched one of them pulling out the washed chili can from the old rusty barrel and throwing it around. The other was poking around the cabinet, which was only two-thirds covered by the tarp. It seemed to have sniffed out a small Tupperware container of cereal that I'd left there. Not really thinking it would do anything more than make me feel better, I shouted as loud as I could. To my surprise, the birds took off across the bay.

Approaching the plateau above the highest cliffs, I was impressed by the screaming noise and force of the wind, and how unstable the cliffs seemed. It looked like the soft grayish tan rock could fall away or avalanche at any moment…as it had clearly done many times before. In spite of my desire to peek over the edge, a great but distant voice was shouting at me to keep back. I was happy to oblige. It was a long, long way down.

The lagoon

Looking over the other side to the northwest I saw the lagoon apparent on the satellite images, then the long bay curving to the darkly impressive headland of Punta Los Machos. Apart from the cliffs beneath me, the bay looked walkable all the way to the point, at least at all but the highest tides.

I watched a brownish bird of prey circling high over the cliffs; it might have been the same one I saw with the "duck." Again, I thought it most likely a peregrine falcon.

After lunch on top, I was taking an easier, longer way down when I noticed that the ravens were back in my camp. As soon as I was out of the wind, I shouted at them once more. They flew off but not so very far. Their respect and wariness were diminishing.

Finally back on the shore, I hurried into camp to see what their big beaks had accomplished. The ravens had gone; but three American oystercatchers were busily poking around the rocks close to the kayak making their characteristic squeaking noise—like squeaking glass. Then gazing up at a cardón, I noticed an osprey perched on top of one of the arms, looking very noble against the blue sky.

Later I went exploring the canyons at the back of the headland and found a dead bird, obviously some kind of bird of prey, possibly an owl. I wondered if it had fallen victim to the falcon. It was headless, but it had impressive talons, and cactus spines were stuck in its feet. It was magnificently attired, largely white underneath with tan spots and flecks of white and gray. I took some digital photos, and thought of Jesus' comment about the lilies of the field: "Even Solomon in all his glory was not arrayed like one of these."

It had been a busy bird day. My Golden *Birds of North America* field guide was earning its passage, and back in camp I was able to leisurely consult the book and positively identify the dead bird as a barn owl.

Barn owl

Next morning, I stuffed my small backpack for a full day exploring south around the bay and up into the canyons above the dramatic cliffs in that direction.

As well as taking all my money and my passport, I brought my GPS, binoculars, maps and satellite images, marine radio, snake bite kit and below the knee protective leggings, flash light, extra batteries, extra socks, windbreaker, Swiss army knife, tweezers for cactus spines, two liters of water and a can of diet cola, snacks, pocket first-aid kit, and antibiotics.

After drinking as much water as I could, I set off wearing two waist packs—one with the camera and all my memory cards, the other with the tape recorder.

While walking around the mile-long bay, my eyes were focused two yards in front, mainly to check for rattlers but also to look out for cacti—again, something I do instinctively in the desert. Walking one way and looking another is never a good idea. I forced myself to stop if I wanted to look up or around or back to my campsite. I stopped often as there was much to see.

The beachcombing was always interesting. "So much wood, so much debris, so much plastic, so many containers, so much rope and netting, I needn't have brought half the rope I did… and quite a few shoes." In places, there seemed to be a tennis shoe or flip flop every ten yards. If you were willing to wear one frayed and sun-bleached shoe by Nike and another by Reebok, you'd never want for fashionable footwear. And as the shipwrecked fishermen from the *Celia Angelina* had observed there were numerous capped soda bottles—some clear, some green—with drinkable quantities of liquid inside.

I saw fresh paw prints on the beach below the high tide line, so they could only be hours old. Wrenching myself away from the beachcombing, I followed them into the dunes and salt flats, where all about, there were crisscrossing lines of small rodent tracks.

Assuming it's true that coyotes were not established on the island, I wondered if the larger paw prints and droppings were from foxes or feral cats. Foxes, like all canines, typically leave oblong prints and evidence of their non-retractable claws, whereas cats leave a more rounded paw print and rarely leave claw marks on the ground when walking. I was inclined to think they were cat prints.

About a hundred yards from the sea, behind the dunes, in the dried mud of the salt flats, I came across some droppings a few inches long and full of greeny-gray fur. Scratch marks beside them looked like a halfhearted attempt at burial.

Cal Sherman, who had first taken me to Guardian Angel, had told me about finding what he thought might be coyote scat and tracks on the island, but he was puzzled because the stride didn't seem

View south to LA Bay and cloud-capped Smith Island.

quite long enough. Anyway, he picked up the scat and brought it back for Antonio Reséndiz to look at. Tony showed it to Michael Rose, the UC Davis researcher whose main field of interest was island coyotes. Cal referred to him as "the coyote man." Michael Rose told Tony it was probably not coyote but fox scat, and he was really interested in talking to Cal about where on the island he had found it and to see the photographs he had taken of the tracks. As Cal recalled, "He wanted to talk to me the next day, unfortunately he was in a boat that overturned and he drowned with several other people before I had a chance to talk to him."

Before his death, Michael Rose had been working closely with Dr. Gary Polis on assessing the degree to which coyote populations along the coast of Baja California and its islands are subsidized by foods that come directly and indirectly from the sea. And the input is enormous. They calculated that an average of about 60 pounds of "detrital algae and animal carrion" washes up along each yard of shoreline every year.

As part of his field work, Michael Rose determined that coyote tracks were on average 4.7 times more likely to be observed each night on the coast than inland... and ten times more scats were counted in transects on the coast compared to equivalent inland sites.

Fox or cat?

Turtle Head

These and other measures allowed Rose to calculate that thanks to the "flow of abundant and diverse resources from the sea," coyotes were four to five times more abundant along the coast than in "adjacent inland areas that do not receive marine input."

I crossed back over the dunes and returned to the shore. There was a dead sea lion, a youngster—maybe three feet in length. It seemed intact apart from where the skin had started sloughing away from the tail. It was discolored an oily red and black and looked to be long dead. But I could detect no smell.

Then I found a mummified sea turtle. It had dried out to a crispy gold and tan. I looked at its high head, its beak, and studied the bones of one of its flippers beneath the parchment skin.

At the far south end of the bay there was an excellent sandy beach and evidence of an old fishcamp. A steep ridge and a long rocky point offered good protection from south winds. I suspected the remains of the camp dated from the summer when the winds tended to be southerly. In the winter, the beach was totally exposed to the more northerly wind and waves, so I quickly ruled out moving there.

Walking out along the rocks to the point, one notices that the cliffs are very different from those at the north end—they are more granitic, with dykes and pegmatites, and sheets of quartzy intrusions, and are much older than the island's almost omnipresent capping of cooled lava. There were two osprey nests high on the southern point. Beneath was an amazing pile of sticks, string, plastic and bones. I thought about climbing up to inspect the nests, but when I noticed that at least one was occupied by an adult bird, I left them alone.

Around the point I headed up a deep canyon which ran straight inland from a short stony beach, then veered south paralleling the coast a kilometer or so in from the cliffs. It was rocky and filled with grasses and clumps of vegetation so I was again wary of rattlers. I took pictures of chollas, cardóns, mammalarias and agaves.

I scraped past the very familiar *torote colorado* elephant tree (*Bursera microphylla*), which released its characteristic strong aromatic smell. Then I came across an even bigger tree that I wasn't familiar with. Its rattling dry leaves got my attention. The leaves were large and elongate, the bark was gray. I took several photos to help identify it.

Ascending to the head of the valley, where much of the surface was decomposed granite, I took note of interesting outcrops of schorl, black and green crystalline rocks, and surprising flat sandy depressions among the vast fields of boulders. After a few trips and scary slides, I put my camera away in case I fell and damaged it.

I climbed on top of a peak that offered a fine view across to LA Bay and of the coast all around. The sea was churning and rippled with white caps. In all its vastness I couldn't

Sideroxylon leucophyllum

see a single boat anywhere. I tried soliciting a radio check in Spanish and English—no reply.

The whole of Humbug Bay stretched in a great sweep up to Punta Los Machos. Only my camp's protecting headland interrupted the curve. With my naked eye I could just make out the abandoned panga and my campsite. I studied it through binoculars. All seemed well. Looking at the channel over to Punta Remedios, the closest point on the Baja peninsula to the island, the seas there were clearly the whitest and most agitated. The north wind was funneling through the restricted gap, partially nullifying the advantages of

Turtle Head

proximity. The Canal de las Ballenas presented a wild and desolate scene, but one of indescribable beauty, as if the Grand Canyon had suddenly been three-quarters filled with the bluest, most life-packed water in the world.

Turning around, the great mountain mass forming the heart of the northern part of the island grabbed my attention. The tallest peak stood over 4300 feet. Looking east, I studied the potential pathways inland to cross to the other coast. But always my eyes came back to the headland sheltering my camp from the full force of the north wind. And as I stared at it… it struck me, it looked just like the head of a turtle, the sweeping bay on either side seeming like a pair of flippers stretching forward. It was such an obvious interpretation, I half expected the entire headland to go swimming over to LA Bay. On the spot, I named it Turtle Head.

High on the cliffs I slowly, cautiously, followed the coast to the south, trying to work my way down to the shore. I descended into an ever deepening valley till coming to a sheer 12-foot drop. There was no safe way down or around.

I made one final climb to the top of another peak, pulled out my binoculars and surveyed the other canyons dropping to the sea. It would likely be an almighty up and down struggle if I had to leave the kayak on the coast and come back to camp overland; I could only hope it would be better right under the cliffs, boulder hopping along the shore.

Next morning, I was lacing up my boots, excited, ready for another hike. I chose to explore inland, towards the sunny uplands, to check out the possibilities for crossing the island. A little less certain about when I'd be back, I wind- and raven-proofed camp, weighing down my tent with extra boxes and gear and a five-gallon water container. I'd probably be out of sight of camp and its sea approaches for some time, but I took comfort from the brisk wind that should deter all but the most determined boaters, and the abundance of clear fresh footprints all around my tent and possessions. No one could claim they thought the campsite was abandoned.

I carried pretty much what I carried the day before, except I left out the bulky leggings and added a couple of flares. Camera in one hand, tape recorder in the other, 200 yards from the beach, I carefully passed clumps of cholla and headed towards a cardón forest. Beneath the thin covering of yellowing grasses, the sterile, cindery soil was soft and yielding. I noticed a number of cylindrical, pint-sized mammalaria cacti covered with tiny hairs and spines. Some bore coronets of little scarlet fruits—maybe a resource if I ran out of fresh fruit and vegetables.

Looking back to the bay, and across to Smith Island and the peninsula, I nearly chickened out. My camp was too easy to spot from the sea, and I had made what was already a good panga landing site even better.

I forced myself on, hiking through a grove of cacti up a gentle, almost imperceptible incline. Small burrows abounded. They were about an inch wide. Some kind of a mouse? Again I thought of Antonio's endemic Angel

Island deer mouse—*Peromyscus guardia*. But whatever was making the burrows was in no great hurry to be photographed.

I followed some narrow trails through the grass, which seemed to bear the impressions of tiny paw prints, but it was hard to make them out because of the disturbing effect of the wind on the dry, lightweight pumice-like soil. There were some larger prints in the gravel. I couldn't be sure if they were made by rabbits, ground squirrels, or what. So far, apart from a few fluttering bats and the occasional beached sea lion, I hadn't seen a single mammal on the island. But something was making all the tracks and trails. The desert must come alive at night.

A pair of ravens had the audacity to land right in front of me and nonchalantly strut just a few yards away. They were probably the same ones harassing my camp earlier. Well, at least that meant they were not harassing it now. I was astounded by their boldness—like they wanted to impress me with how big and shiny they were (how dare you think we're mere crows), and how thick and heavy were their beaks.

There was a real strangeness to this desert island. The cacti and plants and the sounds and the smells were similar to those on the Baja peninsula, but something was different. Perhaps because many of the bushes and cacti were draped with the climbing vine *Vaseyanthus insularis*. Or maybe its strangeness had deeper roots, and had more to do with the spirit and feel of the place.

I saw my first ant nest. As if paying homage to the spirit of the East Pacific Rise, a colony of black ants had made a little round volcano of discarded seed husks and bits of dry grass around their nest entrance. Almost everything looked photogenic. I'd already shot 200 of the 1200-picture capacity of my memory cards. It would be necessary to delete some.

Ridge route to the divide—looking west, back to the peninsula

I found myself in deeper, boulder-choked washes, with slopes of gray, pink and salmon rocks. Occasionally I crossed into other drainage channels to find easier passage, but there was nothing a determined hiker couldn't take in his stride.

About three miles inland as the raven flies, an hour out of sight of the sea and anxious to check my camp, I changed course and almost jogged up a ridge. What a great workout the island had already given me. I looked and felt and probably was several pounds lighter than when I arrived. The midriff was tightening. The spreading zone was contracting.

Higher up, ridges were the way to go. Compared to the canyon bottoms, I was better able to see where I was putting my feet, and was virtually freed from the minor nuisance of seeds and prickles in my socks. At last, as I climbed, I could see the top of Turtle Head emerging from the landscape… and through binoculars I was relieved to survey my camp again. No sign of anyone, or any boats.

Eventually the ridge took me to the top of a high hill. Dead end! Every direction led steeply down before I could rise again. Momentarily disappointed, but otherwise satisfied I sat down, enjoyed a drink and a snack, and just felt really good that the old boy was still in fine shape and, more often than not, ready to just enjoy the moment. It helped that my campsite was still in view.

Climbing to the island divide would have to wait for another day. I doubted that it was much more than a mile ahead. Maybe an easy mile if I chose the right ridge. I made a few mental notes and took a number of pictures of likely-looking approaches, then sauntered slowly back down to my camp.

I went fishing off the rocks, and lost two good lures. Given the enormous tidal range, I was fairly confident that I could recover them both at low tide.

End of a lingcod

(And I did.) With the wind moderating, I grabbed my fishing tackle and paddled out in front of Turtle Head. In thirty feet of water I hooked my first fish, a lingcod.

A live fish in my hands or in my boat becomes a personal thing. I can't help feeling sorry for it. I think fish have a real raw deal; we treat them so cruelly, sticking big hooks into them, leaving them to slowly asphyxiate, things we'd rightfully be arrested for if inflicting on warmer, cuddlier creatures. To end its struggle, I gripped it firmly over the gills and tried to stab it in the head with the long thin blade of my filleting knife, but the blade bounced up and nicked my finger, and didn't seem to do much except make the fish writhe harder and mix its blood with mine.

I stabbed it again right through where I assumed its brain was, and then tried to tell myself, and the fish, that he was insensate or already dead. But neither of us quite believed it. His struggle was too dramatic. The only certainty was he was going to die, and I wanted to make it as quick as possible

Almost as soon as I jumped out of the kayak in the shallows, I grabbed my fileting knife, sawed down through its crunching spine and sliced off its head. Oblivion! All over!

Not quite... I picked up the head by inserting a couple of fingers into its gaping mouth, momentarily gazed into its still clear, spotted eyes, and was about to cast it into the sandy shallows where a couple of gulls were already treading water, no doubt impressed by my new-found fishing prowess. My curses probably impressed them more. The open mouth of the bodiless fish head suddenly clamped down on my fingers, piercing them with dozens of tiny sharp teeth, drawing yet more blood before I could shake it off.

Fast losing my appetite for this never-say-die fish, I raced the dark to skin and filet it, clean my hands, boil the filets, and sprinkle them with lemon juice. I didn't do the best fileting job. The fish was impossibly bony, more trouble than tasty, and I still felt sorry for it.

I finished the fish for breakfast—more to dutifully utilize a wholesome meal than out of any genuine interest. I was craving a bigger, less bony fish... yellowtail steaks fried in butter sounded perfect. My conscience could be placated for that treat.

As the days went by, the moon got bigger and brighter, the tides fell lower revealing more of the bay's rocky shallows and sandy bottom, and then bounced back ever higher as sun and moon swung closer to opposition. I wondered how much higher and lower the sea could go.

I hadn't brought tide charts because I knew, living outdoors on the beach, intimately connected to the phases of the moon, the corresponding tidal pattern would become part of my life. That was a lunatic decision. In a tight situation, I would have appreciated the extra security of knowing precisely when the tide will turn.

Chapter 14

Solace of Marine Biology

*It is easy to remember when we were small and lay on our stomachs beside
a tide pool and our minds and eyes went so deeply into it that size and
identity were lost, and the creeping hermit crab was our size and
the tiny octopus a monster. Then the waving algae covered us and we
hid under a rock at the bottom and leapt out at a fish. It is very possible
that we, and even those who probe space with equations, simply
extend this wonder.*

John Steinbeck—The Log from the Sea of Cortez

After so much strenuous physical activity and exploring, I was ready for
some down time to enjoy the comforts of my camp. The wind dropped. I
recorded: "I've got the shade up and I've got my chair underneath, and what
is really heavenly is just sitting here and doing nothing, just listening to the
silence and relaxing." I studied an isolated cloud sitting above Smith Island.
It was also doing nothing—it seemed strange and lonely, just hovering there
like a white hat in an otherwise clear blue sky.

There was a small plane somewhere high above the Ballenas channel. Even
though I couldn't see it, I turned on my marine radio and monitored channel-
16 for a while.

The low tide provided a marvelous opportunity. Lifting and rolling the
rocks in the lower intertidal was unbelievably productive. The sides of the
rocks were covered in algae and anemones, and gloriously colored sponges.
The crawling, slithering, squirting, flailing world beneath a single boulder
could keep a marine biologist busy a week. Limpets, chitons, bivalves,
gastropods all caught my eye… as did crabs, sea stars, the abundant writhing
brittle stars, sea cucumbers, tube worms, and all the flat worms flowing
mercurially over the rock. Hermit crabs and other boarders were recycling
the suitable abandoned shells. There were even little, big-headed clingfish
(Gobiesox) somehow living under the boulders.

I was able to temporarily fill up a large white plastic bowl and create my
own aquarium for photographic purposes—and how intriguing it all looked
under a modest macro lens, how wondrous to spy on the fascinating detail of
that strange world.

I gently replaced the boulders from around which I had collected, and
carefully slipped the creatures back into the sea. Most of the soft-bodied

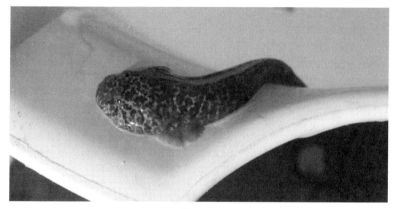

Gobiesox

creatures quickly disappeared again beneath the rocks, those protected by shells or other devices took their time about it. Certainly there were a few casualties, a little collateral damage, but I consulted my conscience and didn't think my disturbing those five or six boulders would make an iota of difference to the multi-billion boulder ecosystem of the island. A few worms and brittle stars might have disagreed. Some happy gulls and fishes were on my side. But losing myself in that adventure in marine biology made a huge difference to me.

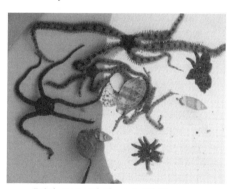

Brittle stars and other intertidal treasures

I recalled when I was a kid in England, a typical inner-city future hooligan. My life revolved around concrete and tarmac, bricks and cuss words, roaming the streets with my mates, minor brushes with the law. I was about ten; never been on vacation; never seen the sea; then I had the good fortune to go on a summer holiday with a friend's family to the "seaside"—two weeks along the wild and wonderful Atlantic coast of North Devon. The ocean backdrop was magnificent. My playground was now rocky shores and tide pools. Hour after hour as the surf rushed and pounded nearby, I found one treasure after another. I was never happier or more absorbed by anything in my life. Naïve and distracted, I ended up with a terrible sunburn and blisters the size of eggs on my legs and back.

It was a mind-expanding turning point in my young life. I wanted to return to those fish and eels and crabs and anemones and the hundreds of other creatures I played with, caught, and studied. The sense of freedom was total. The adventure was something I didn't re-live for years, but it remained with me as a hope that one day I would find myself back there again, on the rocks, by the tide pools, wading the streams, left alone to smell the clean ocean, feel the warm sun and the cooling spray, touch the creatures along the shore, follow my heart and listen. Listen not to the cacophony and the dictates of the inner city, not to the voice of man, or to a fellow cussing kid, but to the voice of nature... and to my own inner voice.

And perhaps all the months and years I've spent alone along the Baja California coastline have been an extension of that dream, that youthful hope... a simple attempt to relive the happiest days of my life.

I completely understood why Japan's Emperor Hirohito, in the midst of a war, with the tide of battle turning violently against his sacred Empire of the Rising Sun would prefer to find escape in the field of marine biology. It is a preoccupation so absorbing and so capable of whisking you into another cosmos... into a timeless and more real universe that will still be extant a hundred million years after the last human has taken his final breath.

As Steinbeck wrote in his Log:

> We had been drifting in some kind of dual world—a parallel realistic world; and the preoccupations of the world we came from, which are considered realistic, were to us filled with mental mirage. Modern economies; war drives; party affiliations and lines; hatreds, political, and social and racial, cannot survive in dignity the perspective of distance.

If total defeat pervaded my life I would be found along some lonely shore, no doubt by the Sea of Cortez, gazing humbly at the wondrous diversity of life, putting everything into a larger perspective.

After returning all my specimens to the sea, I spent the middle part of the day reading about marine biology in the shade.

My mind turned again to the conundrum that was Emperor Hirohito, the 124th emperor of Japan. A small, thin, moustached man, he ascended to his imperial throne in the 1920s, and dutifully settled down to the task of being God-emperor. Some say he was burdened with a child-like innocence. He wanted his reign to be known as *Showa*—Enlightened Peace—because "I have visited the battlefields of the [First] World War, and in the presence of such devastation, I understand the need for concord among nations."

He developed an early passion for natural history, for marine biology in particular. He had a laboratory constructed on his palace grounds in Tokyo, and often collected specimens in and around Sagami Bay, where he had his imperial vacation villa. Shortly after becoming emperor he was given a small bust of Darwin, which graced his study, even through the war years.

Those troubled years found him particularly fascinated by the study of fishes. He perhaps took greater pleasure in them than in his public duties and the delicate task of dealing with the military. Many of his army and navy commanders were exasperated by his scientific endeavors and tactfully chided him for playing with fish while they were playing with fire and grand imperial designs. One of his senior advisors implored him to conduct his marine biology discretely in a way more befitting a god.

And even while Japan was increasingly devastated by war and facing the anathema of total surrender, even in the midst of urging his admirals and generals to further efforts to destroy the enemy, he kept his scientific soul aloof and pursued his studies.

He continued to partake in and lend support to the field of marine biology to the end of his life—Hirohito passed away in 1989—by which time almost 30,000 specimens of marine life had been sent to him from every part of the world. He was a recognized authority on marine hydrozoans—jellyfish and their kin.

It was reported that he was buried with his microscope. His imperial successor, his eldest son, Emperor Akihito, is also a marine biologist. His specialty is the study of gobies, about which he has published 28 papers in the *Japanese Journal of Ichthyology*. He is also co author of several books including *The Fishes of the Japanese Archipelago* and *Fishes of Japan*. His other son, Prince Hitachi, is another specialist in marine biology; his main field being the cancer of fish.

The emperor also intrigued "Unabomber" Ted Kaczynski, who conducted a mail bomb campaign that terrorized academia, airline employees, the business world, and the media from May 1978 till his arrest in April 1996. His targets included anyone he thought working for an establishment and a system that he detested. In his long rambling "manifesto," which was printed in the Washington Post and the New York Times, he states:

> Consider the hypothetical case of a man who can have anything he wants just by wishing for it. Such a man has power, but he will develop serious psychological problems. At first he will have a lot of fun, but by and by he will become acutely bored and demoralized. Eventually he may become clinically depressed. History shows that leisured aristocracies tend to become decadent... But not every leisured aristocrat becomes bored and demoralized. For example, the emperor Hirohito, instead of sinking into decadent hedonism, devoted himself to marine biology, a field in which he became distinguished. When people do not have to exert themselves to satisfy their physical needs they often set up artificial goals for themselves. In many cases they then pursue these goals with the same energy and emotional involvement that they otherwise would have put into the search for physical necessities. Thus the aristocrats of the Roman Empire had their literary pretensions; many European aristocrats a few centuries ago invested tremendous time and energy in hunting,

though they certainly didn't need the meat; other aristocracies have competed for status through elaborate displays of wealth; and a few aristocrats, like Hirohito, have turned to science.

How could it be? Hirohito—on the one bloody hand, up to his wide open eyes in the brutal and vicious business of imperial destiny, on the other enthralled by scientific discovery and fishes, and passionately seeking a reign of enlightened peace and harmony among nations.

During a Cabinet meeting in 1941, with his military commanders and ministers arguing forcefully for the inevitability of war with the U.S. and advocating a preemptive strike against Pearl Harbor, Hirohito brought proceedings to a standstill by suddenly reciting a poem composed by his grandfather, the great Emperor Meiji:

In a world
Where all the seas are brethren
Why then do wind and wave
So stridently clash?

As Herbert Bix a recent biographer of Hirohito put it, the emperor operated with two "conflicting moral visions and norms contained in the Confucian model of the virtuous, peace-loving ruler and the Japanese bushidō model of the ideal warrior... The tension between these two worldviews lay at the heart of everything Hirohito did."

And in the US it seems our current administration operates under a similar tension—that between the Confusion model of peace and virtue and the "mission-accomplished" George W. Bushidō model of the ideal warrior. Let us hope that the tension will be resolved with less damage to the American homeland than that which befell the Japanese.

The wind started to blow stronger. I decided to leave the tarp up to see how much it could take. However, the wind abruptly reversed direction and blew strongly off shore. That was a different story—the gusts got more under the tarp and bowed it violently upwards; something had to give. Not wanting to find out what, I took down the tarp while I was still able.

Feeling ravenous in the sea air, I cooked a wholesome veggie dish and added a full can of "sloppy Joe" sauce which made it disgustingly sweet. I kept adding pasta, and more veggies till the large pan was almost overflowing, but it was still far too sweet for me. I was amazed at the amount of sugar the manufacturers thought appropriate.

The tide had gone way out. Concerned about the return, I dragged the kayak up beside the tent and double tied it to the panga. I slept well till about 2 A.M. when I sat up hoping, almost praying, that was not a boat I could hear. I threw on a heavy jacket, unzipped the door, and went outside to look around.

There was a beautiful full moon. Across the glistening sea, Smith Island and Mike's Mountain (above the town of LA Bay) stood almost as clear as day. Through binoculars I peered around my bay, up at the cardón slopes behind me, out to sea, looking for the slightest movement.

Perhaps martialing my thoughts again… I suddenly recalled a story my father had told me about how, one moonlit night in Italy in 1944, while he was on watch guarding the 7th Armoured Brigade's newly-won front line, a German sniper put a bullet right through his beret and sent it flying. My father was not a big man. He always wished he were a little taller, but afterwards he thought that God had made him just the right height, and he remained throughout his life very contented with his five-foot-five stature.

Up until that moment the story had just been a story, interesting and forgotten, but there on the island, the reality struck me, the full significance of an event that determined both my father's and my existence… the tension, the deadly cat-and-mouse game, the incredible good fortune. The best snipers were not in the habit of missing.

> An American study revealed that in the First World War it took about 7,000 rounds of small arms ammunition to kill a single enemy soldier. By the time of the Vietnam War, this had risen to around 25,000 rounds. The average sniper required 1.3 rounds.
>
> — Gen. J.H. Hay, Jr.
> *Vietnam Studies: Tactical and Material Innovation.*

Mathias Hetzenauer, the top German sniper of the Second World War with hundreds of confirmed kills to his credit, mostly from "penetrating enemy lines at night," recalled after the war, that he could "guarantee" a head shot at 400 meters, and a chest shot at 600 meters, but preferred to get much closer to be certain of a kill with every bullet.

The high tide had filled the sea to within a yard of the tent, and I had the distinct impression that I was being watched as I checked the lines securing the kayak. I hoped it was a sea lion. The tide was so high it didn't take much imagination to see one stealing my shoes from outside the tent door. I moved them back.

Half of the scenarios in my head were ridiculous, but alone and vulnerable I needed to think of everything. If only the American sentinels on the Hawaiian Islands in 1941 were half as vigilant, the Japanese attackers would have had a very different reception.

Chapter 15

Kayak and Current

The person with the fewest possessions is the freest: Thoreau was right.

Paul Theroux

It was Friday the 13th of January. At dawn the temperature was 50°F. In no hurry to get out of my sleeping bag and face the morning chill, I read till it was a warm 75°F in the tent. Finally popping my head outside, I was amazed to see two ravens silently perched high on the big cardón above my campsite, looking like spirit brothers and messengers from beyond.

Paraphrasing Emperor Meiji, I asked myself in a moment of enlightened compassion:

In a world
Where all God's creatures are brethren
Why then do boot and beak
So stridently clash?

Then, in a fit of imperial ferocity, mindful only of the safety of my realm, primed for a knockout preemptive strike, I mumbled "forget this bollocks, I'll **showa** them a thing or two, let's get rid of these guys." I stepped outside thinking to pitch a heavy rock at the nearest raven, but just to be on the safe side (I'd feel bad if I actually hurt it) I threw a piece of pumice instead. It struck one of the fat arms of the cardón, three feet low with more show than solidity. But they got the message; off they went up the canyon.

Then it occurred to me… The "spear" piercing the very green column that I had just struck!!! Maybe some frustrated fisherman who'd lost his hard-earned dinner had hurled it into the cardón hoping to nail the black heart of one of his tormentors?

It was calm in the bay. Further out I could see agitation and white caps on the darker water. I made a quick binoculars check. A sea lion a quarter-mile away. A large "fish boil" beyond. "That's one of the biggest fish boils I've seen… there must be a couple of hundred birds just piling in."

Wispy, streaky clouds promised some sun protection. I was itching to kayak, to go get my yellowtail, and perhaps head south—the one direction I had yet to seriously explore. But mindful of the tide, and as it was Friday the 13th, I decided to keep both feet firmly on the ground and take a morning hike to the south end of the bay.

On the way, I walked into the dunes and hid another gallon of water inside a waist-high bush. As there were dozens of bushes in the area, I fixed the location in my mind—"just in from a half-buried green plastic bucket."

So even if I returned from a hike and found everything stolen, I would still have the "valuables" in my day pack, my hidden bag with all the survival gear, possibly what I'd stashed inside the kayak… and three gallons of water. I was comfortable with that.

Back in camp, all was fine. After celebrating with a nice cup of tea, I discovered my first vegetable losses—needing to cut away half of a jicama (which was becoming moldy outside and brown within) and a few small pieces of celery that had gone brown and soft.

Since my ice had melted, I had been unpacking the coolers at night, exposing everything to the 40-50° air and re-packing it all in the morning. But it was going to be hard to make any of my fruit and vegetables last much into February. Hoping to delay the inevitable, I started drying inside the bins and coolers where they were stored.

Later that day the sea fell temptingly calm. The clouds quickly burned away leaving a perfectly blue sky. Suddenly, Friday the 13th did not look quite so inauspicious. I decided to risk kayaking. For over two-and-a-half miles I eased my way south, occasionally looking over my right shoulder for any sign of wind from the north or west.

The tide was falling and water was draining from the Sea of Cortez like it was dropping over an enormous water fall. I found myself drifting along on an inky black sea, with eddies forming all over. When I put down the paddle to chat on tape, the kayak started slowly spinning in a whirlpool. I headed to what looked like an area of smooth calm water and it turned out to be a vast upwelling which overwhelmed the agitation and horizontal flow. It was fun at first, but I worried that if the current were compounded by any kind of northerly wind I'd be hard pressed to battle against it.

In the summer of 1649, Porter y Casanate—pearl fisher, explorer, and later governor of Sinaloa—sailed up the Sea of Cortez for three months. He reached the Midriff Islands, and possibly Angel de la Guarda, erroneously thinking that he had reached the head of the sea and would soon encounter the open ocean beyond. As he sailed past the island narrows his log recounts:

> I was caught in a current which carried me violently… The choppy appearance of the sea and the churning of the water made it look as though it were a field of rocks… I spent several days sailing up this channel and encountered extraordinary and exceedingly fierce twisting currents that crossed in various places like the courses of deep water rivers. They churned the sea with much noise and with whirlpools, chop and great swells that overcame the ships and worked against the sail and oars, sending us backwards… my flagship ended up spinning around furiously and violently.

He concluded passage through these supposed narrows to the great ocean to the north was not practicable. And he warned that he had been helplessly trapped,

> ...unable to enter or exit through the channel...unable to follow my heading, nor able to tack... If we had not oars it would have been impossible to bear away from the coasts and islands, or to make an exit... For this reason it is called Salsipuedes. (Get-out-if-you can.)

The term stuck to the general area of the Midriff Islands and more specifically to one of the islands in the chain immediately south of Guardian Angel Island. The passage between those islands (which includes Rasa, Partida and the San Lorenzos) and the Baja peninsula bears the name Salsipuedes Channel.

In the early 1700s Jesuit padre Juan de Ugarte was sailing south through the Salsipuedes Channel on the Triumph of the Cross, the first ship built on the peninsula. He also encountered currents that swept the ship back—in six hours they lost eight days progress. He wrote:

> These are not currents like one sees elsewhere in the Gulf, where one scarcely notices a choppiness or a little noise like that produced by a school of fish. These currents create foaming breakers and the noise is like a river that runs through a boulder field.

A high section of cliffs offered few options for landing, so I decided to turn back. It was a hard paddle. I headed in for a break at a short stony beach at the mouth of a narrow cactus-and-boulder strewn canyon.

A sea lion, dried golden brown, was stretched out on a rock eight feet above the water. It started to struggle down on my approach, and then threw itself the final four or five feet into the sea. There was a terrific belly flopping splash—it was too shallow to make a normal, more graceful head-first entry. The sea lion hung around, bug eyed with curiosity, till I ran my kayak up to the pebble beach and stepped off.

The beach wouldn't be a tenable location if the wind and waves kicked up, so after twenty minutes I pulled the kayak into the water and battled back towards camp. I was looking for a better place to pull out and rest when I noticed that some debris on the water, trapped in a large eddy, seemed to be moving north. I paddled over and hitched a ride.

It was now possible for me to take a break from paddling without losing too much ground. I had been sitting in the rear of the kayak with my legs spread a little uncomfortably either side of the large hatch cover. To give my numbed knees a rest I moved to the forward seat position, which is probably the hardest to paddle from, but gives the best view into the sea. The eddy gradually dissipated leaving me surrounded by slack water—a prelude to the turn of the tide.

There were many two-to-three-pound fish swimming just under the surface. Then I saw a single much larger fish moving slowly, deep in the clear blue-black water. I saw it just for a second or two, but it underlined the astounding clarity of the sea around Guardian Angel Island.

Life needs life in an obvious predatory way, but it sometimes makes us more alive by the feelings of joy and fascination it imparts. And there is, alone in the wilderness, an extra joy in the interaction with creatures that are gloriously vivacious, real, spontaneous, and mysterious.

A large turtle in the water let me get within a few yards before it threw down its head, flapped its flippers, and paddled out of sight. I heard the haunting shrill cry of an osprey echoing off the cliffs. Looking ahead I saw a pair of them swooping low over the water. One made an unsuccessful attempt to snatch at a fish breaking the surface in front of me. The osprey came around again and this time seized the fish from the water, shifted its grip in midair, and barely flying, struggled to the top of a cardón to feed.

I then found myself in the midst of a developing fish boil. The dark backs of scores of 10-20 pound yellowtail were breaking the surface, hitting on a school of sardines. Almost immediately, the sea birds were on the scene: California gulls, Heermann's gulls, pelicans, cormorants, terns, grebes. I paddled right through the frenzy.

I could have stayed out there for hours on such a sea, but when I noticed a dark area of surface rippling spreading from the north, I decided to play it safe and paddle hard for the familiar safety of my bay.

Back in camp, I shaved and shampooed, and washed in the sea with a saltwater-lathering biodegradable liquid soap, then sacrificed about two pints of fresh water for a final rinse.

Having been on the island a week I took stock of my situation. I realized that, at the present rate, my water wouldn't last much beyond January. And if I were unable to find more, I could expect to be dead shortly afterwards.

However, what really troubled me was I somehow had just six cans of beer left. My pattern has been to drink one beer and a small glass of vodka every night, or at least that's what I thought it was. Okay there were occasional causes to celebrate, and moments when a little consolation was called for, but taking all that into consideration, something didn't add up. I checked and double-checked all my coolers and containers. How come I had so little of those 30 cans of beer left?

The old paranoia was returning. I kept thinking dark thoughts, and looking suspiciously at those cuervos that had been sticking to me like Velcro, suspecting they were somehow involved.

Next day, with the wind strengthening, making it improbable that a boat would appear, I decided to walk to the north towards Punta Los Machos to do a little more beachcombing. It was overcast; the temperature was ideal for hiking.

I left camp and headed inland around the back of Turtle Head, over a red rhyolite ridge that I came to regard as "the neck," and steeply down to the inland side of the lagoon. The flat, firm, salt-encrusted soil there offered easy walking.

Humbug Bay—looking south to Turtle Head and the high headland beyond my bay.

I made my way back to the shore, to where a long line of cliffs rose above a mostly stony beach. Dozens of aggressive seagulls swooped and noisily mobbed me as my boots bashed pebbles beneath the sheer, unstable-looking cliffs—a mix of rock, sand, and gravel seemingly cemented by bird poop spilling over hundreds of little shelves. It was clearly a favorite gully hang out and nesting area. A pair of ospreys came gliding over the top and hung above me, perhaps curious about what was freaking the gulls.

Harassing gulls aside, I was absorbed by the treasures on the beach. There were interesting bones and shells (including a surprising number of scallop shells, there must have been a camp nearby) and stuff I could use—tons of wood, hundreds of yards of rope, pieces of fishing net, thousands of bottles and containers, a sprinkling of fishing floats (mostly plastic, but some were polystyrene or metal). It occurred to me that I could string the floats together and maybe use them as rollers to move the kayak.

Far enough around the sweeping curve of Humbug Bay to be able to see any boats heading to my campsite, I climbed into a valley to find shelter from the wind while I had a can of diet cola and an orange. The narrow valley floor was stony, busy with blowing trash and confusing to the eye, making me extra wary of rattlers.

Carrying on, I was suddenly surprised by a pair of squeaking oyster-catchers rising up five yards ahead; it was like treading on an annoyingly loud dog toy. And, given the wind and waves, I was even more surprised to see a panga out to sea, three to four miles away, close in to the shelter of Los Machos. It was stopping and starting and circling, but otherwise staying put.

Beyond the seagull cliffs, I came across several shoebox-shaped 30-gallon plastic storage containers. They were either red, white, or blue—an odd coincidence they all ended up there at the mouth of a broad arroyo. I called it Patriot Beach and considered returning by kayak to pick up one or more for use in camp.

A mile ahead, after I'd placed a couple of useful-looking six-foot long ocotillo sticks above the high tide line, I found a collection of yellowing, clear plastic barrels. There was a small lizard apparently trapped inside one. I took a couple of pictures, poured him out, and watched him scurry up the beach and out of sight.

And then the answer to a puzzle... I encountered the remains of the shack that I had expected to see at the site of the panga. It was a partially collapsed structure of ocotillo sticks, and was probably where the sticks I'd found earlier had come from.

So, I was about three miles too far south. And mightily glad of it. The shack shoreline was nothing to get excited about. The beach was rocky, without a launch ramp, and the submerged rocks were covered in viciously-spined little purple sea urchins; and although there was some shelter from the north winds, my bay within a bay, beneath the tall cliffs was far superior.

Up a little side canyon someone had left a tied bunch of seven or eight more of those sun-yellowed plastic barrels. Clearly, with all these barrels and containers, the shack had not too long ago been a place of some activity. What kind of activity I could only guess.

When the wind eased and the panga seemed to be heading to Turtle Head, I decided to turn around and dash back. Thinking back to my previous trips I said:

> I felt more relaxed when I had all my gear on my back or on my burro's back... but now I've got so much stuff left in camp I have to stay mindful of it. Especially as it's so exposed there; if it were hidden it would be okay.

The adventurous souls on the panga finally took off towards LA Bay. I picked up the long sticks and the better of the fishing floats on the way back. The tide was still fairly low. After running the gauntlet of the gulls, I decided to try walking directly under the unstable cliffs of Turtle Head rather than over the "neck."

The rounded green and slippery half-submerged boulders at the base of the cliffs were a real menace. I preferred to walk on the many sections of the cliff that had fallen down, some obviously recently. Most of the rock was the same light-colored volcanic ash I'd seen earlier, but a good deal of it contained layers of small stones so sharp and rough that they provided a good grip even when wet.

After hundreds of yards of scrambling along, looking up anxiously, I finally, gratefully, edged my way around to the sandy shelf leading to my camp, only managing with dry feet because of the low tide. I was in no hurry to do it again. No one would ever know if a hunk of cliff fell on my head.

A fallen hunk of Turtle Head

I slipped out from my daypack, unearthed a cooler, and grabbed a well-deserved cool beer. A nearby oystercatcher, pinkish legs standing "knee-deep" in the sea, was preening itself with its long, straight, orange-red bill. In a final flurry, it threw its head under water, then picked up its wings, and splashed vigorously as if it were washing its snowy white arm pits. He seemed to be really enjoying himself. Cute—the American oystercatcher is definitely one of my favorite birds.

Chapter 16

A Light Over There

No one is so brave that he is not disturbed by something unexpected.

Julius Caesar

The night was calm and mild. Puffy, cotton-wool clouds drifted slowly across the moon, which finally seemed to be past the full. Each night, the waning moon would be rising later and later. Darker nights were ahead. I recalled that the panga had come in when it was moonless, so I wondered, a little pangxiously, what the next days and nights might bring.

The moonlight and the stillness made the peninsula appear deceptively close—astonishingly so. It was easy to imagine kayaking across the channel on such a night.

I was awake till after ten. Before sleeping I scanned the news and talk shows on my AM radio:

> I listened to the radio for over an hour, trying to get the weather… but instead got lots of stuff about Armageddon with Iran, and the problem of obesity in America… so if I can survive those calamities I just have to worry about the druggies and their laden pangas. And as I was dropping off to sleep, I woke with a start thinking, "There's a panga out there." And, of course, there wasn't.

Then I had a strange dream:

> Some French soldier coming out of the mist terrified, fully laden with all his gear, and he came across me and we didn't quite know what to make of each other… I was trying to figure out if he was real, and he was trying to figure if I was real…

Next time I woke, I looked at my watch and was glad to see it was almost dawn. It turned into a calm clear morning. And once again in the rich rosy glow of early day, it looked an easy paddle back to the peninsula, especially to the little guano-covered Isla Alcatraz, due west glowing eerily white in the sunlight. The early warmth of the sun suggested a hot day… a day made for kayaking.

I fished the rising tide with lures, along both points and the bay in between. I kept the pole wedged between my legs with the drag on the reel fairly loose. I found fishing from a kayak works best with lots of wide circling on the rod side to keep the line from running back along the deck. In spite of covering miles over every type of bottom I had few bites and caught nothing. I was amazed, but I wasn't really bothered. A whale spout, a crashing pelican, the rhythm of easy paddling, the little eddies spinning back from the blade, the water on the paddle dripping back into the sea... everything was fascinating.

I was looking at a raft of small grebe-like birds—probably eared grebes—and was intrigued by the way they all instantly threw themselves into a kind of curving dive and disappeared. Then maybe a minute later they rose together surrounded by scores of tiny silvery fish. I could only guess what type of herding activity was going on underwater. Sometimes the grebes were on the surface so briefly, and their disappearance was so sudden, I began to wonder did I really see them? And did I really see the fish?

As Steinbeck and others have noticed, Angel de la Guarda is a fanciful place where just about anything can be believed. In the late nineteenth-century the Gulf of Cortez Land and Fish Company had acquired the rights to settle and develop several islands in the Gulf, including Guardian Angel. An 1872 advertisement claimed:

> It has many hills, although not very high, excellent waterholes, rich forests, fertile farmland, two minerals not yet exploited, and a multitude of animals like deer, wild bulls, mountain goats, pheasants, rabbits, jackrabbits, wild turkeys... the island is a real treasure.

Fortunately the Treasure Island fantasy stayed just that, a fantasy. Today there are many protections in place to prevent the most egregious abuses, but another question troubled me. How is it possible to keep this island from those who would in their zeal manage, regulate, and control it to death? How can we keep it for any reasonable person to enjoy, to interact with nature in all its richness, to go solo and commune with their voices, their God... how to keep it free for anyone with enough gumption to get there?

It remained hot and still. I was really surprised on such a perfect day, a Saturday, that I hadn't seen a single boat. Wondering if the boating fraternity might know something that I didn't, I paddled back into my bay, and then headed quickly to my camp when I saw what appeared to be another dark squall line, possibly indicating a strong north wind. It was a false alarm.

Following a quick lunch, and an even quicker wash in the sea, I put on a short wetsuit and snorkeled briefly. The 65-degree water was still too cool for me.

After warming on a rock in the sun, I launched the kayak, walking it to four-or-five-foot deep water, and then without touching the bottom I pulled myself up, swiveled around, and dropped my butt into one of the seat positions. Over and over I practiced, paddle in hand, pulling myself on board from the front, back and sides. No doubt the buoyancy of the wetsuit helped, but it never took me more than four or five seconds to climb back aboard, even if I had to right the kayak in the process. In fact, thanks to its incredible stability, it was much easier climbing up onto the kayak than falling off or rolling it over. I was more than impressed with the stability of the Cobra Tandem. There in that perfectly calm bay, with a little care I even managed to stand up on it like a surfboard. And it was so easy when beaching to simply step off, or sit on it when launching. The session reaffirmed that my choice of a sit-on-top kayak was the correct one. Re-entering a capsized "sit-inside" would not be such a simple proposition, especially alone, cold, and being battered by a wind-whipped sea.

Satisfied with the results of this testing, I removed the wetsuit and felt plenty warm drying in the sun, allowing my slightly pale skin to get a controlled amount of sunshine. All afternoon it remained sunny and still, with just a few clouds.

A seagull was unenthusiastically pulling up bits of carrot top and potato peeling that I had thrown into the shallows. No doubt, he had reverted to his earlier assessment that unlike most humans, this guy was a lousy fisherman.

A pair of whales cruised by, finbacks or blues, about a mile distant, just off the southern point; it looked like a couple of big hunks of the reef had just separated and swam away. I thought about going out there to take some close-up pictures, but having kayaked miles that morning I managed to resist. Another day I might have gone for it.

The day remained breathless. I was constantly resisting the urge to jump in the kayak and paddle far off shore, and maybe take pictures of the island in the afternoon sunshine. And again, if ever I wanted to try kayaking across the Ballenas channel, conditions seemed perfect—a thrilling night paddle on an oily smooth sea and I'd be back on the peninsula. That was my fantasy.

However, I knew enough not to take the conditions of the moment for granted. The Sea of Cortez is like a charming serial killer; it befriends and seduces you, then suddenly drops all pretense and explodes in heartless overpowering fury.

In the evening, clouds rolled in and produced a memorable sunset, and with them came a strengthening northwest wind which began kicking up a mean surf.

Then after dark, as I was about to settle down and enjoy one of my few remaining beers, I got a shock. There was a light at the southern end of the bay! Just a mile away. I reached for my binoculars; it looked like a campfire and a nearby moving light, possibly a "headlight." The orange fire, the white lavender tinged light—tiny, silent, puzzling. It was an odd dance. How come I never heard or saw anyone arrive? I was disturbed by the mystery.

Whoever it was, I took a little comfort from the fact that they certainly had no qualms about advertising their presence. Do they know I'm here? They must have come in during or after all my cavorting with the kayak.

The wind continued gathering strength, moaning and screaming, lifting the waves and flying around to strike the tent from all sides. At one point I had to go chasing after my folding chair which went tumbling towards the sea. Sitting on the chair, huddled in a thick hooded jacket, I heard on a San Diego radio station that there was a storm and high wind forecast for most of Southern California.

I secured the camp against wind and rain, making ready a couple of large tarps to cover the tent and my baggage. Inside my tent I made sure everything was securely put away in boxes and zipped in bags. I began to appreciate the beached panga for extra protection and, as a last resort, a place to throw stuff if howling chaos struck my campsite.

Then I dragged the kayak up next to the panga, and propped it up on planks even though the tide range was probably diminishing now that the full moon was past.

When the moon rose, I studied the far end of the bay and the beach between to see if anyone was coming. After twenty minutes of seeing nothing unusual except the faint orange glow of the fire and the odd flash from that single light, I retired at 9 P.M. still wondering who was there… just a mile away. Man or woman? Mexican or Gringo? Who was on MY island?

Chapter 17

Nomads

The wretched have no friends.

John Dryden (1678)

When it comes to my Baja sojourns I've always preferred to just disappear, keep a low profile, arrive at my truth, share my feelings as best I can, and move on when the spirit moves me.

Since the initial publication of my first book in England in 1988, I've received hundreds of letters from readers who have found enjoyment and inspiration in my adventures. The comment I hear most is, "I felt like I was there with you as you walked around the coast." Perhaps the single most poignant moment came in a San Diego church when a friend of ours, stricken with multiple sclerosis, came up to me in a wheelchair, thanked me profusely, and said that she felt she had walked beside me the whole way on my 3000 mile journey around the coast.

Bringing such pleasure to your readers is one of the greatest things about being an author. And the wonderful warmth I've known for almost two decades and through three books has been one of the highlights of my life. Another has been all the great hospitality and camaraderie I've experienced south of the border.

On those rare occasions when I do hear something negative I'll try to address the issue if I think there's a legitimate point to be answered. But in the main, certainly in terms of comments that have come to my attention, I've felt myself surrounded by an aura of kindliness and appreciation.

I'd hardly given the Nomad message board much thought since arriving on the island. I'd occasionally wonder if someone might appear and share the experience with me for a while, but I didn't expect it. Mostly I just assumed the thread had faded and died as I hadn't been able to get any messages out.

But there was actually a vigorous debate going on. About three days after I'd arrived on the island Bonni had posted the following update:

Hi David
I'm sending a picture in another email of Graham leaving with his panguero Basilio on Saturday morning.
Graham was headed for the Los Machos area (known to the gringos as Humbug Bay) because Este Ton offered little opportunity for

exploring much of the island interior—steep high mountains all around. Los Machos is north along the west coast of the island, about where it has a pinched off appearance (with indents on both sides), and the lower terrain of the island can be covered on foot and crossed from there. He'll be there for an indefinite period of time, and relocate at some point.

Antonio Reséndiz helped him accomplish a lot with getting the permits and lining up Basilio, the panguero. The enthusiasm of the locals really heartened Graham I know, and several scientific people are wanting him to be their eyes and ears out there...

Roger and Jean at Villa Bahía gave him a great base from which to leave–many thanks to them, and for the picture I'll be sending along.
Bonni

A string of postings followed. Just to give a sample:

In March 05 I met Antonio and my friends and I rented Basilio's boat for a day, great fisherman. He put us into some really good fishing after the bay tour.

The more I read this thread, the more I get jealous! What a cool adventure.

I guess I'm missing something here (yeah - I know Graham's a great guy - we all love him) but the concept of "preparing" to be "marooned" escapes me. I mean aren't the words prepared and marooned anti-themical? Plus he's doing it in the least harsh part of the year - I don't know - why not call it what it is - an adventure with scant provisions (and a big safety net). B

Aren't we kind of getting the cart before the horse here - I mean don't authors normally select some interesting experience in their lives to write a book - rather than saying "I'm going to write a book based on what I'm about to experience."? - and then proceeding to "prepare" and hype. And what's going to happen if nothing interesting happens to Graham - do we still get the book? Will he be putting some extra cream on his tacos so to speak? How do we know that Graham doesn't have half the book written, at least in his mind, already? I don't know - it's sounding more and more like a virtual adventure "guaranteed in advance to please the readers" - as opposed to a real life one. But as usual I'm probably totally out of step on this forum. Best of luck on the book Graham. B.

Just wait for the frickin book, then buy it, read it
and offer your unsolicited review...

Not likely ca'on - I'm too busy living my life in the real world - I can't picture myself reading someone's virtual adventure. But seriously - I hope Graham makes it through ok - I guess you never really know what may happen. B

David, Bonnie and Graham, thanks for sharing the updates with us...
Hopefully we will get to hear some more dispatches in the future. Maybe he
took some corked bottles with him that he can put some messages into...

I believe B's opinion is unique to say the least! Of course that is the best part of
this forum - to be able to be our own unique self. I'd offer that many, many
writers plan and consider topics and experiences for stories ahead of the
writing.

Point well taken John - but then a lot of writers also make their experiences out to be more
than they really are. I guess at some point we just have to trust them - unless we're just
reading for the entertainment value. B

doesn't sound like B...has read any of Grahams books...if he had he would know that
the guy is definitely not a phony...in fact he's quite the opposite as far as I can tell
from the two books of his I've read so far.

His first book 'Into a Desert Place' (c1988) was written AFTER his 3,000
mile walk around the peninsula and it is a must read for all Baja people...

'Journey With a Baja Burro' was about his 1,000 mile walk from Tecate to
Loreto (in 1997) with a burro named Misión to carry his equipment...
following the trail between missions in many places. Again, a great read...
full of history details.

In 'Nearer My DOG to Thee' (c2003) he spent a summer 'marooned' in the Sierra
San Pedro Martir at 8,000 feet, with his dogs... and nearly got struck by lightning
more than once. I am using the word marooned (not Graham) here because he did
not have a vehicle to leave with. Bonni made a few trips up to resupply him.. and
teach him which mushrooms could be eaten (funny chapter). Great details on wild
fires and the California condor... again good historic research on the padres, who
established a mission which is what the sierra was named after.

Whether the chicken was first or the egg, Graham and other authors have always [gone] on an
'adventure' in order to write about it (you could also say that they write about it to go on one)
so that he is able to support himself.

Hmmmm... well if he didn't write about them it would be a great loss of
entertainment and education for the rest of us Baja and adventure seeking
folks...

Posting from Bonni
Hi David–First of all, thank you so much for everything you are doing for
Graham. I hadn't looked at the Baja Nomad website for a while, and it seems

to have really grown into something awesome. Graham had asked me before I left him in LA Bay to check it out…! I tried to clarify Graham's location (Los Machos) on Guardian Angel Island for the readers who were wondering, especially hoping that if anyone was "happening" upon that area with a marine radio, they could contact him. … He only has a 5-watt, hand-held, AA-battery powered radio that can't reach LA Bay. He will be monitoring certain standard channels, and only if he hears a boat or plane in his vicinity, in order to save on batteries… In the past, on his other trips, I generally have heard from him via the people he encounters along the way who are kind enough to give me a call or put a letter in the mail from him when they get back to the States. On one of his last nights recently in LA Bay, he was at a restaurant in town with Roger and Jean (owners of Villa Bahía), when a couple came up to him there and said they were the folks who sent me a Valentine's Day letter he had asked them to post while he was on his burro trip (in 1998)... My best reassurance on this trip is that amongst the fishermen out of LA Bay, with Tony's and Basilio's assistance, any important news he gets out to them will filter down to me. The ejido people were very supportive and interested in his project, but full of warnings, especially about the fat rattlesnakes that might be active all year long. Mike Essary has set a date with Graham in early February when he plans to fly over the camp, speak with him via radio, and possibly drop some things off his plane. If I get any news, I'll send it along to you.

HI BONNI! Thanks for the note. I haven't had the pleasure of meeting you yet, but I have met su esposo, Graham, and have really enjoyed his books very much! I just wish I could share a rattlesnake kebob with him out there overlooking the bay! (con salsa picante) Best of luck 2 both of you.

This post now qualifies as a trip report if we can expect continuing episodes of "Survivor, La Guardia". Why not post this riveting account of man vs. the elements over there? Of course, I'm sure it won't have the commercial impact desired on THAT board......are we to look forward to two months of pre-sale pimping of the next book here? I'm with you B.......21st Century American television has twisted the meaning of the word "reality".

I am really stoked...on the updates of Grahams latest adventure… after reading a couple of his books I feel like I almost know the guy and now to be able to read about his latest adventure on here is a real treat...I think Graham's adventures are a real inspiration to anyone who wants to explore some of the more remote areas of Baja

By the way, Graham is really a super nice fellow... He would be honored to spend time with any of you Baja loving kin!

Graham in person is a real kick in the burro! A very real, funny, person. The DesertExplorers.org had him as our annual Rendezvous speaker twice.

I'm with B. This whole thing is hokey.

Graham, Best of luck in your current endeavor. I've always enjoyed your books and stories. I've been around the Guardian but never set foot on it. Too damn hostile and no cable TV. The last time I know of anyone spending any time on it, one died after 4 days and the other two barely survived. Anybody remember that fateful encounter? … Some people should start their own thread and title it "Armchair Whiners". If you don't like the subject and can't say something Nice, Don't say anything at all.

Please don't misunderstand me. I think this "adventure" is a lot different than some of his others. Pardon me and others for pointing it out. Sorry if it's not a "feel good" post. Let's not confuse opposing points of view with whining - we're all friends here. In fact it might surprise you that some of us are just the opposite of armchairers - in fact our motive is to keep the forum real.

I don't happen to have read any of Graham's books - maybe my point of view would be different if I had. This week I'm going to pick one up - I should have it done in a few days. As I've said before - I would hope that the bottom line on this forum should be reality - and when it looks to me like someone is hyping something a little much then I'm going to call them on it... Sorry if it irks you. Any suggestions on which book I should start out on? I'm thinking "Into a Desert Place". B

Chapter 18

Machete-Swinging Crazed Lunatic

*Every time I see an adult on a bicycle, I no longer despair
for the future of the human race.*

H.G. Wells

Throughout the night I was treated to the sounds of moaning wind, booming surf, raking stones, flying sand and gravel, and a creaking, tugging tent.

Every time I woke, I went outside to look around and secure what I could. Dark ominous clouds obscured most of the stars. Had I covered the bag well enough in the canyon? If there was heavy rain I would have to go up in the night and wrap it better… maybe move it.

No earthly pangas would appear on such a night. So even though there was a stranger or strangers on my beach, and a real chance of a raging storm, I was surprisingly relaxed. In fact, I was more concerned for whoever had camped there at the exposed south end.

It's 1 A.M. and it's still a wild night… the kind of night you could have got yourself killed. I was earlier fantasizing this is the perfect night to paddle back across the channel because it was so calm and flat all day, so who would expect this at the end of it? At least it's very mild—the temperature is now 63°F. I wonder how my neighbor is faring at the other end of the bay. Enormously bright out there.

I just woke up from a dream. I was at a royal funeral in England. We were all on the beach in this beautiful little bay, the royal family and me… and suddenly a huge wave came up and swept a whole bunch of people and everything out to sea. I woke up and thought I'd better check the kayak.

By 3:30 A.M. there was a strong surf breaking over the pebble barrier, threatening my tent. After each particularly noisy rush of water and stones, I poked my head out for a look. It was five o'clock in the morning before I was finally convinced that the tide had turned.

At 6:30 A.M., the wind was gusting even stronger. I lingered in the wildly snapping tent, tired and thoughtful, doubting that my neighbor will be going anywhere in this wind. Maybe he needs help? I'll have to pay him a visit.

I looked at him again in the rich morning light.

Definitely looks like a gringo. I can see a yellow tent and someone dressed in blue—almost like a wetsuit or a uniform. Hard to imagine he would leave as the sea is so wild and clouds are coming from the west and pouring over the mountains into LA Bay. Otherwise it's sunny, so I believe there's no chance for rain… It will be a little odd talking to someone after eight days alone. I hope he's not a machete-swinging crazed lunatic.

So much for the maxim: windy days are hiking days! Ironically, it was too windy. With everything tugging and straining and threatening to rip and roll, I was reluctant to leave the camp.

At 9 A.M.—the wind was still blasting, and my little beachhead seemed as precarious as ever, but my curiosity was too great. I secured the camp as best I could, then dressed in a sweater and long pants, hurriedly hiked around the bay wondering if my neighbor was about to get the surprise of his or her life.

As I drew closer I could see he was probably a gringo, a guy. A hundred yards to go… He was walking the beach, on top of the pebble berm, picking up things. I wasn't sure if he'd seen me across the bay or even knew I was approaching. I looked back to my campsite and realized how difficult it was to spot anything.

He looked up. I waved. And a few seconds later I was introducing myself to Gary, a Canadian kayaker from Victoria, B.C. He had paddled over to the island a couple of days earlier, had gone to Este Ton, and then headed down to the southern tip before making his way back north. He said he saw a panga in Este Ton as he paddled back past the entrance.

In the general ramble of our initial conversation I discovered that he was a very experienced kayaker, indeed a kayaking instructor and trip leader. He had wanted to paddle around the island, but with this wild weather he realized that wasn't going to happen. As he stood there in his sandals, I formed the opinion that he was a quiet, pleasant, thoughtful fellow. I was relieved that he seemed no crazier than I was… at least no machete swinging so far.

He had launched from Antonio's *Campo Archelón* in LA Bay. He heard about me from Tony and from other people in town who'd described me as "the writer," but he'd been led to believe that I was on the other side of the island!

As we chatted, the wind seemed to be moderating somewhat. It should be a perfect "inland day." We agreed to hike together later that morning. I arranged to meet him 500 yards in from the shore about two-thirds over toward my camp. I walked back to get ready and do the necessary "proofing."

Gary Doran beginning hike inland

We actually hooked up maybe 1000 yards in from the beach; and I was surprised to see that he was still in sandals—it looked like a lot of vulnerable toe and foot to present to all the desert fangs and spines.

Our goal was to climb to the middle of the island and see the other coast. We started up a broad, easy, grassy valley, then headed into a steep-sided arroyo where our way was disputed by several large boulders, including one the size of a two-car-garage, that had effectively plugged the canyon. It looked like it had recently fallen from a pinnacle of rock. Another boulder just like it stood precarious on its pinnacle, ready to roll down too. We detoured into another valley and carried on climbing.

Soon tiring of that, I rediscovered what I'd learned earlier—ridges were the safest way to go. The ascent was gradual, the way unencumbered, the footholds less precarious, and the views spectacular. Gary was good company. I think we both enjoyed finding out about each other's lives and adventures. And he too was convinced that he could hear pangas day and night, and began wondering if they were actually there. It was gratifying to think that maybe I was not as deaf or mad as I'd feared.

Our progress had been steady with no major setbacks. Scrambling up a final steep slope of loose gravel and rubble we were welcomed by a lovely fresh breeze and a place on the great divide offering a splendid view of both coasts.

Relating the view to our maps and Google satellite images, we identified a lagoon and Punta Pulpito a few miles to the north, and Punta Rocoso to the south.

Gary gave me a few pointers about VHF radio etiquette. Requesting a radio check on Channel 16, I was delighted to make loud and clear contact with a boater in Puerto Don Juan—an anchorage at least 20 miles away on the peninsula, just south of LA Bay.

We made it down just before dark, and agreed to meet again the next day, to kayak if calm, and hike if not. We arranged to discuss it by VHF radio at 7 A.M., and parted company close to where we'd met about 1000 yards inland, heading back to our respective ends of the bay.

It was too late to cook. As the evening progressed, the wind didn't die as I'd hoped, but strengthened and veered from a norté into a wild and worrisome westy. I lost some of the protection of the northern point. The

Fallen boulders plug the narrow canyon

straining rainfly began lifting and tugging against the weight inside the tent, moving across the poles, making horrible creaking and groaning noises. The tent seemed on the verge of ripping apart as flying sheets of sand and gravel audibly lashed its walls, and a fine mist of grit blew through its large mesh panel sides. That particular design of Coleman tent had been a poor choice for these conditions. Inside the tent, I again put everything away in boxes and bags and lidded buckets. I expected a tough night, but took comfort from not being alone, and from a brilliant moon rise.

I cocooned myself deep in my sleeping bag, not so much because of the cold, but rather to stop the tent from bashing my head and the grit from flying in with me. My lips and teeth, and every bag and container inside the tent were covered with grit; the tent would need a good clean out when the storm abated.

I slept better than I should have and woke to a windy morning. The surf was wild and Pacific-like. Making our radio rendezvous, Gary and I agreed that it was too windy to leave our camps.

When the wind finally moderated we went for a less ambitious afternoon hike, a few miles hiking up valleys and over hills; it was just a good excuse really to continue chatting and enjoying each other's company. We stopped

Pacific-style surf pounds Turtle Head

at my camp and I showed him my setup and the Cobra Tandem. Gary had a fast, sit-inside, sea kayak... and all the knowledge, equipment, and experience to keep himself safe, or at least as safe as a solo kayaker could ever be in these waters.

He was planning on crossing the Canal de las Ballenas and returning to the Baja peninsula side the following morning which, given the state of the sea, made me a little nervous. He offered to take a letter out for me and mail it to

Gary Doran—the night before paddling back to the peninsula

my wife, then as an afterthought, offered to download all the pictures I had stored on the memory card in my digital camera to his iPod and put them on a CD disk and also send that to Bonni. That was welcome insurance.

After he returned to his campsite, I penned a few paragraphs to Bonni and hurriedly composed a website update. Then I walked over to his end of the bay just before dark. It was odd, but exciting, to be leaving my camp so late knowing I'd be returning by starlight or moonlight. At least I wouldn't have to worry about muggers or mountain lions, rattlesnakes or coyotes... or even ghost pangas. I took Gary some extra drinking water, a little fresh fruit, and a Walkman radio so he could listen to the latest weather forecast for Southern California.

Gary made me a cup of hot chocolate, and gave me his Google satellite maps of the island, more or less the same ones I had but his were on sturdier, coated, photographic paper.

He outlined that his goal the next morning was to make Smith Island and camp there before returning the following day to LA Bay. An emergency Plan B was to shoot straight across the "narrows" to Punta Remedios or Bahía Guadalupe, but that would put him way north of the town facing a much longer overall journey and a long haul down the coast.

I could sense he was nervous about crossing back. He said, "I really want to get this done. I want to do it. Get it over with." I felt for him as he wrestled with his fears.

Concerned that his desire to put the crossing behind him might cloud his judgment and lead him to act precipitously when patience might be a wiser option, I told him I had plenty of food and water and everything necessary if he needed to stay and ride out the storm.

But if he left, I agreed to monitor my VHF radio all morning, and try to make contact on the hour, every hour. The unspoken assumption was I'd be there to raise the alarm and try to convey a message to the peninsula if he got into trouble.

Gary's presence on the island had been like a vacation and a revelation for me, and had me once more reflecting on the importance of company, and its contribution to enjoying and relaxing in the wilderness. My solo trips definitely had a down side.

I walked back to my tent in the cold dark. The moon wasn't yet up. But the stars and bioluminescence generously lent what light they could to speed my way along the wave lashed shore. There was almost no need to use my flashlight. I was surprisingly unconcerned for myself, but the roar of the surf made me anxious for Gary. I was deeply impressed by his courage; and grateful that his presence on the island had emboldened me.

Chapter 19

Unexpected Challenge

Alone, alone, all, all alone;
Alone on a wide, wide sea.

Samuel Taylor Coleridge

I was outside the tent before 6 A.M. Looking through my binoculars I could see no sign of Gary or his gear on the beach. The wind seemed much diminished, but it was hard to be sure; it had shifted back to the north and I was now protected from its full force. The seas were still intimidating. The rolling waves and white caps looked awesome out in the channel.

Scanning the sea, I saw a group of about six sea lions, probably juveniles, jumping 50 yards from the shore, hurrying out of the bay... and beyond them, a pod of dolphins; they looked huge through the binoculars, like whales. But there was no sign of a kayak.

I tried to raise Gary on the radio—no reply. He must have gone. I pictured Gary dropping into the troughs and rising on the crests of the waves, paddling hard for the salvation of Smith Island.

The ravens came early. For once, I welcomed them, hoping it might be a sign of returning good weather. I was about to brush my teeth; my toothbrush was horribly gritty, so looking out to sea, somewhat distracted, I mindlessly poured a cup of water over the bristles to clean them. I was astounded when I realized what I'd done. What a stupid waste of fresh water. I should have used sea water.

I tried the radio again at 7 A.M. And again failed to make contact.

> I'm a little anxious. The wind is picking up; nothing he can't handle as yet, but it's what it portends. He's not answering the radio, so I kind of think he left early and he has gone a long way... If he left by say 5 o'clock, it's gone 7 now, he'll be beyond the mid point... The wind is sweeping down from north to south. I have an anxious feeling in the pit of my stomach... and I don't really feel too much like breakfast... I need to climb into the hills to try to make contact and be ready to relay a message if necessary.

Aided by the low tide, with VHF radio in hand, switched-on, and new batteries, I hurried over to Gary's camp to see if he'd left a note. Not

Long way back to the peninsula

expecting to be gone more than a couple of hours, I didn't take much else apart from my camera, tape-recorder, money, passport, and a quart of water.

At Gary's Beach I saw his prints and the mark where he dragged his kayak down to the water. He'd left the Walkman radio, but there was no message, no time of departure.

I climbed into the volcanic hills at the south end, trying to not rip my skin on the ocotillos or impale myself on any of the numerous bunches of sharp-pointed agaves. Monitoring the radio, I picked up several conversations from the peninsula, but nothing from Gary.

Long way back to camp

Rhyolite boulders and agaves

Standing on a ridge with a clear line of sight to Smith Island, I tried calling again at 8 A.M. During a burst of static I distinctly heard, "This is Gary on channel 16." I'm not sure he heard any of my replies. He sounded relaxed enough though. I was ecstatic. Surely he was safe on Smith Island or close to it.

But then I was troubled by doubts. I couldn't help but picture Gary out of his kayak, in the chilling water, battered by huge waves. Hoping to make the next hour slot and perhaps find out for certain how he was doing I climbed higher, towards the tallest peak, working my way up what became a dangerous slope of rubble and large boulders.

The sky had largely cleared, and the sun was beating down, making me increasingly wary of rattlers. I tried to stay on top of the rhyolite rocks and granite and not put a hand or a foot near any brush or shadows. In spite of my urgency, it started looking like I wouldn't make it to the top of the mountain by nine o'clock—I'd be stuck in a steep valley with another peak between me and LA Bay.

Fearing I'd be late with the call, I scrambled up a slope of massive granite boulders stacked so steep a major avalanche was a real possibility. In one tight gully I was momentarily perched over a sheer drop, one foot on a loose boulder, one hand hanging on to a precariously rooted elephant tree. It was a no-way-back, gamble all on the next move, moment. Fortunately, everything held, and I was able to pull myself up and out of danger.

Ironically, I was doing exactly what I had urged Gary not to do—acting precipitously to allay anxiety! He was probably perfectly safe while I was putting myself in real danger. And I began to notice an odd sensation, a weakness, in my right knee—like I had torn or was about to tear something!

After struggling to the top of the mountain, I rested awhile on a smooth, flat rhyolite rock. A pair of ospreys circling above sent their shrill cries into the air. Otherwise, wind aside, the silence was striking. My mouth was so dry I needed to take a long drink before I could try the radio. My calls to Gary went unanswered.

I scanned the sea with my binoculars for any sign of a kayak, any speck of color. At sea level it sometimes looks deceptively easy to just paddle to the peninsula, but you're really only seeing the closer part of the channel and the land rising beyond. I could now see and gauge the true expanse of open

A promising way down?

water that one has to cover. Mile after mile it looked an intimidating challenge for a kayaker.

At 10 A.M., I tried calling again. There was still no reply from Gary, but I picked up several Spanish conversations, presumably from boats and LA Bay. Again I relaxed and was sure all was well. I speculated that he might have paddled around to the other side of Smith Island to camp.

Gazing in every direction I had to consider my own next move. I certainly was not going down the same way I came up. But no other direction looked particularly inviting. I ruled out heading down towards the coast. There were also intimidating drop-offs north and south. So I found myself trailblazing inland with no food, very little water, not even a jacket, and my right knee feeling like something was about to give.

The best walking was on top of the volcanic boulders, and often that involved leaping one to another over ground packed with stiff needle-pointed agaves. One slip into a bunch of those and you would be in serious danger of poking a major blood vessel and bleeding to death.

So, mindful of my dubious knee, I stepped down from the top of the rocks and slowly, patiently, began working my way between them, treading cautiously among the agaves, the diminutive elephant trees, and all the scraping twigs and grasses.

"I've got all kinds of spiky and sticky things in my socks making for uncomfortable walking, but until I see I'm on a downward course I can't be bothered to take off my boots and pick all the seeds out."

The wind was picking up. I tried to turn north, to drop into the large wash meeting my bay, but several times after starting what looked like relatively easy descents, I found myself thwarted by sudden sheer drops and had to retreat back up the way I came.

It was frustrating. I wanted to head north and I was going south and east; I wanted to go down and I was heading up. It was hot. My water bottle felt alarmingly light. I took the inevitable tired step and collapsed to the ground, just missing becoming an agave pin cushion.

Needing to turn this around quickly, I set off down a steep ridge even though the valleys on either side were falling sharply too. There was no safe way down into them. The ridge suddenly ended; a sheer 50-foot drop confronted me. I retreated upwards yet again till I came to a steep slope of loose stones and slates. I had already ruled it out as too risky a path down, but this time I chose to go that way "because at least the fall won't kill me." Well, it didn't kill me, but after a couple of scary tumbles and back slides my weakened knee started to audibly click!

I was now in a tight valley choked with huge granite boulders. Some I crawled under, others I climbed over, most I squeezed around. Too fearful of a long exhausting uphill retreat, and too anxious to know if I could get down, I had "no time" to put on sunscreen or even sip water.

As I descended there was gradually more sand and less rock beneath my feet; the canyon started opening out, and eventually disgorged me into the wash behind the beach at the south end.

It was after 2 P.M. by the time I got back to camp. What an unexpected ordeal. My boots were almost destroyed; the soles were working loose and were useless for any more long hikes. I was left with just my backup pair.

The clicking knee was a real worry. It might have been done in by the strenuous hiking and climbing, but all the campsite squatting and crouching to clean clothes and utensils in the sea hadn't helped, nor the way the large hatch cover in the kayak had forced my legs into a slightly unnatural wide stance. I could only hope it would sort itself out with rest.

To aid my recovery I resorted to a lazy afternoon reading and a little medicinal vodka. Come sundown, while cooking a wholesome mucho veggie dish and enjoying the solace of a warming fire by a calming sea, I looked back to the now pink and purple mountains from which I'd escaped. I wondered how Gary was doing. I missed knowing he was at the other end of the beach.

Sunset—first night on island

Campsite—Humbug Bay

Gary Doran on the island divide.

All are welcome at my camp

Baja blue heaven

Looking down to "Turtle Head" and Punta Los Machos

American oystercatcher

Raven keeping an eye on me

Este Ton

Beautiful day, beautiful coastline

Wary chuckwalla about to crawl into the rocks

Campsite Este Ton—after rain

Sunset—looking south to Las Animas

From the shore to the mountains—north of Este Ton

Coast south of Este Ton

Endemic prickly poppy

Endemic penstemon

Last look back at Guardian Angel

Chapter 20

Crossing

*We shall find peace. We shall hear angels. We shall see
the sky sparkling with diamonds.*

Anton Chekhov

For several days it was warm, calm, and sunny—truly lovely January weather. I treated myself to a life of ease—poking around in the shallows, reading in the shade, meditating, showering, cutting my toe nails, shaving, doing simple chores like getting all the sand and grit out of the tent, taking stock, and checking on my hidden bag and water containers. I estimated I had 19 gallons of water left.

I watched the high-flying jets heading north-south or vice versa, leaving their parallel vapor trails. Occasionally two would cross, to leave a white on blue Cross of Saint Andrew in the sky. Not surprisingly, none ever went east-west out into the Pacific.

> There is a side of me that just enjoys pottering around, lying in the sun, being lazy and fishing and all that stuff. And that side will be happy to just stay here in camp for several more weeks and then go home. But how can I write a book about that? I'm struggling with that side that doesn't want to take any risks, that doesn't want to have anything bad happen, doesn't want to go too far out to sea, doesn't want to hike too far… just wants to basically go on vacation here… That will be the test of a real writer; can he write about nothing???

Well, I had severe doubts about that, so I elected to stop using my knee as an excuse, get off my ass and finally walk across the island. Not willing to leave my camp "abandoned" for too long, it would have to be a day trip—a flat-out "sprint."

It was a perfect hiking morning—almost certainly too windy for pangas, but not blowing to the point of threatening my campsite. After adding a couple of flares to my stuffed daypack, I left at 9 A.M. wearing my reserve boots. I took essentially the same route to the ridge as I did with Gary.

In a steep little gully, conscious I'm in short sleeves and shorts, I hurried by a bush that was noisily swarming with bees. And I started to notice more and more ant nests with their volcano-like entrances.

I was glad to climb back on to a ridge. And, at last, standing on the island divide, I could easily see mainland Mexico. With my binoculars I scanned the sea and the island's east coast for any sign of boats or fishermen. There might have been an old boat or a structure inside the lagoon at Punta Pulpito, but that was miles to the north. I wondered if it was the remains of the panga that Ed Gillet had written about. Otherwise the scene was delightfully empty. A lonely shore beckoned.

My knee felt fine. I studied my options and fixed a rough timetable in my mind. "It's 11:20 A.M. I can probably be at the water by 1:30. If I turn around at two that will give me three hours to get back." Then I picked what looked like the "easiest" way down the other side: descending a spur dotted with large elephant trees into an almost circular cauldron, then through a mile of rubbly canyon leading out to a gently sloping plain, and finally hiking maybe a mile or a little over, down to the shore.

It was time for action. With the GPS clipped to my belt, I stepped and slid down the steep slope. After leaving a full water bottle at the base of the spur, by an obvious elephant tree, I took a photograph of the "correct" slope and recorded, "I'll be a happy man if I see that water bottle again." I fixed in my mind to climb back to the ridge on the spur with the most elephant trees. I had reached out for them a few times on my descent.

Way down to the east coast

I was hurrying, but also needed to be careful. Miles of mountain and rock would separate me from my camp. "This is not a good place to get lost or have an incident of any kind." I didn't trust my memory. Under stress or when the light changes, it can all look very different. I took digital pictures, marked GPS positions, and described my route on tape. Moreover, I stamped my boot prints in the gravel and soft ground, and put up a few "ducks," or little rock piles, on salient boulders.

I also tried to ram into my memory all the important twists and turns in case I lost the tape-recorder or the GPS or camera.

> Coming back up, keep to the right. It almost seems like a too narrow canyon. The wider one looks like it's going straight up to the ridge. It might be. It might be going into a complete mess. So at this point keep right, keep right, don't be tempted to go up what looks like the obvious way straight ahead.

Backup on backup, I was covering every contingency, completely focused on minimizing risks and avoiding trouble. And that's been the pattern of my life. A master of the art of staying safe. I've never broken a bone, never spent a day in hospital. I've been driving for 35 years, never had an accident or a ticket. Yet because I take very few unnecessary risks, I feel I can on occasion take an extraordinary risk and stand a good chance of getting away with it. At least I have so far.

The canyon dropped steeper than I expected, and remained choked with boulders and bushes. I was carefully watching the time. "Make a single mistake, take one wrong turn, and I'm going to be walking in the dark. Now that's a scary prospect."

Finally, as I made my way out of the valley and around the south side of a mountain, I caught a glimpse of the sea and felt the welcome cooling breeze. The wind was hitting the east coast hard. A good surf was foaming over the rocks. It looked so close, but I suspected it was further than it looked, at least another mile. I stopped to take a GPS position of the canyon mouth. While I waited for the GPS receiver to lock onto the satellites and come up with my position, I took a few sips of water, looked around, noted paw prints and dried fur-filled poop, then rubbed some desert lavender between my fingers and inhaled the splendidly soothing scent.

"On my left as I go down there's some very dramatic basalt slopes probably 600-800 feet high... When I return there is no other canyon I could

East coast cardón.
Looking north to Punta Pulpito

possibly enter first."

"I left after nine and its going to be after one by the time I get down to the water. That's four hours at a pretty good clip, so that means I'll have to keep moving to get back by five. I'll have half an hour of poor light between five and five-thirty but basically it's dark by five o'clock. And I have my slightly less clear 'react to light' glasses. Great for the sun but not so good for twilight or dark."

There were a few clouds building right above the center of the island; I hoped they didn't signify anything too horrible. But I welcomed the prospect of shade as the way to the sea turned out to be a lot further than it looked. I was actually on a sloping plateau and had to drop down into a wide, hidden canyon. It was almost 1:00 P.M. and it looked like I was still half-a-mile from the coast. It was so close; I had to do it now. Punta Pulpito was miles off to the left; Punta Rocoso stood dramatically to the right.

I walked over a bank of stones to gaze into the wide bay. It was a lovely coast. "Here I am on the other side. The seagulls are giving me the welcome. A lot of sea birds here… probably haven't seen anybody for a while. I'll beachcomb and catch my breath... then I've got to go back." I wanted to stay all day.

There was a sea lion skull on the beach beside an old Reebok shoe. Or at least I hoped it was a sea lion skull, otherwise there was an extraordinary predator there on the island with me. I picked up a couple of small, rounded pastel-pink-and-green rocks to take back to Bonni. The pair slotted together nicely.

I stayed on that fascinating coast just half an hour, then reluctantly, knowing too well what was before me, picked up my backpack, ensured all the pockets were closed, tightened the straps, triple checked I had everything… then the retreat began. "This will really test my knee. I've got a long uphill stretch till I get to the ridge. Two and a half miles in a straight line, more like four with all the twisting and the canyons."

A route further north looked so much easier, but I did not want to risk attempting it "blind." I went back the way I knew, using all the information I had laboriously gathered to guide me home. I had to keep moving. Initially, at least, I would try to rely on my memory and follow my tracks. Only if I had doubts would I resort to the photos, tape-recorder, or the GPS.

It was hot. The clouds were in the wrong place. The sun was pouring into the valleys before me. I was walking uphill, but I didn't allow myself a drink, not so much to conserve water, though that was a factor, but more to conserve time. Every moment seemed precious as I thought about the difficulties of trying to return to camp in the dark. I had just 1.5 quarts of water left. I could have instantly drunk half of it. It was sobering to have so little water so far from camp! I felt "naked," like I had misplaced something. "Every so often I check the camera is there, the GPS is there, radio is there, because going back is not an option."

The unexpected came in the form of a hard sharp piece of branch that went right through the sole of my boot and broke off pressing against my foot. I pulled it out. It didn't seem to have punctured my flesh—certainly no blood was pouring out—so I was not inclined to take off the boot and look at the damage.

There was no room for further surprises. But fifteen minutes later, I felt a deep shooting pain in my foot. Instant involuntary limping. I lowered myself onto a boulder and looked under the pierced boot. Another piece of wood had penetrated the same hole in the sole and broken off inside. I could feel it poking into my sock but I kept on going. Surely I was close; I was determined not to stop till I reached the water and the wall leading up to the divide. Heading into what I hoped was the last arroyo, I twisted and turned around the rocks like a fleeing serpent.

> It's bouldery, shadowy, overgrown, I'm walking into the sun, so I've got to be more careful of rattlesnakes. This wouldn't be a good place to get nailed because I'm right in the middle of the peninsula and down a steep grade from the ridge.

Looking back to the island spine

It was reassuring to see the couple of ducks I'd left on prominent rocks. I knocked them off. Away from the coasts there was absolutely no sign a human being had ever existed. I wanted to keep it that way.

At last I found the water bottle. In sore need of a rest, I took off my boots and socks, removed all the seeds and stones, gouged out the imbedded piece of wood, and had a good, long drink. I hadn't had a drop since I left the beach.

In all, I allowed myself a twenty-minute break. My goal had been to make the ridge by 3 P.M. I would be about 15 minutes late.

When I finally, with the help of the elephant trees, struggled to the top and caught my breath, it started to feel cold. That kept me moving in spite of the tremendous views and photo opportunities in the rich light. I headed down a little way to get out of the breeze before looking at my campsite with binoculars. It was hard to see because of the glare off the water. I could only make out the tent dome—a golden nugget in a blinding sea of liquid gold.

By four o'clock, I was off the ridges and making my way down a mile wide wash through a maze of cactus and rubble. The worst was behind me. I started to feel more relaxed as the increasing coolness made a snake encounter less likely. With countless pathways before me, and often making decisions a hundred yards ahead, I was amazed that without any conscious intent I found myself following my steps almost all the way back. Was it the "logic" of the lie of the land, I wondered, or some kind of subconscious memory or tracking skill, or some fantastic psychic ability I could call on in the wilderness?

Flushed with satisfaction, I cautioned myself against complacency. The final mile was straight into the sun so I was trying not to walk into a face-ripping ocotillo branch or stub a toe on one of the many little chollas hidden in the grass. And I still had to find out if the camp was okay. The glare through the binoculars was even more blinding. There could be a dozen pangas and a hundred drug runners waiting for me and I wouldn't know; but they could see me coming for miles in the colorful clarity of the desert's early evening.

I arrived back about five. An empty bay. All was as I'd left it—the kayak, tent, supplies under the tarp! In spite of the wind, the inside of the tent was not too gritty.

So nine to five, quite a work day—definitely not a vacation. My knee had come through fine; living with the odd click didn't seem a great hardship. I opened up camp and pulled off the tarp to see what there was to eat. The breeze had almost died. I was too tired to produce anything elaborate, and ate straight out of an "emergency" can.

Certain I'd lost a couple of pounds, I felt I'd earned the right to put my feet up, enjoy my penultimate beer, and ponder another outrageous Sea of Cortez sunset.

But no drink, no drug, no mall, nothing that could be bought or sold could have given me the satisfaction I felt that evening as I looked back on the day, and watched the stars slowly take over the sky. I was simply, idiotically happy!

I sat out and read a little, making use of the red light on my headlamp. It protected my night vision, was less visible out to sea, and didn't seem to attract bugs. A white light often attracted an annoying ticker-tape parade of moths and other insects.

It was so dark beyond the book, every source of light demanded attention and seared into my consciousness: the flashing lights of airplanes and the twinkling starlight on the dark water, the subtle glow from LA Bay and the grander mesmerizing glow of the Milky Way. I was curious about a low bright star just beneath and slightly preceding Orion. It left a "starpath" across the water. I mused that the light on the water had made it from the star, across space, to the Sea of Cortez, and then into my eye. Of all the directions that light could have gone, it found its way to me. What were the odds? Back home in San Diego, with too much "noise," with focus constantly distracted, I probably wouldn't have given it a photon's worth of consideration, but there alone on the island there was something personal, something miraculous about it.

While admiring the statuesque black solidity of a large cardón silhouetted against the stellar brilliance of the heavens, I saw a bright shooting star, ranging right across the sky, falling slowly, casting shadows; it looked like it landed at the southern end of LA Bay, but was probably hundreds of miles beyond and likely never even reached the earth.

Inside my tent by 8.45 P.M., I was making a quick review of the day's pictures, deleting the bad ones and those taken just for navigation… I then fell into a sound sleep with the camera beside me.

I was woken by the tent's tugging movement after midnight. There had been warnings on the radio about gusty winds for Southern California. A little not overly-concerned corner of my endorphin-loaded brain was running a few wild and windy night scenarios, and placing on some mental shelf a plan of action. But everything was in perspective. A howling gale could take everything I had in camp and I knew I'd deal with it.

I felt nothing could rob me of this contentment. Even if it was the martyr's joy; I was resigned, squarely back on the path. Peace pervaded the universe. No matter what the state of our troubled world… I had faith in peace, faith in a God of love and light who commended the peacemakers, and commanded us to always be willing to take the first risky step. I was encouraged, in every sense.

Chapter 21

Slaughter in the Shallows

Fish say, they have their stream and pond;
But is there anything beyond?
...Oh! Never fly conceals a hook,
Fish say, in the Eternal Brook...

Rupert Brooke - Heaven

After a late lunch I went up to the shade cactus with my chair intending to read, when I heard a louder than normal racket from the shore birds. A hundred yards away, the sea was exploding with small fish—a "fish boil." Larger predator fish, probably yellowtail, were driving them to the surface and eager birds were gathering from all over to join in the slaughter.

The pelicans rained in with loud splashes, then sat on the water, beaks lunging down, and almost every time they came up with something to swallow. A few made a halfhearted two or three flap attempt to take off before ramming their beaks back down.

Some gulls were trying their own diving, but were never going to be as effective as the pelicans. Others were harassing the pelicans, getting in their faces, hoping they'd drop something. They must have been getting some scraps as they were really excited.

Birds attacking a school of small fish

Still trying to catch a yellowtail

And then (suddenly I'm really excited) right off the rocks, by my beached kayak, a mass of large shiny brown backs were breaking the surface as they pursued the "bait fish" into the shallows. It looked like you could literally walk on fish, or throw a stone and hit one, or leap in manly and gather a bunch.

I hurried down, grabbed a fishing pole with lure attached and cast into the melee. There was an immediate rod-bending hit. But the reel drag wasn't set tight enough. I couldn't drive the hook home. By the time I got my second cast in the water most of the large fish had moved out of range. I tried in vain to drop my lure in front of one of the stragglers.

The fish hung around in the bay so long I decided to go out on the kayak. I threw in my fishing pole, a knife, a pair of pliers, and everything else I needed to boat a fish. As soon as I was on the water, I could better see what the big fish were after. There were tens of thousands of anchovy-like, silvery fish gulping at the surface, creating an effect reminiscent of raindrops battering the sea.

I went out 200, 500, 1000 yards; the bickering birds and the boiling splashing of the big fish constantly moving in front of me.

Looking across at Smith Island, I could see as plain as day without binoculars a miles-long line of black humps breaking the smooth surface. Whales! Probably finbacks. Right in front of the island and for two or three miles to the north of it, there was one blow after another—white exhalations of vapor hanging in the air and catching the sunlight. It was a sizeable pod, moving south. I watched five simultaneous spouts spread over a huge area.

I was tempted to paddle further off into the channel, but looking around I was out way beyond my comfort zone. My valuables were back in camp. I hadn't raven-proofed. So I sensibly headed back in. Seeing all was well on shore, I was happy to enjoy another lazy afternoon drifting and fishing inside the bay, which was dotted with birds. They were resting, full, bellies gorged with dead or dying fish, drifting, content, just like me.

And in my lazy drifting, I soon hooked, and released, three fish. A poor old bass, I just nicked his eye with the hook. I nearly killed it for bait even though it only weighed a pound or so, then I thought what the hell, it can probably live with one good eye. I also hooked a triggerfish and a yellowfin croaker and returned them gently to their homes 30 feet below.

I approached the rocks at the south end of the bay. Groups of Heerman's gulls paddled slowly in the water as I eased by. Forty or fifty satiated pelicans rested on the rocks, many in breeding colors. I could have almost reached out and touched them with my paddle, but they weren't too bothered and kept preening, "yawning," clapping their beaks, and scratching their necks with their feet.

Back in camp the tide was so low I left the kayak on the exposed sand 50 yards from my boat ramp till I could bring it up with the rising sea.

At the tail end of twilight, the yellowtail returned with the tide, right off my beach. I deemed it too late to have to deal with all the messy fuss of cleaning and fileting, so I settled for just watching and appreciating the show, a show that has been running for hundreds of thousands, if not millions of years.

Next day, the Sea of Cortez continued in its mellow mood. I went out early in search of the elusive yellowtail. Baitfish once more spotted the sea like rain. Knowing the currents would be wicked, the camp was every-proofed and I had everything I needed in and on the kayak, just in case I couldn't battle back.

The birds were working a half-mile out. As I arrived nearly every bird took off and flew elsewhere, leaving me floating above deep black water speckled with shiny scales and dissipating clouds of bird droppings. Two sea lions occasionally poked their heads up to check me out. But there was no sign of a fish anywhere. The melee had eerily disappeared.

I gave up and paddled to the north, always the safest direction, running ashore occasionally to pick up any colorful or interesting items in the driftwood. Looking down in eight feet of water, I floated over a sandy bottom strewn with living, dark-brown sand dollars, and suddenly found myself on top of another big school of yellowtail. They started circling the kayak. My rod was out of reach, wedged under a crate and a stack of wood at the front of the kayak. By the time I got forward, freed it, and managed to get a lure in the water, they were gone. A pity I wasn't trolling when I passed over them— it would almost certainly have been fat yellowtail steaks for dinner.

Chapter 22

Out of Beer

Grief may be joy misunderstood
Elizabeth Barrett Browning

Two week vacations probably wouldn't work for me. I had been on the island two weeks and I was just beginning to truly relax and enjoy the experience.

I'd settled into a very satisfying routine—an active "expedition" day followed by a day of reading, camp chores and rest. And many of the latter turned into days of considerable activity.

> I washed myself and my socks in the sea, tended to my camera, tape recorder, and fishing reels, and generally cleaned up the fishcamp. I gathered up rusty cans, old batteries, and a few pieces of metal and moved it all to a single pile of trash tucked away in a little hidden gully. I also buried some in a two-foot-deep hole. Then I spread shingle, broken shell, and fine gravel around my tent to help keep down the gritty dust that kept invading it. I wasn't sure it would be effective but it looked attractive… What fun to have time to do all this stuff, very relaxing.

And every part of the day brought its own simple pleasures—from the first cup of coffee (instant decaf) in the morning, to putting on shorts and T-shirt as the day warmed, to stargazing and satellite watching before retiring to my tent around 9 P.M. and sinking tired and exhausted into my cozy sleeping bag after listening to the radio or reviewing my digital pictures.

It was always a delight getting acquainted with the local wildlife… most of it anyway. A small greenish gray bird was a frequent visitor to my camp. It seemed to enjoy hanging around, hopping in and out of the salt tolerant shrubs close to shore. I made a tentative identification that it was some kind of a warbler.

However, there were sad, philosophical moments too, especially when I found myself facing the end… my last can of beer. For the first time I began to seriously ponder how I'd get off the island.

January 21st—Wearing my "backup" boots, after running the gauntlet of the gulls, I hiked north along the beach to Los Machos. I wanted to check out the "narrows" on a windy day, and feel the venturi effect. On the way, I found another green plastic crate perfect for holding gear or as a table support. I left it beneath the cliffs till I could kayak over to get it.

I also found what looked like a slab of bacon—a large hunk of fibrous meat beneath a thick "pork" skin. What was it? A piece of sea lion? Whale? Whale shark? I wasn't sure but, as for perpetrators, orcas were high on my list of suspicious characters.

One beach seemed packed with skulls—pelican, dolphin, sea lion. But perhaps the most interesting was the delicate skull of a smaller carnivore. It might have been a cat. I picked it up and carefully folded it in some tissue to take back.

Approaching Punta Los Machos, there were long stretches where steep walls of rounded rocks rose from the sea like man-made ramparts. Maybe summer storms, blasting from the south, had thrown them up. On top, an undulating cobblestone and shingle platform stretched way back from the shore. So even though the bay was calm and well-sheltered from the prevailing nortés, there was no place to comfortably camp close to the water, and there was no easy beaching of a boat. Perhaps that's what put the humbug in Humbug Bay.

Yet, in that impossible looking sea of rocks, someone had skillfully made a bed of planks and slates—perhaps after an emergency need to anchor or pull up a panga and wait out a storm.

The cliffs of Punta Los Machos were exceedingly colorful—composed either of sulfur-yellow layers of volcanic ash surrounded by zones of red and orange, or dangerously loose, sharp, angular red, black, and brown volcanic rocks. And there was the inevitable cap of reddish-brown basalt, which from a distance looked as if some mighty Mexican Vulcan had smeared the island with great swathes of refried pinto beans.

I walked out to where I could feel the full force of the gusting wind. Standing like Heathcliffe on the blasting crag, I confirmed that beyond the sheltered waters of the bay, the nine-mile-wide straits between Punta Los Machos and Punta Los Remedios were inordinately white capped, wild, and foamy.

Returning to the calm behind the point, I enjoyed a snack and a soda and then began an energized urgent retreat. I needed to hurry to get by all the places where the rising tide could force me to take an uncertain detour inland.

> I was just walking past a little cave-like entrance at the base of the cliffs and a great blue heron flew out right at my feet and took off. I had just found a large fishing lure and I was walking along looking at that and you can imagine how I jumped to see this big bird suddenly shooting out.

My feet felt pummeled as if someone had been beating the soles all day, and several toes were feeling like they might be becoming blistered. But I was in too much of a hurry to bother removing my boots and take a look.

Hunk of flesh   *"My rest a stone"*

Punta Los Machos

Back in camp, the wind was blowing and the tent was flapping and snapping more than I expected. But by 6:30 P.M. calm was restored. Beneath the clear skies the temperature gradually dropped to 44°F.

Feeling ever more relaxed as I massaged and warmed my feet over the fire, I started to really revel in the sense that this was my island and appreciate what a privilege it was in this crowded, over-regulated world to have so much freedom to explore and wander it at will.

Two days later, I was exploring and wandering inland, up a wide and deep south-east trending incision into the island's backbone. It was going to be a hot January day—and was already 80°F in the shade at 8 A.M. In no particular hurry, I made a slow and patient ascent, bird book in hand, plant field guide in my pack, binoculars around my neck. A welcome breeze was soon followed by strong wind gusts, which made it increasingly unlikely that I would have any visitors.

It was a snaky day. No matter how fascinating I found the cardóns and flowering plants, or how absorbed I was with a particular photograph, I kept one eye open for rattlers. And that eye got bigger and bigger the further up I climbed.

I never tired of picking and rolling the fragrant flowers of the desert lavender between my fingers. It was such an evocative scent. I remembered how amazed I was as a young street urchin walking past a hedge of lavender and thinking, "My God that's the same scent in our shampoo and bathroom soap." Lavender must have been a favorite of my mother's. Throughout her life, there was always lavender in some cosmetic or toiletry in our house. If she won bath salts playing bingo, and she had a choice… we'd all be smelling of English Lavender for the next six weeks. It had never occurred to my

Another canyon to explore

young street-wise, nature- naive mind that the aroma derived from a bush or a flower. Scents surely were manufactured and came from a factory or the corner shop!

Mid-morning, I climbed on to a ridge stretching halfway across the valley and looked back to camp through the binoculars. Satisfied all was well, I

Colorful rock beds

sauntered up the canyon feeling like a prospector as I surveyed the ground and examined all the interesting rocks and minerals.

Crystal rock

"Teddy bear" cholla

There was a pink wall to my left, an amazing dyke of greenish rock cutting across the valley floor, an incredible boulder of white crystalline material so heavy and hard I couldn't break it with a rock hammer. Then among the pastel orange rocks scattered all about, I found and photographed an uncommon "teddy bear" cholla.

The flat, gravelly floor of the canyon made for surprisingly unproblematic walking at first. "Just so easy, a gorgeous hike made more beautiful because there is absolutely no sign of anything man-made."

As I ascended, I got other occasional glimpses back to my campsite. How sensible was I being? I had no more than three liters of water. I had left no note in camp, no indication of my plans. But I had a flare, my VHF radio, and the GPS. That seemed extravagantly sensible compared to what I carried on my cavalier charge around the coast of Baja in the early 1980s.

A mile up, the main valley narrowed and turned east. A smaller side canyon continued south. The wind died. The junction of the canyons fell perfectly still. After removing my hat and shirt, I enjoyed a peaceful lunch sitting on a large boulder watching and listening to phainopeplas and black-throated sparrows flitting between the bushes.

Suddenly, a hummingbird appeared before me looking like it wanted to land in my red hair. Startled, I leaned my head back, initially out of concern and then so I could focus on its gorgeous iridescence. As I was looking at its tiny eyes and admiring its perfect poise, the hum of its wings was drowned out by a wild gust of wind that kicked up a mini tornado of dust and leaves and started all the bushes swaying. In seconds all was still again. The hummer was gone. My hat and shirt had blown 50 feet away. Weird. If at that moment I'd been dialoging with the divine, I'd have been a true believer.

I pushed on up the rocky main canyon. Peripherally I was aware of blue sky, green cacti and bright orange-red basalt boulders. But my focus was now more than ever on what was a yard or two in front of me. I took in every stick, shadow and shrub.

Deep in the mountains, the valley split in three directions. I chose the broadest. It was an easy path of cinders for about 100 yards, and then I had to traverse another basalt boulder field.

Suspecting I was nearing the divide, I pushed on thinking every new ridge and high point would grant me a view of the other coast... but it was not to be. Running out of time and nerve, I turned back and made a rapid descent till I could see my campsite again.

I was back in camp an hour before sundown. The wind was still gusting around the bay, but all seemed well. I rubbed antibiotic ointment on a few scratches and cuts, then after allowing myself a warming shot of vodka, I rather enjoyed a well-deserved, mild, shorts and T-shirt sunset.

Fill-in flash on a magnificent sunset.

Chapter 23

The Tides That
Try Men's Souls

We shall not cease from exploration
And the end of all our exploring
Will be to arrive where we started
And know the place for the first time

T.S. Eliot

It was a mostly cloudy morning. Thin streaking bands of color trended from the north of the island to LA Bay. The sea was calm with just surface rippling.

I pulled the kayak down to the water and paddled south for a couple of hours studying the shoreline. Given a low tide and if the surf wasn't too bad, I was confident that I could walk back beneath the cliffs if necessary.

Back in camp it was almost 80°F. I washed myself in the sea, rinsed off with warm sea water from my solar shower bag, and then enjoyed a final rinse

Returning from a foray to the south

with half-a-pint of fresh water. Part of me felt the fresh water rinse was an unjustifiable extravagance, but I was comfortable (or complacent) enough to do it anyway.

The sea remained so temptingly flat, I kayaked out again, down to the southern end of the bay, drifting close to the rocks to admire the birds and the Sally lightfoot crabs happily picking at the seaweed.

I landed at Gary's Beach. Wandering around, I picked up a piece of green net, a yellow rope, and a small sea-scrubbed plank that could serve as a good cutting board.

Hearing a throbbing noise, I looked up and was amazed to see a large yellow helicopter heading south, going point to point across the bay. I stood still on the beach beside the blue kayak. I wasn't sure if the crew noticed me, but I suspected it might have been some kind of anti-narcotics surveillance.

That evening, beside my small fire, I recorded: "If I do have visitors tonight it could well be the military; I'm half expecting it. So I ought to have all my documents at hand." A dozen pelicans worked the bay as I added:

> I've been here two and a half weeks. I haven't seen a scorpion, a mouse, a mosquito, a noseeum, hardly a fly, certainly no nuisance flies… just absolutely perfect. There are not many places in the world so amenable to camping. Gorgeous. Not a rattlesnake of course. Nothing. And I've hardly seen an ant anywhere around the camp. This is such a good time of year.

After dark, sitting on the chair outside, warm and cozy, I was listening to a news program on my radio when there was a simultaneous burst of static and a flash in the sky to the southeast. That was followed by two or three more in quick succession. A lightning storm? Rain?

I was not altogether confident in my tent with its large mesh side-panels. A combination of wind and rain would likely produce a soggy mess inside. I rolled up a tarp and pegged one side of it to the ground by the tent, so I could quickly unfurl it over the top to help divert some water.

The flashes continued, backlighting the mountainous core of the island, but there wasn't a cloud in the sky, and no discernable sound of thunder. The silent storm was far to the east, over mainland Mexico. I remained outside reading and enjoying the still, pleasant air. Suddenly, a whistling waft of cool air came from the island center and the night turned instantly cold. I was glad to finally zip myself inside the tent and wriggle down into my sleeping bag.

About 1:30 A.M. I was woken by the sound of the surf rising and the wind tugging the tent. The flashes continued. For most of the rest of the night I lay awake, watching, waiting, deep in thought.

I recalled people and events of my life with an astounding clarity, like it all happened yesterday and I was the same person as I was then. The recollections seemed extraordinarily real, shockingly so… more real than the present; like I could just step back through time and space and pick up my life from that point. It gave me an insight into what it must be like to have Alzheimer's—to live a previous reality that seems more tangible than the blurred and fleeting present.

Next morning, no sooner had I stepped out of the tent than three ravens landed to make their totem appearance on the arms of the usual cardón cactus. To make sure it was a token appearance, I let them know that this was the pumiced land, and they were not welcome.

Filling my kettle, finishing one of my five-gallon water containers, and surveying the diminished levels in the other containers brought home to me the sobering realization that, at the present rate, I'd be completely out of water in a week… or two if I used the water purely for drinking.

The sunrise painted the Baja peninsula peaks a beautiful orange-pink; I watched as the warm, radiant color visibly crept down the rugged mountain slopes. Smith Island seemed to be once more a volcano streaming glowing lava from its flat top all the way down to the reflecting fiery sea. It was a sea of uncertainty. Vast patches of smooth oily surface alternated with patches of incipient ripple and chop. Calm or wind-whipped? I waited to see which way it would go.

It went for another easygoing kayaking day. I was happily aboard, fishing near the south end when the helicopter went over about the same time, following the same line. Even though I was a sitting duck on the kayak, I instinctively froze, hoping not to be seen. And if they were checking out the north-protected bays, as they should be if diligently looking for drug runners, they'd be sure to spot my tent and tarps around the old panga.

After unloading the kayak and a quick soaping dip in the sea, I put on my boots and hiked a little way inland. Resting on a woman-sized warm rock, I stared at my camp and across the channel to the peninsula, and was assaulted by a sudden surprise bout of loneliness. I wondered how everything was at home. Home! It sounded idyllic. Home. Safe in a warm bed, or watching TV with Penny and Pedro cuddled beside me, and Bonni back from a hard day working in the hospital, kindly bringing them a "cookie" and me an ice-cold beer.

Some folks might have a very nice cozy co-dependent relationship. Ours was more of the go-dependent variety. It seemed to thrive if one of us could go away occasionally. Certainly, I really missed and appreciated Bonni most when I had to fetch my own beer… and Penny and Pedro, of course, found it very annoying being constantly disturbed as I got up. Yes, our relationship was like the sun and the moon—constant, complementing, eternal, but ironically at its brightest, fullest, and most glorious when apart.

I had been on the island nearly three weeks—five weeks remaining! It seemed so long. I fantasized concocting some excuse, wimping out, going home, and later returning to the island with a friend or two, maybe a Mexican fisherman, and about 2160 cans of beer. I did not want to be alone. But I knew the mood would pass—as it had on a dozen or so previous solo adventures—

and then so much sweeter would be the homecoming. If, of course, Bonni hadn't changed the locks by then.

I decided to go up the canyon before dark to take stock of what I'd hurriedly put inside the survival bag, and maybe wrap and raise it a little better in case of a downpour. And when I saw what was inside I went into paroxysms. Paroxysms of joy! Halleluiah! Sweeter than homecoming! Come back ravens, all is forgiven! Absence makes the heart grow fonder! I nearly fell flat on my face as I skipped down the gully, two forgotten cans of beer in hand. It turned into a calm evening. And after dark, after a nice warm beer (O.K. two warm beers), for the first time, apart from a faint glow, I saw direct evidence of human activity on the Baja peninsula—fireworks or flares from LA Bay. There must have been drinking and celebration going on there as well.

I woke about 12:40 A.M. and stepped outside the tent to a calm, still night. As I stood there peeing into the gently lapping waves I was surprised and enthralled by two things.

The first was to see that the tide was so high I could have made quite a splash by diving off the back of the panga and going for a swim. The second was to see a glowing electric Jell-O green where the stream of recycled beer met the sea. Glorious bioluminescence! My own fireworks display right there at my feet. To prolong the display I threw stones into the sea and marveled at the splashes and the waves of ghostly light.

Saturday, January 28—I guessed it was the day before the new moon. It was 49°F at dawn. The wind was calm so I elected to kayak. It was a long drag to the sea because the tide was so far out, but at least the lower part of it was over sand.

I headed south to fish beneath the cliffs, had a few good bites, saw a turtle, picked up planks for extra rollers, then in the face of a gathering chop I returned to the safety of the bay to see that the tide had risen faster and higher than I expected. Many of my launch planks had floated back off into the plankton, which necessitated a quick paddle around the bay to retrieve them from the surf or the shore.

After lunch, a fierce northwest wind kicked up. I deliberately launched into a wild sea, taking nothing except a stowed dry bag with a few basics. Then off a sandy beach within my bay, a five minute walk from camp, where I could easily retrieve the kayak and the paddle, I practiced battling the wind gusts and testing the kayak's ability to deal with the churning waves, the worst of which came roaring over the bow and more so over the side if I got even halfway broadside to them. One cold breaking wave landed right in my lap and took my breath away—and almost my testicles (I'm sure the fickle fish that laughed at my lures would have been fighting over them)—but I somehow stayed in the boat and the boat somehow stayed upright. Great stability. But there's the downside of a sit-on-top kayak—in such conditions you have no spray skirt protecting you and keeping you dry below the waist.

Before ending up in the water and getting clobbered by the kayak, I pulled away from the shore and sat resting, moving up and down, bow directly into the wind. Even above the noise of the wind and the surf I heard a panga, a very real one. It came flying around Turtle Head, and then in one almost cavalier graceful movement the motor throttled down as the bow swung sharply around to face the open sea. In that position, the boat rode the swells. It was a busy scene onboard. The two occupants gave no indication that they had seen me. I assumed they were seeking shelter while they secured their load. After a couple of minutes frantic activity they suddenly took off and gunned it towards the peninsula, casting aside a shower of spray with every crash of the bow.

All afternoon, I thought I could hear the wooden thud of a boat on the water, the banging and slapping of a panga flying over the waves. The sound continued into the evening. It sounded like there was a flotilla of fast boats out there.

I was reading by headlamp after a fantastic sunset. Hearing the noise again, I turned off my red light and peered into the blackness. Then I looked through binoculars. Nothing. I didn't think it was my imagination... but when I started to hear the persistent sound of a telephone ringing I was forced to believe it was all in my head.

Back to reading, still tense and expectant, suddenly there was a loud WHOOOSH like a missile the size of a telephone pole going by and away. I was off my seat so quick, ready to take to the hills, when I caught sight of a dark, winged form ghosting across the stars. I guessed it was a nocturnal bird—an owl or a nighthawk which had probably swooped down to check out some movement I'd made.

Before retreating to my sleeping bag, I raised a foot high wall of gravel with my shoe to protect the low corner of the tent and then slept soundly for several hours till I was woken by the dramatically loud noise of a sea lion breathing. In my half awake state I was reaching around to feel for it in the tent. It wasn't far away however. By starlight I could make out the sea lion's head poking from the water, then as my eyes adjusted I saw the eerie glow around its body as it glided through the shallows.

The water was just a sea lion's length from my little gravel barrier. If it hadn't been such a calm night I would have been dashing around trying to get all my gear out from the tent to save what I could.

Chapter 24

Over the New Moon

*Wealth was everywhere. For a pittance I'd found paradise. It was the same
with all my long lonely journeys—the point would come when having
gone through the stresses and trials, fears and doubts, I'd at last feel whole,
complete, relaxed, tuned-in, needing no one, but basking in every warm
and giving human, animal, and spiritual encounter.*

Graham Mackintosh—Nearer My Dog to Thee

Sunday, January 29—No rest day for me. I had learned to live with my knee and the other aches and pains. With a little shot of adrenalin, pain and exhaustion seemed of little consequence, especially on the trail, separated from camp. Perhaps all the camp concern was a mental device to get me dashing "effortlessly" home. Without the anxiety I'd probably be way more lead-footed, spending too much time sitting in the shade, feeling lazy and sorry for myself.

I decided to walk south, close to the coast, to search again for the elusive inland trail—a fast and safe way back regardless of the tide and the surf. It was warm. I hiked along the shore then snaked my way up a valley onto a ridge that led to a peak that was about 1000 feet above the sea. The view was spectacular, affording occasional glimpses back to Turtle Head, and south to all the great canyons I would have to cross.

I pulled out my VHF radio and tried to call several people I knew in LA Bay including Antonio at Campo Archelón, and Roger at Villa Bahía, but there was no reply. Then I tried requesting a radio check from all stations. I was surprised to get a clear strong signal from a man who requested we switch from channel 16 to 18; I complied but I couldn't raise him there. A little while later I got him again on 16 and this time he said go to 80, "eight-O." Again he wasn't there. With that, I gave up. Possibly he had a place towards the south end of LA Bay which I could just line-of-sight on. The town itself was still mostly behind Smith Island.

Walking high above the cliffs and taking forever to traverse the first of the deep, boulder-choked cross canyons, I finally concluded this "over-the-top" route was impractical, if not impossible. It would take so long and be so hazardous I might as well (if I couldn't come back by kayak) wait out the tide and walk and wade back beneath the cliffs.

I returned to my camp at 4:30 carrying more netting, a fishing lure, and one of the planks that had washed away earlier. It had been a hard physical day. I was beginning to feel almost skinny. I must have lost eight or ten pounds already. It was easy and "effortless" to lose weight with such a lifestyle—my Baja diet.

At sunset I took my mug of tea to the base of the cliffs by Turtle Head to look west for any sign of a "new" moon, which would indicate that the tidal range had begun to diminish. I was disappointed—not even the slimmest sliver!

Well, of course, barring a solar eclipse, I wouldn't see the "real" new moon anyway. The new moon was a theoretical rather than an experiential concept, the calculated moment of moon-sun "togetherness," the very opposite of opposition. I always thought it would be much more reasonable to call that "new moon" moment of togetherness "No moon," because when you actually see a tiny arc of a "new" moon in the early evening sky, then the new moon has already passed. Certainly, I always felt a little foolish getting excited, looking up and proclaiming, "Yes, yes, the new moon," when there was absolutely no moon to be seen.

New moon, no moon, whatever we call it, sun and moon are "together" in the sky—united in their gravitational effects, creating the most extreme tides.

At 9 P.M., I retired anxiously to the tent knowing that I was possibly facing an even higher tide that night. The kayak was up tied beside the panga and raised on a platform of planks. I woke at 2 A.M. and was disturbed to see the surf running to within a yard of the tent and beginning to wash under the kayak. I wished I'd brought those tide charts. I didn't know if the tide level would be the same, higher or lower than the previous night. I would just have to wait and see, so I resorted to the radio for an hour or so; one ear on the program, the other on the noise of the waves outside.

> Listening to radio news and talk shows; mostly about the election of Hamas in the Palestinian territories. Amazing how that threw so many of these opinionated… commentators who didn't know what to make of it, or who to blame, and this whole philosophy that free peoples don't make war and sanction acts of terrorism is so naïve.

Every twenty minutes or so, I ventured out to look around. Finally, at 3:30 A.M., I gratefully accepted that the tide was falling. I could switch off the radio and sleep. If I didn't see the moon the next day I resolved to move the tent… I guessed that would take me about two hours. But it had already cost me about five times that in lost sleep.

Next morning, I climbed to the island divide and explored along it where I could see both the peninsula and the coastline of mainland Mexico. Even up there I was impressed by the number of ravens, but not once did I see a vulture. Most unusual, and a stark contrast to the situation on the peninsula where vultures abounded.

Looking southwest back to the peninsula

I made my way back to camp and put up the tarp shade so I could stay out of the warm afternoon sun. While sitting there, scanning with my binoculars, I was amazed at the amount of plastic that had suddenly appeared in the sea, especially soda bottles and colorful liter and half-liter (outboard motor) oil containers that the fishermen must have discarded without a second's thought. There was everything that would float: pill bottles, buckets, milk jugs, balloons, Styrofoam, bits of boat and driftwood. Hard to believe someone hadn't dumped a huge barge of trash into the Sea of Cortez. But it was obviously just the extreme high tides washing all the stuff from the shore; and over time most of it would be re-deposited. The sea and the beaches were in danger of becoming a vast unsightly trash dump. Definitely not what Steinbeck had encountered.

The afternoon tide came right up the launch ramp. I could have just pushed the kayak from its platform into the sea, but I kept to the shade, reading and occasionally gazing at the sacrilege that humankind had casually inflicted on the stunning beauty before me. And there, like a whispered warning of impending fiery destruction, Mother Nature had sprinkled the waters with great globs of pumice, her volcanic floating rock.

At 3 P.M., beneath thin clouds that promised an interesting sunset, I watched shadows forming in the canyons, then slowly pouring down the valleys that I had earlier descended. It was easy to imagine the hand of night

laying claim to the land and clawing the world into darkness.

Then YES, YES, YES!!! Hope. At dusk, a little slice of moon. Another cycle. A reprieve. The tides will diminish; the currents will slacken; the nights will be brighter. It was enough for now. I was content.

Looking southeast towards the mainland

Chapter 25

Manna from Heaven and Sea

*The higher goal of spiritual living is not to amass
a wealth of information, but to face sacred moments.*

Rabbi Abraham Heschel

The beginning of February brought warm, calm days and gentle southerly breezes. Kayaking and fishing were particularly delightful in such conditions, leading me to range ever further out from shore and away from my safe, comfortable base.

I was paddling north beyond "the shack," taking note of the number of stingrays and shovel nosed sharks scurrying along the bottom when I glanced up and was amazed by what appeared to be a huge wave down at the south end of the island, stretching right across the Ballenas Channel like an approaching tsunami or tidal bore. I checked it with my binoculars and it looked just as real and mysterious… a mighty flood apparently bearing down on me.

I paddled in towards a sandy beach and stopped about 75 yards from shore. I didn't want to be too far out in case I ended up swimming, and I didn't want to be too close to a tumbling surf zone. I pulled out the binoculars again. The rampart of water was still there and there were several long, undulating lines of birds flying above. I noted that the visage of the land behind was broken, indistinct, and partially eaten away.

When the wave never got any closer, I landed, scrambled up a steep stony bank, and after several minutes with binoculars trained on the strange phenomenon, concluded it was most likely an illusion—this time an illusion of my eyes rather than my ears—one more example of the strange play of light and reality in the Gulf of California. I picked up some driftwood and paddled back to camp.

Minutes after returning and unloading, I pushed off again and paddled south. I landed beneath the cliffs to take pictures of interesting flowers, crystal-packed pegmatites and other rock formations. The water was literally flat calm and mirror-like—a hovering bee would have disturbed the surface like a helicopter. The sea was as blue as the sky; separating the two realms nigh impossible to the baffled eye. It was mesmerizing, like floating in space. Which way was up? Which was down? If I leaned too far over, would I be dropping into my reflection, or would it and the sea be rushing up to join me? Everything became wildly unreal. Every dip of the paddle, every swirl, every returning drip, every amplified sound... a miracle.

I was lost in a peaceful, trance-like state. Beyond fear. Beyond doubt. Compassion was universal. And in that state, Baja whispered, called to me as

Cactus-choked valley

she had promised. I was part of its every rock, every bird, every creature. We could melt into each other at will. And in that perfect state of belonging and brotherhood... there was ecstasy.

I drifted towards a little rocky cove where a great valley met the shore. Coming into the shallows, I glided by a large navy-blue fish indifferent to my presence. I stepped into the sea and stood over it. The shallow water was so clear, it was easy to imagine the fish was hovering in mid-air, like a blimp slowly moving across a tree canopy beneath. But its gills were opening and closing and its fins were gently waving to keep its position in the water. Expecting it to take off any moment in startled flight, I eventually reached down breaking the surface as slowly as I could, hoping not to break the spell. Gently touching its sides I realized it had no fear of me at all. I could have picked it up.

My mind struggled to separate my reflection from the fish. I closed my eyes, and in the utter silence and the peace, I had the sensation that I was

A moment of clarity—Gulf opaleye

being touched, held, gently raised up. It was surely a glimpse into paradise, where the lion shall lay down with the lamb, and where love and brotherhood were so deep the lion would lay down his life for the lamb.

When I opened my eyes again and looked at the fish, I noticed there were two small, light-greenish patches on its back, the larger of which looked like an angel, arms raised, beckoning, with flowing robes the milky green color of nighttime bioluminescence.

Needing respite from such dizzying possibilities, and wanting to feel *terra firma* beneath my feet, I left the fish in the shade of my kayak, which was half-pulled onto the stony shore, and walked off to explore the beach.

I found a long-dead, dried-out turtle, and high up under some cliffs, a hopeless tangle of heavy fishing net. I tried to extricate it from the rocks and driftwood but instead got out my knife and cut away a section that was almost heavier than I could pick up. The mesh material was a kind of rope. I folded it on top of the kayak, eager to get it back to camp to add to my collection of pieces of net. They were proving to be some of the most useful items there on the island, especially for camouflaging, weighing things down, and holding them together.

My return was aided by an incoming tide and a gently rising southerly breeze. The breeze stiffened in proportion as I tired, carrying me swiftly home. So minimal were my exertions it was easy to imagine I was being towed by sea lions and dolphins. My only regret on such a magical day—that I hadn't set off earlier and had the courage to venture even further.

Back in camp and back into a more down-to-earth mindset, I began to wonder about the fish. Maybe it was so sluggish and indifferent because it was old and dying, and maybe the green patches on its back were really a fungal infection. In one sense, that interpretation was intellectually more satisfying, but in another, it seemed devastatingly dishonest to the truth of the feelings I had experienced.

I also began to wonder about the wisdom of cutting up the fishing net. Even though it was partially buried and looked to have been there a while, it was a very expensive net and if the owners were searching for it and seen what I'd done, they might want to cut a few hunks out of me.

Then at dusk, while I was out at the point taking several self-timer pictures of myself silhouetted by a glorious flaming sunset, I was amazed to see a panga appear at the south end of the bay. After a while hovering off the rocks, it landed on Gary's Beach and soon afterward there was a fire over there. The evening was so quiet I could hear voices and all kinds of odd bangs and booms. One of the guys had a very nasty cough. I tried hard not to give myself away.

An hour later, just about dark, they fired up their motor, rounded the southern point and disappeared. I had very mixed feelings: paranoid pangxiety of course, a nagging net guilt and, a little surprisingly, taking comfort from their presence.

Just before midnight, I thought I heard a motor "out there." But it sounded different, deep and throbbing like a boat larger than a panga. I heard it start and die several times and then... silence.

February 3rd—Another gorgeous day. I headed out on the kayak with two rods to go fishing. I looked towards the south end of the bay and thought about it, but I decided to try my luck running under Turtle Head and up beyond the lagoon. While there, I did a little beachcombing and shell collecting then returned to fishing for a while, but my heart wasn't in it; I was feeling too connected to the fish and was glad I didn't catch anything. A strengthening north wind made it even more uncomfortable, so I reeled in the line and headed back to camp.

While unloading the wood, I saw a dark shape in the water at the south end of the bay. A whale. The body was huge; by contrast the dorsal fin was tiny. It was either a blue or a finback; either way it was absolutely the largest or the second-largest creature ever to have roamed the planet. And it was right there, a few minutes paddle away and heading closer. I left everything on the rocks—fishing poles, tackle box, beachcombing finds—grabbed my camera and pushed the kayak back in and paddled in that direction. Like Captain Ahab, I was too wrapped up in the chase to ask if this is a good idea. The waves were bigger than I would normally hazard, but when you are set on a course, it's easy to rationalize away every doubt or inconvenience. I told myself this was a great opportunity to build my confidence in these seas.

Being so low in the water I only occasionally saw the dark back of the whale, but I headed for the unmistakable columns of spray lingering, drifting south. But on the "final approach" the great leviathan disappeared. I rode the shimmering waves up and down, turning, gazing in every direction, but it had vanished. I looked down into the blue water, half-expecting to be suddenly raised into the sky by an island of black.

After ten or fifteen minutes bobbing and circling and getting occasionally slapped by cold water, I came to my senses and decided to head back. Now paddling hard into the wind, I moved closer to shore and followed the curve of the bay into the welcome protection of Turtle Head.

The wind moderated a little. It wasn't too cold, so I bathed, shaved, and washed my hair, then took an afternoon nap inside my tent where it was a lovely, warm-up, sweaty 120°F.

The temperature and the dreamy, relaxed time-out helped focus my mind. I had just four gallons of water left; that's about three days comfortable supply... and after that "I'll probably be dead in another three days if I don't start taking action NOW."

Chapter 26

Still A Bad Joke

As he brews, so shall he drink.

Ben Johnson

I had a plastic inflatable solar still packed away in camp… but the kettle, tubing and corks comprising my main still were up the canyon in the hidden "survival" bag. I hiked up to collect what I needed.

After half filling the kettle with sea water, I placed it on my fire and waited for it to boil and send over the precious steam, which of course was pure distilled water. All I had to do was condense as much of the steam as possible through a long arrangement of copper and plastic tubing. The salt stays behind in the kettle. Simple enough. I hadn't done this for years, but I was confident I'd soon be making a very comfortable yield.

Well, it took me several hours to make a little over a pint, and I probably sweated out more than that just tending the large fire and dashing around trying to keep the smoke from getting in my eyes. If I wasn't going to be tied down 15 hours a day, I had to make the still more efficient.

I then unpacked and examined the solar still which had been given to me by a couple of young entrepreneurs years before. It was a last-second decision to take it. I thought it was modeled on the solar still I had carried and used on my 1983-85 trip, which I could inflate, pour seawater inside, and just leave in the sea or on the beach, and effortlessly collect a pint or so of

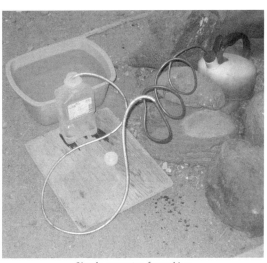

Simple apparatus for making drinking water from the sea

drinking water at the end of the day. However, this one was critically different, requiring much more set up and maintenance. It came in two parts, was held together with patches of Velcro, and was designed to rest on the water, anchored to some object, with sea water being absorbed from beneath and evaporating into the cone above and then condensing on the wall of the cone. I had my doubts about the design as soon as I looked at it.

It was supposedly for use in life and death situations where ease of use and clarity of instructions were at a premium. I think I have a reasonable command of English, yet I struggled to make sense of how to use it. It was so Mickey Mouse and impractical, I cringed imagining some poor African or Indonesian peasant desperate for a drop of fresh water, cursing the company that mocked and tortured him so. No wonder the company went out of business. I cast it aside as a bad joke, keeping the salt-and-mineral-supplement powder that came with it.

The temperature was well into the eighties. Before chaining myself to the kettle still, I went for a late afternoon, final mind-clearing hike. That was a mistake. Back in camp, I was so thirsty I drank nearly a pint of water. Food didn't interest me, but I forced myself to down a bowl of cereal, with minimal water and powdered milk, and chew a few leaves of uncooked cabbage.

I arranged some rocks to contain a two-part fire—an optional larger fire to supply warmth, light and a continuous source of hot coals, and a smaller side-fire for the kettle. I tended the still all evening, listening to the kettle boiling and the steam bubbling through the tubing.

It was another disappointment to make just under a pint in two hours. At 8 P.M. I was too tired to do more. I stood at the tent door gazing at the ever present volcanic cone of Smith Island—an image burned forever in my mind. The half moon shone brightly. The temperature was beginning to drop... it was now 60°F. I caught up with my diary and was soon asleep.

February 5th—Superbowl Sunday. Most of North America might be concerned this day about making ten yards... all I could think about was water and how to make another ten milliliters.

There was plenty of wood left around my bay to fuel the fires, but easier pickings were on the farther beaches. Before getting the still going again, I took advantage of a cool, calm morning to kayak around Turtle Head to gather some from the near-virgin stacks on the other side.

The kettle was soon boiling away on its little fire. In spite of my initial derision for the solar still, and knowing this was almost certainly a waste of time, I tried to set it up and get it working. I read the instructions again and again, but after a couple of hour's investment, I reconfirmed my opinion that it was simply a terrible design. Tubes fell off, the Velcro patches were poorly aligned, it never inflated as it should have, and the wind threatened to blow it away and knock it down.

And as I was trying to blow it up, I heard a pair of whales breathing. Two more blues or finbacks were cruising north, just half a mile away. I was a little deflated to think I could have been out there with them if I wasn't tied to the stills.

The solar still might have yielded something under ideal laboratory conditions, but in "the field" with waves, the tide rising and falling, and the wind gusting, it was a disaster. It would bring tears to the eyes of an NFL linebacker. And that was about the only way it was ever going to yield a drop of anything.

I kept the components handy for use as a waterproof plastic hat… or for possible rain collection.

During the day, I couldn't listen to the game as AM radio reception wasn't strong enough on my little Walkman. But towards dusk, in between still duties, I picked up snatches of the last quarter.

And after a long day—my reward, about three pints of very plastic-tasting drinking water. The cost—with all the bending and crouching, my back was beginning to seize and the noise in my right knee was beginning to sound like a creaking bed in the middle of a particularly lively love-making session.

I crawled stiff and exhausted into the tent before 8 P.M. After getting snug and comfortable, a strong wind kicked up out of nowhere. I had to go back outside to secure everything. Even though I hadn't had any booze for quite a while, it had been a sobering day. I fell asleep yielding to negative thoughts like there's not much point being on the island if all I'm doing is chaining myself to the still and making barely enough water to stay alive. And that was being optimistic. So far, in spite of my industry and best efforts, I had been using MORE water than I was making. My precious cushion was diminishing. I had less than three gallons left.

The solar still proves useless—thinking of my wife cheered me up

Chapter 27

My Own Personal Guardian Angel

As cold waters to a thirsty soul, so is good news from a far country.

Proverbs 25:25

Monday, February 6th—I got the kettle still going again, and made a few changes. I removed the length of plastic tubing (which considerably improved the taste), and then concentrated on cooling the steam as efficiently as possible by immersing and drenching as much of the copper tubing in cold seawater as I could. To combat any negative thoughts, I also tried to occupy my mind better while tending the still. I listened to tapes, read a little, kept binoculars handy to birdwatch, and simply gazed about, making the best of a bad situation. My morning's yield—another pint of water.

As this was a potential Mike flyover day, I also had to be ready in case he appeared to make that parachute drop. If all went well, I assumed I'd have to paddle out to collect the package from the sea. But I was not really sure what to expect. The more I thought about it, the more dangerous it sounded... throwing a heavy pack out the door or window of a small plane! I just hoped the parachute didn't tangle in the tail and bring the plane down.

A couple of planes flew over during the day; each time I immediately backed away from the bubbling still and turned on my VHF radio. Nothing. Then about 3:30 P.M., just as I'm thinking "this ain't ever gonna happen," a plane was flying north, overhead, lower than the others. I turned on the radio and heard Mike calling me. We switched to Channel 18. The signal was not perfect, and Mike was having trouble hearing me inside the noisy cockpit, so conversation was kept to a minimum. He asked where I was in relation to the lagoon. I repeated a couple of times, "I'm in the bay immediately south of the lagoon, just the other side of the headland."

He said he'd climb higher, circle to the south, and his companion in the plane would try to drop the parachute in the middle of the bay. I grabbed a paddle and lifejacket, readied the kayak and ran it down to the sea on the planks.

I was so busy getting the kayak in the water I didn't realize they'd already dropped the package... apparently close to shore. I might not have seen it anyway as I was looking into the sun. Mike said the parachute was checkered black and white and the bag was black. He told me it contained a letter from Bonni.

I thanked Mike profusely. He said he will try to come over in a fishing boat the next day or two and bring fruit, treats and a few more supplies. This is getting better. I mentioned water, telling him I'm operating stills and making drinking water from the sea. Again I had to repeat it a couple of times so I hoped he understood. I said, "Adios, over and out," as he turned and headed back to LA Bay.

It seemed a reasonable assumption that the parachute and parcel would (if it floats) wash up towards the south end of the bay as there was a strong northwest onshore wind blowing.

I pulled the kayak back up the ramp, grabbed my binoculars and a light daypack and hurried along the shore. I'd only have an hour and a half to search by daylight. I was almost running, peering ahead, in the surf, among the pebbles, looking for anything wedged in the larger rocks. I began to doubt that I'd find it… and if it washed ashore south of the bay, it would be tough to recover it from the rocks before the waves broke it apart beneath the cliffs.

Two-thirds of the way around the bay, I saw a dark object on a gravel beach. It was definitely something washed up, something black… and yes, there's the chute attached to it, being washed by the waves. I was relieved and excited. And surprised when I picked it up—it weighed 20 pounds or more. What was inside? I had guessed Bonni and Mike might send a six-pack or a twelve-pack of beer, but this was way too "solid" and round. After taking photographs I returned ecstatic to camp, deciding to open it there. It took a long 20 minutes.

Two thumbs way up

CIA mini-parachute?

I placed the bag on a large flat board resting on a crate and opened it with ritualistic respect. I unzipped the black bag and pulled out a heavy inner package wrapped in a sodden white towel. I carefully hung the black bag and parachute to dry on my clothes line. It was clearly a purpose-designed chute, probably from a Special Forces catalog or CIA surplus store, and it had fulfilled its purpose perfectly. I wanted to get it safely back to Mike. It must have been very expensive.

The white towel was covering a layer of clear bubble wrap, taped tightly with duct tape. I pulled at it anxiously. And inside all was dry. The first thing out was the letter from Bonni in a Ziploc bag.

When I finally unwrapped the main package I got a huge surprise—it contained a single steel barrel of Heineken beer. And there was also a little bottle of schnapps, a bag of chocolate chips, and a package of Kit-Kats. The chocolate treats were clearly Bonni's suggestion. She knew my favorites. Everything had arrived in great shape—dry and undamaged. The schnapps was a gift from Mike and the large "mini keg" was probably his idea. Much more sturdy than a twelve-pack of cans.

There was a little note from Mike:

Graham,
If you're reading this it's a good chance my plan worked! Enjoy the beer—your own mini keg on La Guarda. Bonni told me your favorite chocolates—don't blame me if they're wrong.
Enjoy the schnapps too—one of my favorite Swiss drinks. Hopefully see you by panga tomorrow or the day after.
Mike.

After a few more photographs of this, my first-ever parachute re-supply—everyone should have one at least once in their life—I made ready for evening.

I opened Bonni's long letter with a little trepidation, hoping all was well at home, having heard nothing for nearly a month. I was grateful that no disaster had struck the family. And there was a delightfully loving Valentine's card; it will probably be the most memorable of my life.

Then Bonni included this note that she had sent to the Nomad discussion board. It was posted online February 1.

This is some infill for the readers who are interested in following Graham's trip to Isla Angel de la Guarda. The letter that Gary (the primo kayaker) sent me is all I've heard from Graham, not surprisingly. We trust he is doing well and I am personally very stoked about this trip.

From my years being with Graham, I know how many people take the time to tell him what his books mean to them. There is also never any denying how many people do not like his brand of travel or writing. He agrees with dissension!

No one thinks he is out there trying to thwart death every day. As for the idea of being "marooned," this thread opens with a copy of a personal Christmas email to David K. From the next letter, which Graham actually wrote to Baja Nomad readers, he's used quotes to show the humor intended with the word. Sorry that got lost. Mentioning his book intentions took on a life of its own, too.

Today I'm bringing a letter for Graham to Mike, who will be flying over the island around Feb. 6. His "drop" is limited to about 20 pounds (beer and chocolate!) as weight is very tight on a light plane and they are en route from parts elsewhere in Baja. Like he indicated in his post, Mike is doing this for mostly his own experience–but it will sure be appreciated. He will let us know what the latest is on Graham when he can.

Two other friends are going to join Graham for about a week around Feb. 22. They will also be able to let me know any news from him when they return. He has his foibles to be sure, but is not hiding them and making any great claims. Anyone is welcome in his camp to enjoy with him some of the best that Baja, or even the world, has to offer. He is one lucky person to be out there.

Thanks to all the people who have expressed support for Graham. He realizes completely how he has been helped by so many people he's encountered, or possibly doesn't even know, over the years. Will let you know what's up when I hear.

Bonni

I was surprised and delighted that I might have some friends joining me. However, reading between the lines, it was clear that Bonni was dealing with an undercurrent, perhaps a flood of negativity on the Nomad message board… I could only assume some folks were ridiculing my use of the word "marooned," saying my trip was futile and of no interest, my writing stinks, and I'm a shameless pimper of a new worthless book.

Well, there's an element of truth in all that. But an element can be as small as an atom or make up the core of the planet! I was too happy marooned with my mini keg of beer to care much. I just hoped Bonni wasn't upset by anything too over-the-top.

What Bonni was alluding to was a string of Nomad postings that included these exchanges after the letter I'd given to Gary had been posted on line:

Graham letter from the island!
Monday, January 16, 2006
Position: 29° 15.568 N
113° 25.933 W

I'm just getting a quick note out with a Canadian kayaker. His name is Gary. Real nice guy. He paddled into my bay 2 days ago, and we've been hiking and exploring together the last two days.

Yesterday, we reached a point in the middle of the island offering a fantastic view of the other coast. I'll try to reach it before I leave here. Weather has been generally warm with some lovely days perfect for kayaking, but yesterday and especially today have been real blasters, with Pacific-size surf in places. I'll need to get the sand and grit from my tent when it stops.

Generally I've been out of radio range, but in the mountains I made contact with presumably a boater south of the Bay of LA, in Puerto Don Juan. So if I climb high enough I can probably make contact with someone.

I have plenty of everything and all's well. I've lost a pound or two already. There are lots of animal tracks, and scat with fur inside. Probably not coyotes—might be feral cats? If so, there are a lot of them. Otherwise, not sure what they are.

I'm camped at the north end of this bay within Humbug Bay. There's an abandoned panga there which has been incorporated into my campsite. Driftwood abounds in the bay—so fires will be no problem. It was wonderful to have a week of bright moonlit nights, but now I'll be doing more stargazing. The beachcombing is great, and I'm always finding a crate or a plank to add to my comforts.

Gary is camped a mile away at the south end of the bay and I'll be heading over there with this letter just before dark. Then I'll come back by flashlight. He has agreed to let me download my pictures so far to his *I-pod*, and when he gets back to Victoria, B.C., he'll make a CD and send it to Bonni.

There's a resident hawk on this point and it's killing a lot of birds. I saw it flying off with the blooded carcass of a webbed-foot bird, probably a duck. Also I've found the remains of a duck on the beach and a barn owl in a little canyon above my campsite. Every day, for companions, I have sea lions, oystercatchers and ospreys. Great bird watching here, and looking at the seashore creatures is wonderful.

Crows are the only nuisance so far. They love to poke around my camp when I'm gone, and check everything out with their sharp beaks. The fishermen who brought me over warned me about them. So I need to "crow-proof" my camp when I'm away.

So all's well and I'm very content among all this beauty and peace, but I did get a surprise, actually quite a shock on the first night. About 1:30 A.M. I heard a motor; a panga came in after the moon had set and began shining a powerful light on my tent. I thought it best not to emerge so they wouldn't know it was just me inside. Besides, I was sleeping naked in my sleeping bag. So I was frantically getting dressed and shining my light back so they knew I was inside. Luckily they went elsewhere. Not sure who they were, but I doubt that they were fishing! After that, I've slept dressed every night.

I'm going to head over to give this to Gary. So no more for now. I'll keep this campsite for a week or two more, maybe longer as I'm getting so cozy and settled. It's sheltered from all but the worst weather like today. Moving will be difficult as I have so much food and water and equipment. Only regret I didn't bring more beer. Such a super way to salute the sunset. Miss you all.   Graham

The postings went like this:

> *thanks David for the updates on Graham...very cool to hear what's happening on that big island*

Hey, cool update! I hope we get some more as time rolls by. Wish I was there.

Graham sounds like he has ants in his pants. Seriously though, I'd worry bout those "runners" around there. I'd also like to meet that hardy Canadian he met out there complete with IPOD! My kinda guy

Well, let's hope that something dangerous–or at least interesting–shows up, and pretty soon. So far, this adventure is every bit as exciting as a 10th-grader's essay on "How I Spent My Summer Vacation."

He's still alive???? How is this possible?? Aren't the daytime highs, like, in the 70s and humidity in the 40s? And CROWS, too!!!

C'mon, now, he MUST have earned "immunity" in a competition with that member of the KAYAK tribe he encountered, no? Or did members of the PANGA tribe come to his aid? Predicted next episode of Survivor: La Guardia...........SNAKES!!!

I read his book on the walk down the peninsula with Misión the burro and liked most of it OK. I may read the into a desert place epic but that read about spending time alone with his dogs on the mountain for 3 months........sorry Graham.....too boring for me, not my cup a joe.

good luck on the isla. maybe you'll find some pirate's treasure or some other stash!! watch out for the motta runners though, they hi speed it on converted PT boats at nite headed for El Golfo where they unload. scary dudes amigo, Cuidado!

The third book has chapters on the condor program in Baja, Mexican wild fire management we could learn from, eating wild mushrooms and how easy one could eat the wrong ones... other things certain mushrooms do... the observatory across the canyon from Diablo mountain... the padres mission the mountain range is named after... almost being struck by lightning (see tree hit near his tent), and more... you cannot judge a book by its cover...

That mushroom on the cover ... amanita muscaria or better known as the Fly Agaric are very common in forests. These mushrooms contain alkaloids that cause mind expanding hallucinations. They also contain toxins that will make you ill.

I read that Graham was eating mushrooms in the Sierra San Pedro Martir of Baja. He was smart enough not to trust his own limited knowledge and eat unidentified mushrooms. So he relied on his wife to show him which mushrooms to pick and consume.

Either his wife is an accomplished mycologist or they are both crazy. Even experts have trouble identifying many fungus which share common traits. Sometimes it takes a chemical reagent or microscopy in order to delineate them.

But if Graham ate the pictured mushroom than it might account for his toughness and determination and his way out trips....

Way back when in the northern latitudes of Europe when Norsemen fought dearly for their lands they drew upon the gods to help them in their conquests.

They also drew upon reindeer and mushrooms to bolden their warriors. It is said that the reindeer would eat the Fly agaric and it would thereby spike their urine. The warriors would collect this urine and drink it before battle. The stimulant and highly intoxicating beverage made for a fearsome warrior.

AS the men charged the enemy stark naked and screaming wildly the enemy would be convinced they were of evil making and would usually high-tail it.

Does anyone know if there's any water on the island? While back I was talking with Ruben Daggett and he mentioned there was some kind of oasis with palm trees on the east side? Is this true...

I just finished "Into a Desert Place" - I was going to submit an unsolicited review - but on second thought it'd probably upset some of folks on this board - besides that stuff is all subjective anyway. B

I didn't enjoy the first book. I started it thinking "he must be a likeable chap because folks are always helping him out". Which progressed to "thank goodness that ranchero was nice enough to give him water. Good thing that panguero passed by when he did. Nice of the couple to give him a ride, and that guy to send the message to his wife". Towards the end, "ok, who's going to bail him out next?"
I would enjoy a book by a person who carefully plans and invests in their own equipment which allows them to be as self-sufficient as possible on a excursion to remote parts of Baja.

I felt the same way about the prose and his "way" of barely getting by with out the hapless luck and help of the indigents, well put.
But Graham's a great guy who I'd never bash personally, maybe critique his work under fair game laws, and I'd welcome campfire tales with him anytime.

what a shame....to see what started out as such a cool thread degenerate into name-calling and grade school B.S....the way I see it is that a few people don't deem what Graham is doing as having any importance and maybe even believe that they themselves could do what he does or something even better...but after reading his first two books I am quite sure there are things he has done on his travels that almost no one on this forum would even consider, the fact that what he's currently doing is probably less dangerous and life threatening doesn't change that...I actually find it kind of ironic that people on the internet are rousting a guy who's actually out there on an adventure that many of us could only dream of doing....I guess they're right when they say "Some go while others watch" and some of those watching are such attention deprived folks that all they can do is go on the internet and put the guy down...really makes no sense

Just registered - looks interesting. But I have to say a few of you have the wrong impression about Graham. I've spent quite a bit of time with him - in San Pedro Martir delivering condors, in LA Bay on a film shoot, and have listened to his plans and reasons for his trip to Isla Guarda. He has to make a living like we all do, but his "real" motivation is experiencing unusual aspects of Baja and then sharing his experiences. But then, there is always spin on any person/situation on message boards. Thought you all might like some first person input. Dropping off some basics for Graham by plane next week - more for the experience than the need, but those are the things that make life exciting! (Mike Essary)

Jesus, there's a lot of bitching here. If you don't like it don't read it. Who gives a sh-t. His books are entertaining and that's it. They are not going to win any literary prizes but they are a nice escape for when I can't make it myself... Try reading one too many Hemingway books and then pass judgment.

David, I am really interested in any updates from Graham. If you choose not to keep adding them here, please send them to me via email or pass my addy along to Bonni. I'm not sure what the deal is with this forum? Seems like every other thread I read is people bashing each other...

Really - honestly now - doesn't the concept of airlifting supplies to our "marooned" Graham kind of make you smile.

It's just one man's journal, basically, that he writes up that we can choose to buy or not.......... way less harmful than Entertainment Tonight.
I just think all the indignation is way overdone. I'll stay out of it after this because it is just becoming a novella now. Frankly, I could give a F–k.

Anybody with the nads to walk 3K through Baja has got to have some interesting stories to tell. I've driven through most of it and I can tell you, I sure as heck would not want to walk it.

In the literary class of Steinbeck or Hemmingway?......decidedly not. just my pea pecker brain's opinion! he documents well like a college level geography text, good for sleeping.....but as a riviting adventure story teller......uh uh. And Bonni must be a saint.

Like I said some time ago, my dog has spent more time in Baja than most of the people on this board. This... is a place for a very few people to share their experiences and the rest to talk about them - or pick them apart. I tired of the criticism, sarcasm and unlimited anonymous opinions (ad nauseum) long ago.
... a lot of these folks will just never have anything more to do than spew forth their whiney liberal crapola as they seek to label and defame the few adventurers left with something to share. That is why we are drawn to the desert to eliminate the din of global whining for just a few precious moments of tranquility...
It still amazes me what people will write behind the veil of a keyboard that they would never have the balls to say to you or I in person...

...the guy up above talking about how uncool someones posts are is just spewing wasted jibberish, why he even bothers to post such nonsense is hard to understand...sounds like he belongs on a highschool chat forum rather than a place where people who are stoked on Baja adventures meet up and tell tall tales …don't let a few nay-sayers ruin it for the rest of us...keep posting those updates on Graham, I for one cant wait to hear more about his adventure

Well after getting back from Baja yesterday I am just getting to my nomads reading.

I have just been issued one of only two permits to camp on the islands in the Bay of LA and the Islas Encantadas. We had to pay a lot extra to get the permits from Ensenada. I know that the only other outfit in Baja legally able to put feet on the islands is located in Bay of LA. I have no idea who it is but he is probably the one helping out Graham's adventure. I for one am glad to see all of this press coming out about spending time on the islands, maybe it will spark up some business for tours to the islands.

As far as I know the islands in the northern Cortez are protected under the biosphere laws and there is no people allowed on them unless they hold the proper permits, and carry them on the trip. Much like the islands in La Paz and other parts of Mexico when you bring tourists to them you have to give the government the fee per person. That is the little wrist band you get. These fees are separate from a fishing license.

On my license it names the islands that I am able to camp on. Of all of the islands in the Bay of LA there are only a few that are set aside for campers with guides.

I went through the hassle to get the permits when I was approached by some Yoga people who wanted to do fasting and cleansing meditation in the middle of nowhere. I got the permits to make sure I was completely legal for such a client, as it seems more people do yoga than spearfish

Besides packing food for a bunch of people that are not going to eat is a no-brainer

Anyways, Graham couldn't have picked a better time to hang out if you ask me. I have never met the guy, but I can understand why he is loco for Baja....If I ever meet him I'm gonna tell him "Dude, I got major bookings off of your island adventure thing...."

I started with Baja burro but actually recommend starting with "Desert Place"... the interaction between the wandering Brit and the local Mexicans makes for some great stories especially when he gets out in some of the more remote spots like the Calamajue fish camp or some of the ranches up in the high desert...I don't want to give away too much of the story but I think the real beauty of Graham's tale lies within these relationships he forms with the local folks by just showing up in their "neck of the woods"...

I don't know Graham, but he seems to be applying the same approach to finding adventure and danger in Baja California that Uncle Erle [Stanley Gardner] used successfully. Nothing wrong with that. At least he isn't irritating resort owners by expecting them to provide free board and room for himself and a lot of camp followers.

It only gets harder to find that exclusive untamed and unvisited place. The proximity to the U.S. is obviously a great advantage. In fact that's what appeals to our family is the fact that we can actually drive to our paradise. I do think he's got some large cajones even though he is (physically) well supported in his efforts. Graham, being such of one with the earth most likely leaves a very soft footprint where he treads. This is good. He also has great compassion as he showed with his canine escapades. If he has good fortune in his solo endeavors so be it, he's earning it. He is counting on an audience however, but then, who isn't! I am curious about others who have spent extended periods on that island

How about an interview with 2 brothers who have paddled..yup, paddled... and spent almost all their lives in places like the one GM is visiting? Go to the south end of Coyote Bay between Sta. Barbera Cove and Coyote campbeach and you will find Kino and his brother at their fish camp most winters. Now they are not adventurers in the sense we use or even doing something they consider dangerous. They are just fishermen living on islands and bare coasts for the last 50 years or so. We have boat-dropped them a thing or two over the last 30. It's their life. Wonder what they would think about writing a book?

Now that sounds like a book worth reading!

...those panga brothers are/were legends in their own right. Talk about basic tough! I will try to get you some photos and a history of them for your Baja book interest. But there are many just like them scattered around the Cortez. They have always been there...families of fisherfolk, just melting into the scenery...unnoticed and unheralded.

Well, I'm half way through the desert place book right now. I've been to the area he's in above LA bay in a boat. And on most of the land. So, it's been very interesting to me. As far as I'm concerned it is good to hear what his thoughts were during the process of going down the coast. I know some seem to not like his style of writing and all I have to say about that is....to each his own. So far he's held my interest pretty well. Still have a long way to go though.

Well, I was blissfully ignorant of all this as I spent the evening writing an update for Nomad and my website, and if Mike came early it would have to double as a news update for my wife.

Monday February 6, 2006

Forgive me if I get silly or sentimental, but as I write this by moonlight I'm looking up at a lovely 1.3 gallons of Heineken beer, which was delivered by Mike Essary via parachute about 3:30 this afternoon. I didn't even have to kayak out to get it; some wild wind and waves drove it quickly to shore. All it took was a half-mile hike around the bay. And suddenly I have a care package of beer and mucho chocolate. I drank my last can of beer about ten days ago...so I'm enjoying this evening.

Ironically, I have almost as much beer as water! In fact, I've spent most of the last 3 days making drinking water by distilling seawater—a slow and tedious process providing about a cup an hour and necessitating constant tending and supervision of the still. Luckily, there is an abundance of driftwood for fuel.

The weather has generally been warmer than I expected. Over the last week the temperature has dropped only to about the mid-fifties at night and climbed to around 80° in the day. If I'm not hiking or kayaking, I generally seek the shade of a large cardón cactus on the slope above my campsite. If the wind isn't too strong, I'll rig up a shade with a tarp.

January was delightful: not a mosquito or a no-see-um, no scorpions, hardly even a fly or an ant. I've tended to intersperse an active day hiking or kayaking with a "rest" day birdwatching or turning over rocks, or just reading and meditating.

I've hiked across the island to beachcomb on the east coast, and I've enjoyed hiking the ridges of the island divide, which offers spectacular views of both coasts.

Any calm day is an invitation to kayak up and down the coast. Several times I've found myself surrounded by schools of yellowtail—usually when I haven't my fishing pole with me. Sea lions are plentiful, and I've seen several turtles and fin back whales. Some of the rock formations in the cliffs are astoundingly beautiful, and several times I've gone ashore to photograph an interesting vein or unusual wildflower.

Here in camp, I've become part of the community for the local gulls and oystercatchers—if I'm quiet, the latter birds will waddle along the shore just a few yards away, prodding beneath the rocks with their long orange-red beaks.

What I enjoy about camping in such a place is the beauty and the peace that so readily descends if one will be still and let it. I find my mind drifting to thoughts of family and friends and all the blessings they have given me. I have never felt more spiritual and connected than when I'm at peace on a Baja beach.

And it comes as a shock when I then turn on my radio at night to catch up on the news, and to listen to all the anger and negativity expressed on the political talk shows north of the border. Sad!

Maybe I'm getting older and a little less bolder, maybe I'm getting lazy, but I sure enjoy the great sense of discovery one can have in a place like Isla Angel de la Guarda. Armed only with binoculars and a hand lens, and a few field guides, I could be very content for quite a while. Some of the best days I've had have been right here on "my" beach marveling at all there is to see beneath the rocks.

Until Mike's flyover, I'd only spoken to one person in the month since I came out here, and that was Gary from British Columbia, who kayaked out for a few days. There is no way I'd kayak all that way—I've rarely gone more than one half-mile from shore. I spent the night at his campfire before he paddled back, and he was clearly anxious about the journey. He was well gone by first light. Sharing his anxiety, I climbed a nearby peak and willed the wind to stay down for his crossing. By the time he would have been close to Smith Island, we managed to exchange a few words by radio; I was jubilant to know he was safe. What a courageous young man.

Yes, I'm getting older and a little less ambitious. I'm happy to find a place of peace… to enjoy the privilege of this island, to have so much of it for myself, if for just a little while.

As I look up I can see Sirius, and Orion, and half a moon, and there, manna from heaven, a very large can of Heineken. Maybe I can allow myself just one more little beaker.

And then I get to thinking back through the years, back to my "moment" of madness, to my walk around the coast of Baja, back to all the kindness and hospitality, to friendships made by campfire and casa. Simple memories from over 20 years ago, as vivid as yesterday.

Many of these fleeting friends have passed on, but they'll live forever in my heart. What luck and joy I've found in this land. It's easy to believe that, out here, I have my own personal Guardian Angel.

Thank you,

Graham

When that posting finally made it to Nomad, the thread went in this direction:

Extremely (no simply) well said.

Graham certainly has a way with words, I think he's describing the way a lot of us feel on some of those deserted Baja beaches.

I've done the entire west side of that island in my puny 12' Valco. Including both ends. Is that Refugio he's staying at? That place is very nice. Funny he should mention his experiences 20 years ago while I'm reading about them. Good luck to him. I envy him today.

Thanks David for posting Grahams updates

Thanks Graham for letting us in on your wonderful Baja Feelings. You paint a pretty picture

I agree, I wish I could maroon myself for longer periods of time. Maybe someday...

10 days without a beer?? what madness! is there no civility on that island? could never do that, the man must be a shaman

The day after my parachute drop, I woke at first light and began a personal note to my family. I wanted so much to thank Bonni for all she was doing in my absence: typing and relaying my updates, adding her own clarifications, and having to read any put downs... not to mention her sending the Valentine's Card and helping arrange the re-supply.

It became suddenly windy. I thought there was no chance Mike would go fishing today, so I broke off the writing, and went outside to start the still again. I had made almost half a pint, the kettle was boiling away, a little steam was rising and escaping from the end of the tube.

And with the day gray and cool and the wind gusting, I looked up and was surprised to see a panga at the south end, a large "superpanga." It made its way across to my sheltered corner. There were four people aboard; all were in yellow waterproofs. The panga had a huge 225 hp Honda motor at the back. One of the folks up front was holding a video camera to his eye. It had

Mike and Igor with Swedish friend Lennart and boat assistant behind

to be Mike. Another person at the back seemed to be taking pictures with an SLR camera—I guessed that had to be Mike's "co-pilot," who I learned was Lennart Waje from Sweden.

They were glad to be in the shelter of my bay. The waves outside looked very uncomfortable. I couldn't believe Mike would come over on such a day. I told him I'd retrieved the beer and thanked him profusely. He was jubilant over the success of the air drop. His whoop of delight nearly brought down Turtle Head.

After changing into shorts, I waded out waist-deep to pick up six gallons of water that Mike had brought for me. The boat skipper, bison-built Igor Galván, a graduate of the Technological Institute in Ensenada, is the son of the owner of Guillermo's RV park in town, and can often be found there providing information to tourists and helping out in the restaurant. He offered me another gallon bottle of water. A total of seven gallons more! Security aside, that was like a gift of a week's freedom to explore and enjoy the island.

Photo by Lennart Waje

Bags of goodies

I waded out two or three more times to pick up several bags of tortillas, cakes, chocolates, a small bottle of brandy, two six-packs of beer, fresh fruit and veggies. Wow! For a moment I almost despaired looking at the amount of chocolate I had.

I gave Mike a couple of empty water containers in exchange for the one he'd brought over, and the letter for Nomad... to which I scribbled a final hurried paragraph for Bonni as the boat held position, anchored just off my launch ramp. I could have whipped myself with a stingray for not composing a proper thank you and better expressing my appreciation, especially after salivating over all the extra goodies Mike had brought over. The letter was sealed in a Ziploc bag as they were going fishing—fishing in THIS!

It was half in my mind that if Mike came over I'd ask to be taken to Este Ton. But it was too rough and might get rougher. I was going nowhere. I asked Igor, who had a good command of English, about the season for noseeums—he said April and May were usually the bad months. I was reassured that I may miss those buggers entirely.

They headed north, around Turtle Head, probably to fish in the shelter of Los Machos. I put the extra goodies away and decided I could give up making water for a while. After enjoying fresh fruit for breakfast, I climbed Turtle Head with radio in hand to see if I could spot Igor's boat. But on top, I could hardly stand in the screaming and whistling wind. It was so loud, I doubted I could even hold a conver-sation. There was

Very little water—but plenty beer, fruit, juice, and treats

no sign of a panga and it was getting increasingly rough out there.

I made my way down for an early lunch and a couple of treats washed down with a few little beakers of beer. Then slowly, in the midst of this sudden abundance, I started to feel sad and listless. A headache was coming on.

My Spartan diet, not drinking alcohol, and the sensible shrinking of my supplies and waistline had actually made me feel pretty good… now, ironically, I was feeling almost threatened by all the refined sugars, trans fats, larded tortillas, and the other fiberless dietary disasters. It was enough to give one fibrillations.

The specter of lazy overindulgence raised its ugly head. I needed to keep pushing myself, stiff back, clicking knee or no. Like a dutiful grunt I went for a long walk in the desert, at least a couple of clicks. Once out of water I'd be "grounded" again by the need to operate the still and conserve perspiration.

Months later, after I'd returned to San Diego, I had a chance to catch up with Mike and get the full story of the "special forces" parachute drop:

> [Mike] How do you drop something out of a small plane? I looked on the internet… Try to find lessons on making parachutes and air drops on the internet and you'll never learn much, just military stuff and pictures of parachutes thirty feet long, which wasn't going to work. So I talked to some of my pilot buddies and the only thing they'd heard about was pilots dropping bowling balls out of airplanes in the desert just for fun, to see how deep they sink. But no one had dropped a parachute.
>
> Bonni told me you wanted beer, and I happened to be at Costco and lo and behold Costco had a Heineken 5-liter keg. Perfect. Structurally very sound, it's round, it should be able to withstand it.

Then I went out and got some of your favorite chocolates. Bonni had dropped off the letter. I bought a bunch of bubble wrap, so I had the package—it weighs maybe 15 pounds.

Now I needed a delivery system. So I found a duffel bag that I thought was big enough. I figured I'd drop it in the water. And I need something to tie it to a chute so I bought 100 feet of parachute cord which you can use for tents or whatever, it's a thin cord.

Then I visited a sports store and said to the salesman, "Do you have any golf umbrellas? Not a little rain umbrella but something big." So he takes me to the golf section, and there's 20 different umbrellas. The reason I picked the one I did was it was cheap, only about $15. I spent more on the beer.

I asked, "Does the frame come off?" The guy said, "What are you talking about?" I said, "I want to use it for a parachute." And the guy goes, "For you?" And I go, "No, not for me. I'm dropping a package."

So I brought it home, disassembled the umbrella... and then I started figuring out how much parachute cord I needed. Again, there's no literature on it. Is it three feet? Too short. Twenty feet? Seems too long. So I tied eight 10-feet pieces of parachute cord to the umbrella. Then I packed everything in bubble wrap, put it in the duffel bag, zipped it up and tied four cords to each handle of the duffel bag.

And then I thought, "How do you deploy this thing?" Do I just wrap it up and throw it out the window? There's no literature on it. Cindy, my wife, watched me play around for about two hours, folding up this parachute in different configurations, and the best I find was you start with the cords, lay them down on top of each other very carefully, then take the chute and layer it down back and forth, back and forth... So how do I hold it together? Cellophane tape! It would hold it down but it would let it go pretty quickly too.

I got a different piece of parachute cord and I tied it to the very tip in a slip knot that would slide off the top. I tried it in the house a couple of times, and it deployed fine.

Now I've got your package and a delivery system... and my friend Lennart arrives from Sweden. I wanted to fly him down to Mexico to do some fishing and to see the gray whales. His wife didn't want him to fly with me because she doesn't like small planes, and she's back in Sweden. His son, who was about 15 at the time, actually flew with me first, and I can remember Lennart's comment, "Well I'll be damned—if my son can fly with you, I can fly with you."

We flew to Yuma, Guaymas, then San Carlos and over to Mulegé. In Mulegé I'm telling him, "We're going to fly to Guerrero Negro to see the whales then we're going to drop this parachute."

And this is the first Lennart really knew about it. And he goes, "What do I need to do?"

I said, "Well, I'm flying. So you need to open the window, tie this thing to your wrist and chuck it out." He was like, "No way."

Well we've had a couple of cocktails at the bar, so we tested it there. I said, "Tie this around your wrist, jerk on it really hard, and see what happens." So he jerks on it and the cellophane tape tears, and the parachute stretches all the way out, and the knot on the end of the parachute slips off. I said, "See it works." And he says, "You want me to tie it to my wrist in a plane and throw it out a window going 100 mph." And I go, "Yes, that's exactly what I want you to do."

There were some other pilots down there in Mulegé and they were watching us while we were doing this, and they were saying, "It's not going to work; there's no way! It's going to rip the cord; it's going to rip the umbrella; it's going to rip his arm off; it's going to drop like a rock; the guy's going to have a crater instead of a can of beer; there's no way it's going to work."

So the next day we leave Mulegé and fly to Guerrero Negro and we do our whale tour, and then we're coming back to Bahía de los Angeles. And we go to where I have your GPS coordinates. My intentions were to get in touch with you, and then I'd drop down to about 500 feet. Unfortunately, when we got to the island… there was a 30 mph north-northwest wind that day. A horrible wind. The plane was bouncing like a ping-pong ball in a washing machine.

Another problem is talking to you, which is on a VHF marine radio, which means it doesn't go through my headphones or microphone. I've got to take my headphones off in a plane and all small planes are fairly noisy, so I'm trying to hear you and talk to you… and we don't even have the window open yet. When we open it, it's twice as bad.

Finally we get hold of you, and now I realize that my initial plan of dropping down to 500 feet in your bay, especially as there's a mountain over 500 feet at the north end, and one at the south end maybe 1000-feet, is not going to work unless I dive bomb down, which I don't want to do. The plane is literally bouncing all over the place. After we spoke to you, I told Lennart, "We're going to drop down to 1500 feet and I'm going to come back around and head north. I'm going to try to position myself about fifty yards off shore and I'm going to tell you when to throw it."

He goes, "You're going to tell me when to throw it?" And I go, "Yes, open the window." Normally the windows in a Cessna only open so far, but I'd disconnected this one screw and it opens up. The good news is when you're flying at that speed the wind holds it up.

Unfortunately, the bad news is that when you've got the window up the wind is coming in at 100 mph... I've circled around and am dropping down another 500 feet to 1500 feet. We're trying to talk to you, but it's intermittent at best. I'm just offshore heading right towards your camp; we could see the panga. I'm honestly a little nervous because I've never thrown anything out of a plane before and I'm fighting this plane with the windows open, and then I've got to deal with Lennart.

He says, "What do I do?" I say, "Tie it to your wrist." So he ties the ripcord to his wrist and he's holding this package and he says, "How do you want me to throw it." I say, "Lift it up to the window and push it down."

There's a strut right out the window for the wing and there's also the elevator in the back, so I'm having visions of, and he did too, of throwing it out the window and the damned thing ripping the tail off the plane. But if you think about parachutists who jump out of planes all the time, they jump straight out and they don't hit the tail, well almost never do you hear about it.

So, I'm yelling at the radio, "OK Graham we're going to make our drop." We're at the south end of your little bay, and we're heading north. I've slowed down, but I couldn't slow down too much, with the turbulence the plane is bouncing all over. My ground speed, because we're going into the wind, is not too bad, about 70 mph, but air speed we were up over 100 mph. I couldn't get the control I needed at less than that. I wanted to do this, but I wanted to live.

I remember we're all ready and Lennart is holding this satchel. And I'm looking at my instruments and I'm flying the plane and he goes, "Now?" And I say, "Not Yet." About five seconds go by and he goes, "Now?" And I go, "No. Not yet." The third time he goes, "Now?" I'm like, "Yes, NOW." He goes, "NOW?" And I go, "YES, NOW." And were going back and forth in this tense conversation and I go, "Push it out." So he throws this thing out, and out of the corner of my eye I can see the chute deploy.

My initial thought when I was planning this was I could put the plane into a hard left bank and I could turn around and we'd be able to see the thing drop down. But in that weather there is no way I could do that serious of a bank at that speed and that altitude. So I put it into a left bank as much as I can and I radio, "Graham we dropped it." And that's when you came on and said, "You dropped it already?" So we didn't see it land. I knew it opened, but I didn't know if the parachute ripped off...

I powered up and climbed up to altitude, and talked to you, and you said that you needed water. And I said we'd be back in a boat with supplies. We were trying to talk to you for a while but we lost you in literally a couple of minutes. I don't know why because were up high with a direct line of sight.

Anyway, Lennart was relieved his arm was still there, and the package didn't hit the plane.

[Graham] Would you have been surprised if it had hit the plane?

[Mike] No! But the worst concern I had was if the chute got caught and tore off in the stabilizer or the elevator. I would have had an interesting flying approach back with the wind blowing like a banshee and the turbulence, and then we'd have to land at Bahía.

[Graham] Tell me about the boat ride over to the island with Igor.

[Mike] When we were leaving LA Bay we were in shorts. Igor said, "You might want to put some rain slickers on." I said, "What do you mean?" He said, "Trust me."

Literally, as soon as we started crossing the Canal de Ballenas, it was probably six foot swells and Igor is a great captain and he's very good with his boat. We were still making 10-15 knots through it, kind of going cross to the waves. At some points you couldn't even breath, there was so much water in your face. We were drenched the whole way over... until we got to your bay and were really protected.

[Graham] And where did you go when you left me?

[Mike] We buckled up and battened down the hatches and held on as Igor powered back to LA Bay, back to the inside islands; and it was a lot quicker because we were heading more with the waves; we were making 15-17 knots with the wind coming off our right rear quarter. The bad news was that once we got there, apart from one yellowtail strike that Lennart got on a jig, we had no hits. We couldn't even find lingcod; you can always find those. I wasn't that upset because I had accomplished what I had wanted, which was to get over to see you and make sure the parachute deployed, and make sure you had water and food and stuff. Well, we wanted to fish too, but that was secondary. But Igor is such a fanatic; he was so pissed off because we weren't catching any fish. We wanted to go home. We said, "Igor it's okay." And he would say, "No, I've got another spot." He kept us out there probably an hour-and-a-half longer than we wanted to stay out, and we still got no fish. So it was not a good fishing day, but it was a very successful re-supply day.

Chapter 28

The Un-Magnificent Seven

I am a brother to dragons, and a companion to owls,
My skin is black upon me, and my bones are burned with heat.

Job 30:29-30

February 8th started warm and calm. Assuming it would be the most likely day that Mike and Lennart would be flying back to San Diego, I took note of a couple of light planes flying over the island heading north, and both times I switched on my radio in case Mike might have had a final message or question for me.

I kayaked, fished, and beachcombed in the morning, then hiked, explored, and photographed all afternoon. I made it back to camp just before dark, feeling uplifted again by all the exercise and the simple joys of being alone in the wilderness.

That evening, lightning flashes over the peninsula and warm, strong, southerly winds reminded me how exposed I was in that direction. Rain was likely. I readied all my basins and buckets and spare tarps to catch as much rainwater as I could. The tarp under the tent was sticking out a few inches all around; I folded the edges out of sight so the tarp wouldn't channel water beneath. Then I put everything that was inside the tent away in bags and containers. If the wind permitted, I'd try to cover the tent with the large rolled-up tarp that I had staked to the ground along one side; a rectangle of heavy rocks was in place around the tent ready to weigh it down. And given a heavy enough downpour, I was planning to dump the first salty washings off the kayak so I could use the gallons that might collect on top—another advantage to having a sit-on-top.

A few drops spattered the tent. In spite of me lying awake for two hours primed and ready, waiting for the downpour, nothing more fell. But a story I heard on a San Diego radio station floored me like a thunderbolt. Two light planes had collided in midair just east of San Diego, raining flaming debris on the suburbs below. The report mentioned that two single-engine Cessnas were involved and all aboard the two planes were killed. I tried to tell myself Mike and Lennart couldn't have been involved, the odds were too great.

Finally falling asleep, I slept till dawn. It was still 80% cloudy. Many of the clouds away to the south had curtains of rain trailing beneath them, but as so often happens in the desert, the rain never made it to the ground.

Over the island the sky seemed to be clearing. In fact, it became another blue sky, sunny day. And even though the strong wind was moderating, I doubted there would be much boating activity after such an unsettled night, so I elected to go hiking.

The Lagoon from "Turtle Neck"

I was ready by 9 A.M. The tent was secure. The campsite was clean and organized. A tarp covered all my boxes and anything that might excite raven attention. The kayak was tied high.

To go north I headed around the back of Turtle Head and made my way over the basalt boulders and then down to the sea by the lagoon.

There was a surprising amount of seaweed and weed fragments rolling in the surf along the beach. And for the first time the water next to shore looked dirty, a kind of mustard yellow.

I found five fishing floats which I left in a barrel, and a ten-foot-long, sturdy wooden pole, perfect for enhancing my shade setup. I placed it above the high tide line, beneath the cliffs, and carried on intending to collect the best of my finds on the way back.

After accidentally treading on and smashing a light bulb—fortunately no glass worked its way into my foot—I began deliberately smashing some of the older tin cans and plastic bottles on the beach; they just disintegrated into dust and tiny pieces. In time, if not overwhelmed, Baja could deal with, and has been dealing with a certain amount of trash, at least in the sense of removing it from view, but the volume was now staggering and growing.

Given the precarious state of my boots, I took added interest in all the Reeboks and Nikes stranded among the driftwood. With duct tape, string and bungees, I was confident that I could fashion many of them back into suitably sturdy footwear. No matter how ridiculous they might look to worldly eyes, I knew that having put my soul into it, I would take great pride in wearing such recycled creations, and deem it a joyful badge of rebellion against the wastefulness of conspicuous consumption and the manipulation of the advertising industry—a healing step for a wounded world.

After I'd walked an hour or so, the wind dropped to nothing; the sea was calming and clarifying by the minute. It was a totally different day from what I had expected—calm enough now for comfortable kayaking. And it felt warm, especially as I was wearing a long-sleeved black T-shirt.

Approaching the location of the shack, I recalled the first time I'd walked that far—it seemed like a whopping three miles of separation from the security of my camp. Now those miles seemed almost insignificant, just the ready preamble to a much greater perambulation. I was fitter and lighter, and most importantly I no longer felt ill-at-ease in an alien environment. This was my world, my back yard.

Seven north-flying oystercatchers overtook me and landed just ahead on the beach making their strident squeaking. Before, I had only seen them in twos and threes. Such was my mindset I was looking for significance in the number. Seven? Why seven?

At the remains of the shack, I rested awhile and then decided to set off inland, up an arroyo to explore some high mountains to the north. It was breathless and hot. My pace became a slow steady plod rather than my usual brisk aerobic stroll. I sought out the shade of a large cardón, and was amazed to find there a much-decayed and possibly very old wood and canvas carrying bag. Satisfied that there was nothing inside, I pushed on determined to get as far into the mountains as possible.

One-and-a-half miles up from the shore, I enjoyed a protracted lunch on a large flat boulder shaded by a juvenile, multi-armed cardón. The boulder served as both table and chair. Then, still pacing myself in the heat, I entered a narrowing and deepening canyon wending north.

I climbed onto a ridge where there was a welcome breeze and I was able to look back along the coast. I could just see Turtle Head and the southern end of my bay. It was about 1 P.M.

Cardón provides shade

And gazing down, I was jolted by the sight of two pangas coming from the south, heading purposefully into the bay. They disappeared behind Turtle Head. My first thought—it must be friends coming out to join me. I pulled out my marine VHF radio, monitored channel 16, then immediately turned around and started back.

I retreated as much as possible on the ridge lines. The boats hadn't emerged. The visitors must be at my campsite. And then it entered my head, they could be Mexican fishermen from the mainland, or maybe drug runners!

Even flat out I was still a good hour and a half, maybe two hours from camp. So I was relieved to see the pangas coming back into view and heading over to Gary's Beach and landing there. Through my binoculars I could see several figures on shore.

Back by the water, following the long curve of Humbug Bay, I watched as one of the boats began motoring back towards my campsite. A minute later the other followed in its wake. So much for my not getting any aerobic exercise—spurred on by anxiety, ignoring the heat, I was charging back as fast as my sinking boots could move on the angled, pebbly shore.

The pole, fishing floats, and other items I'd marked for pick up would have to wait. I dashed past the lagoon. When I reached Turtle Head, the tide looked to be lower than average, so I decided to continue under the cliffs, rather than go the slower way over the top. I skipped over dry rocks, slid and clawed my way past wet and slimy rocks and traversed the larger more recently downed slabs and boulders. After getting four-fifths of the way around the point, I thought I might make it and be just moments from seeing who the visitors were and what they were doing in my camp, when I was confronted by surging water two or three feet deep slapping against a smooth, slightly overhanging cliff wall.

I was too fired up to go all the way back around, so without hesitation, still wearing boots, I stepped into the sea, jamming my feet between the slippery seaweed-covered boulders, and with the waves washing my thighs I reached behind to make sure my daypack which had everything important to me—tapes, binoculars, money, passport, camera, camera memory cards—wasn't getting wet.

Fifty, forty, thirty yards to go… I stepped over the final boulders, up onto the sandy shelf on the other side and hurried to greet the strangers. First, I saw the two pangas anchored and tied to shore near my launch ramp. My tent was still up at least, and my clothesline. But otherwise I hardly recognized the place—my neat orderly campsite now looked more like a Tijuana shanty town with buckets and barrels and boxes and clothes strewn everywhere. The fresh salty smell of the Sea of Cortez had been replaced by the smell of diesel, burning wood and plastic, and the sweet pungent aroma of marijuana. And as I stepped into the view of a group of mostly grizzled and grimacing Mexicans sitting and squatting around a small rock-ringed fire pit, the sound of the surf and the birds was suddenly overwhelmed by a cacophony of rasping coughs and inane laughter.

What greeted my return

I counted seven of them. Seven! One motioned for me to come closer. Smiling and clutching what looked like a flame thrower, he struck a match and lit a kind of pilot light in the end. Two or three of the others stood up and smartly backed away. "Do you like *carne asada*?" He asked.

Chapter 29

No Law Out Here

A poet could not but be gay, in such a jocund company.
William Wordsworth

Red-faced from sun and exertion, I must have already looked like a piece of roast meat. Several of the strangers were grimacing like they were in pain or expecting a fire cracker to burst in their face. One coughed uncontrollably. The man with the flame thrower was pointing the business end in almost every direction as he picked up a few pieces of driftwood and threw them on the seemingly defunct fire. Then, WHOOOOSH! A funnel of flame shot out and instantly the fire pit was burning brightly. A car hubcap—filled with shredded beef, onions, tomatoes, and chilies—was placed on top. One of them held up a packet of flour tortillas and gestured for me to help myself.

Before doing so, I exchanged my wet socks and boots for tennis shoes, left them in the sun to dry, uncovered and opened one of my plastic containers and fished out a bag of tortillas, some chocolates, some cakes, and a six pack of beer. I grabbed one of the cans for myself and offered the rest to my new, very close neighbors.

I introduced myself; they said they were all from mainland Mexico, from Bahía Kino, a medium-sized fishing and tourist center on the Sonoran side of the Sea of Cortez.

As I finished lunch and delighted in sinking tired into my chair by the remains of their fire, an even stronger whiff of marijuana reached my nostrils. One of the younger ones, in between coughs, kindly offered me a hit. I declined, saying I was English and we preferred beer.

"*Mota*! It's very cheap in Mexico." He added.

I said I didn't want any trouble with the law.

"There's no law out here." He spluttered.

As they heard about my situation, they offered me extra water if I needed and even a ride in a panga if I wanted to shift location. I mentioned Este Ton. The young fishermen, he might have been 19 or 20, said he was recently there and was attacked by a cat. He had to fend it off with an oar. The cat supposedly had strange round eyes and long fangs... like a vampire. "Dracula Cat" he called it. I don't think he was being entirely light-hearted. He shuddered as he said the name "Dracula."

Apparently they were planning to go diving that night, but first they all proceeded to wander away and find places to nap. Some of the fishermen went up to the large cardón where they said they'd found my water and soda—clearly not the best place to hide it. They fell asleep on stones, on the salt-encrusted sandy soil, on top of sleeping bags, under blankets—a motley, mota-mellowed, snoring, coughing collection. I had the odd feeling of walking around my camp trying not to disturb them.

Late afternoon, I made a fire and set a kettle on top for coffee, lifting it off just before it started its screaming whistle. I then sat quietly and read and caught up with my journal.

My companions slowly stirred and gravitated to their kitchen. A few twigs and pieces of driftwood were thrown into their fire area. There was another WHOOOOSH! The flame thrower, attached to a propane cylinder, started the fire, but also ignited a nearby bush. The burning bush caused great merriment.

I walked over with a flotation cushion I'd found. "For you," I said, and left it on the ground. A grateful fisherman picked it up and put it on top of a small barrel to make a more comfy seat. They offered me a cup of hot chocolate which I poured into my half-emptied coffee mug.

Out came the mota again. I spoke to the oldest man. He seemed the least under the influence. He said he was born in Bahía Kino and had three kids. However, a fierce-looking fellow did most of the talking… he looked like Sitting Bull on a bad day. I wondered if he was a Seri, the notorious tribe long associated with Tiburón Island. Tales of their murderous cannibal ways were widely circulated. I'm sure most were exaggerated. But more than once the Mexican government conducted punitive expeditions to the island after the alleged murders of shipwrecked mariners or other visitors. He confirmed that they intended to go diving if it stayed calm.

A couple of the more lively ones were filling gasoline tanks on the boats and pouring diesel or two-stroke mix into the diving compressor… the smell of the fuels lingered powerfully. When the flame thrower was used to rejuvenate the fire, I half expected we'd all go up in a vast conflagration. The wood they were burning was oily, and resinous, and filled the air with acrid, choking black smoke.

Otherwise, it was a beautiful still evening. I walked out to the point to tape the day's events, but even a hundred yards away I felt the need to whisper.

Instead of anyone going fishing or diving, nearly all the guys drifted from the kitchen into a large sweat lodge-like tent they'd erected. Only smoke, coughs, raucous laughter and giggles emerged. It was comical and charming. A radio put out Mexican music, the volume of which was continuously turned up and down as someone had something to stay. Later, yawns and tired voices wafted over. Someone said, "I want eggs." I doubted that they would be going anywhere.

When reception allowed, I listened to a San Diego news station to get an update on the midair collision and to try to find out the names of those killed. Although no names were given out, I heard that both planes had just taken off from the same El Cajon airport, which put my mind at rest about Mike and Lennart being involved. They were heading for a different airport— Montgomery Field in San Diego.

However, Lennart's wife in Sweden, who hadn't wanted her husband to fly in a small plane, was far from rested. She knew something that I didn't. She had heard on Swedish television, about the time that she was expecting Mike and Lennart to be returning to California, that there had been an accident involving two small planes above San Diego... and at least one of the victims was thought to be Swedish!

As Mike told me later:

> We found out that literally right before we had got back, that these two planes in El Cajon had collided, there was one guy on one plane and two people on another plane and they all died. We find out that the two people on the plane were from the Scandinavian Aviation School in El Cajon, out of Gillespie Field.
>
> Before Lennart and I flew on this trip, because I wanted him to get comfortable about being in a plane, I booked him an introductory flight [with] the SAS in Gillespie Field. And for $69 you get an hour flight. So we went over to this school and we met everybody. Lennart is talking to them in Swedish.
>
> So we go up in a Cessna 172 like we were going to fly, and I was sitting in the back seat. We're flying around for an hour and Lennart is doing the usual things when people don't know how to fly; he's going up and down, left and right. So we gave him an introductory flight and he gets used to it, and we talk to the instructor, the guy's a great guy, I give him my card and he gives me his, and we talk about getting in touch, and all that stuff.
>
> When we get back we hear about this accident and we start checking into it and... they published in the newspaper that it was two instructors from the SAS that had been in one of the planes that crashed. One of the guys was acting as a student in the left seat with the other instructor in the right seat because he was doing further training, maybe for commercial. And it was one of the pilots that we had just flown with the week before; probably in the same plane that he was in when he crashed. We find out that he was in his mid-twenties. I had the guy's business card. He was a nice guy, a really good instructor... I was sitting in the back seat thinking this guy is doing a good job. And literally eight days later, he's dead. It was very depressing. I don't think it was his fault.

I drifted off in my tent, just yards from the pangas, and all the barrels, crates, air hoses, gas bottles, and rope.

Next morning, I woke to the sounds of the birds and the sea... then music, coughing, and the noise of the hub cap being scraped clean, no doubt for fried eggs. I whispered to the tape recorder, "I hope the *federales* don't descend on our beach, round us all up, guilty and innocent alike." Este Ton, even with its blood-sucking vampire cats, was beginning to sound like a great option.

The two pangas left loaded with all the fishermen bar one, who stayed in camp. Seeing me pulling my kayak over plank and roller, he hurried over to help me carry it to the water. What thoughtful, hospitable folks. As I kayaked out of the bay and headed towards Los Machos to pick up my beach finds, a gentle southerly breeze produced waves from that direction. But other waves were coming from the north and the west, and when seen against the reflection of the high shoreline they all seemed to fuse into a surreal crisscross pattern of blues, reds and tans—the surface of the sea woven into a magical carpet of tartan. I wondered if I'd absorbed too much second-hand smoke.

The two pangas were working close in to Los Machos. At least two of the men were diving, gathering from the sea bottom. The throbbing noise of their air compressors carried miles, sounding like distant gasoline lawnmowers—a couple of little pistons aggressively laying claim to a wilderness. I was soon so used to the sound that when it stopped the sudden silence was striking.

I paddled far out, and was amazed at how far. I was so less cautious because help was at hand. In spite of all their "faults," I was so relaxed to be with them.

The panga motors growled into life. The boats doubled back to the south. The occupants threw a few friendly waves in the direction of my blue kayak. Now alone, I was fishing more than a half mile from shore increasingly aware of my vulnerability, more watchful, surveying the horizon, analyzing the movement of the water, the incipient breezes… when suddenly a series of rolling waves from the west hit the kayak, nearly causing me to paddle furiously to the beach. Then I realized it must have been the wakes from the passing pangas.

I made several landings under the cliffs to seek out more treasures. Passing Turtle Head I was thinking about the determined way I had been wading around it to check on the pangueros. I thought back to my 1980s walk around the coast, to the many times I just HAD to get by some awesome stretch of cliffs. Doing it NOW, NOW, NOW! Pumped up, resolute. Climb, wade, swim, boots on, boots off, falls, cuts, bruises, scrapes—nothing mattered except getting by. That's how this very "easy going" super couch potato got it done. (And it was probably at least partly why my knee was now clicking and squeaking.)

On such a perfect day I didn't want to return to camp, not even to drop off the beach finds; instead I continued south on my kayak towards where the pangas had anchored. I watched the divers occasionally returning to the surface, and overheard the little conversations with those aboard.

The light wind continued from the south, just ruffling the water. After the fishermen passed me again heading back to camp, I paddled closer to shore and floated among the submerged granite boulders. It was cloudless and warm. I ventured along beneath the cliffs almost two miles from my bay, observing, experiencing, drifting, living.

The current which had been slack was now beginning to run against my return. And when I saw an ominous dark line to the north, out in the channel, I decided to retreat in face of my old fear of battling wind AND current, which to me was as inveterate a fear as a twentieth-century Teuton's terror of war on two fronts. The wind did indeed pick up to a stiff breeze, but *"Gott mit uns"* it came from the south and blew me to the safety of my bay.

It was strange drifting slowly back to my once lonely campsite and seeing so much activity... boats and tents and barrels, so much blue where it shouldn't be. I couldn't imagine what I'd do in camp all afternoon. Socialize? Practice Spanish? If they're all sleeping, I'd feel awkward wandering around trying not to make too much noise. I'd just have to go with the flow.

About half a mile from camp, I heard the boats tied at anchor making a drumming sound with the slapping of the waves. Then there was a strange roar. Surf? No, it was the flame thrower again. Back on shore, I saw they were boiling sea cucumbers in large metal pots, and then preserving them in salt. When all was done, they had two large plastic drums full of them.

This and every activity was interspersed with coughing and laughing and the smell of weed... before all seven succumbed to their afternoon siesta.

Salting boiled sea cucumbers

Resisting irritation and resentment, I seized the opportunity to venture into the desert where, just knowing they were there in camp, I was able to relax and focus on photography and flights of fancy. Trusting my neighbors completely, I ambled around in no particular hurry. It was amazing how a little personal contact, a little getting-to-know, a little open-mindedness could dispel a too-easily-erected Everest of paranoia. These were fine people, like the incredibly kind and generous Baja Californios I had come to know so well.

It was a lovely warm evening. I sat on a rock amid the cardóns—camera and binoculars in my lap—reveling in the near silent beauty of the island, meditating on my occasional need to isolate myself from others, both physically and mentally. I pondered the reasons why and the downside of that separation; and yet how, in my isolation, I always ended up feeling more connected, more appreciative of company, and more excited about the bonds of common humanity.

And just as powerfully, I always felt more connected to my past, perhaps to an imagined future, to my family, especially my parents. Paralleling my father's close call with the sniper, out of the blue I recalled a story my mother told me of a fortunate escape that she'd had during the Second World War.

On the afternoon of January 14th, 1944, before embarking on a shift at a local "sten gun" factory, she was inside the Davis Theatre in Croydon, south of London, watching *Two Señoritas*, a Joan Davis film, when a large bomb, one of two "blockbusters" dropped from a German plane, came crashing through the roof, landing towards the front of the theatre, amongst the packed moviegoers. It killed seven people; another twenty or so were seriously injured. It could have been much, much worse. The bomb failed to explode. My mother was sitting about eight rows back. Initially, she had chosen a seat that much closer to the screen, but on impulse, just before the show, she decided to change seats. The Davis was one of the biggest movie theatres in England and could seat

Smoke from motor… and maybe mota

over 3700 people. The audience that afternoon was estimated to be close to 2000. I had heard my mother talking about it with my father's brother when I was growing up. I remember my uncle saying how he'd heard what had happened and hurried to the scene to find my mother wandering the High Street outside, dazed, shocked and covered in oil and dust.

I'll never know why that bomb failed to explode. I wondered if it might have been sabotage by some slave worker or an act of resistance by a courageous German fighting evil the only way he or she could. I pondered and meditated, and thanked him or her, just in case.

Suddenly, I too felt the urgent need to move. In spite of my greater feeling of security with my new friends, perhaps even because of it, I had to move on. My psychic juices were flowing. The certainty was intriguing, liberating, energizing. I could visualize it. I would soon be in Este Ton.

When I returned to the camp, everyone was shaking off their sleepiness. They said they were going out that night for sure, but they all looked very unenthusiastic. I wondered if they'd change their minds again. Eventually however, they got into their yellow waterproof overalls, put on their boots, pulled the boats in to shore, loaded whatever they needed, and about 6:30 P.M. all seven of them were aboard and ready.

I took some photographs before they left. Depending on what they deemed appropriate, they lined up (joints clasped behind their backs) beaming huge smiles or standing stiffly serious and dignified. They were initially shy about photos, especially "compromising" pictures, but I reassured them I wouldn't plaster their faces in my writings.

The outboards coughed and clattered to life, and then the two boats headed out of the bay, trailing smoke and laughter.

I had to admire their courage to be out on the water at night, diving in the cold blackness, dealing with the terrors of the deep to feed their families. Who could begrudge them their puff of marijuana? Quite honestly, I was more disgusted by all the politicos, north and south of the border, who find money effortlessly flowing into their receiving hands, daring to lecture these decent hardworking folks about what they could and couldn't smoke. Even though I don't indulge, I wouldn't begrudge them. They were adults, working at an incredibly difficult job.

They had left their fire burning with all kinds of plastic trash bubbling away. In the nearly still air, the toxic smell was overpowering. I found myself coughing like they were. When they motored out of sight, I poured a little seawater on the flames to knock it down.

I walked around the bay and gathered up the water I'd hidden—I had a total of 5 gallons left. Then I headed up the canyon for my survival bag, an interesting experience by moonlight. A hundred yards from camp I happened on the turd temple where the ground and bushes thereabouts were liberally decorated with rosettes and streamers of white tissue, and the multifarious objects of veneration were deposited for all to ponder.

It always amazes me that they don't attempt to bury or at least cover their poop. I also thought about the state of the campsite, the trash and the fumes, and felt saddened, although tolerant. It was hard sweaty work bringing down the bag.

Before I retired to the tent, I took my chair over to their fire so they could use it when they returned, and also a stack of driftwood so they'd have plenty of "smokeless fuel." I had mixed feelings, but I was full of admiration, almost affection, for these folks. It was kind of fun to see them enjoying themselves so, and a little bit contagious. Meeting them had been a privilege. And while their real pangas were out there, no ghost pangas haunted the sea or my mind. I slept soundly.

Well, at least till 2 A.M. When I woke I was amazed by how bright it was. The moon was overhead, approaching fullness. Hearing a faint radio sound, I checked it wasn't coming from my headphones; then looking out the tent I saw two fires on Gary's Beach and realized that I was hearing the fishermen singing and playing their music while they were boiling the cucumbers and the rest of their harvest. If I had woken to hear all the activity, and didn't know who they were, I would have thought a bunch of savages were gleefully cooking a missionary or two. Maybe they were over there because there was more wood, or perhaps they wanted to avoid disturbing me.

Just before 4 A.M. I woke again; they weren't back, but I was conscious of more singing, shouting, and banging. They were still on their beach. And before I could drop off to sleep, I heard one of the pangas approaching, and a minute later the other was also racing back across the bay. The two fires were still burning.

They came ashore, and mercifully after a little activity and a few more puffs of mota, all was silence.

Chapter 30

That Place

If I could pray to move, prayers would move me.

William Shakespeare (Julius Caesar)

Naturally I was the first awake. The temperature was a comfortable 64°F at 6:30 A.M. Before I emerged, I tidied and packed away everything inside the tent. Outside, I quietly made coffee and breakfast, and started gathering all my stuff together.

When they finally started rousing, around 9 A.M., I let them know I would love a ride to Este Ton and I'd like to take up their offer of a few gallons of water. After a few nods and reassuring coughs and comments about *mas tarde* and a little in-gossip about the wind, I waited to see what would transpire.

Not much—until two more pangas came roaring in. Now there were four pangas and another seven or eight fishermen. There was a gathering of old friends on the beach—comradeship enhanced by *mucho mota* and a few beers. Dive gear, camping gear, and barrels were being unloaded. It was obvious the new guys were staying. I was beginning to feel a little out of place, and maybe a little less secure about these more reticent arrivals "who knew not Joseph."

Before they all got too wasted, I reminded those who did know Joseph of his wish to go to Este Ton. One of them shook his head and muttered something about the wind; then probably thinking that getting rid of me would free up some prime real estate, replied with a thumb and finger held real close like he was imitating a tiny spark plug gap. "*Un rato,*" he said, which literally means "in a little while," but in the flexible thinking of most Mexican fishermen could mean anything from a few seconds, to a few days, to ha ha ha, maybe when Baja California is sliding past Seattle!

Say no more. In my strangely optimistic mood, that was clearly a "Yes." I took down my tent, and thanks to my earlier foresight I was soon ready. And unmistakably so, even through a cloud of mota. It was windy and getting windier. I didn't get direct or pushy. If they felt comfortable taking me, I'd trust their judgment. If not, I'd move my camp towards the point. To help them see sweet reason, I gave out a few chocolate bars and a packet of Oreos.

Three of the fishermen conferred and began looking purposeful. One of them started pulling a panga towards the shore. Another presented me with the gift of an arrow head he said he had carved on another of the Midriff islands, Isla San Lorenzo. A third poured about five gallons of water into one of my empty containers. I was ecstatic. They were going to take me. I helped the fishermen lift the kayak onto the boat.

With everything stowed under hatches or on deck, I took some final group pictures. Then we were off, me and two of the nicer guys, the younger one of the pair spoke fairly decent English. We ran south aided by a gathering tail wind, which made for some choppy waves and noisy crashes. The kayak was just resting on top of the panga, and I'd put a few heavy "launch ramp"

Ten mile run to Este Ton

planks on top of it, so I was watchful lest something came flying back knocking my teeth out. The skipper was clearly in a hurry, probably because the wind was definitely kicking up and he'd have to return into it. I took as many pictures of the coast as I could—as far as the crazy crashes and showers of spray permitted.

It was a rugged, colorful, barren shoreline; I studied and noted each valley, beach, and bay—many would have offered more seclusion and been perfect for a kayaker. But Este Ton had called. And I'd committed myself by saying in my last message to Bonni, that if I wasn't at Humbug Bay I'd be in Este Ton. I hoped it would be deserted.

We scared a flock of pelicans off a rocky point and they all flew straight across our bow; it was a miracle of apparent dead stops in midair and flaring acrobatics that we didn't run down a bunch of them.

I recognized the colorful mountains looming above Este Ton that I had seen with Cal when I came over in his little boat. The bay entrance faced south so we had to run past a serious reef and turn sharply back in. No wonder Cal missed it on his first visit to the island. Este Ton looked even more magnificent than I remembered. And, yes, yes, yes, the round, 200-yard-wide bay was empty. I could worry about the paranoia later. I was ready for the stress, the gamble, the ghost pangas. Haunt me, baby! I wanted and needed to be alone again. I was *mota-vated*.

There was one obvious little sandy beach on the eastern side of the cove. It was flanked by basalt and granite slopes and a rocky shoreline, and was in serious danger of completely disappearing during the highest tides which, unfortunately, were due with the full moon over the next couple of days. The other beaches around the bay were pebbly and more exposed to the wind.

So we headed for the sandy beach first, and as we approached, the younger English-speaking fishermen pointed to a large flat rock above the

Arrival Este Ton

beach and said that is where he'd seen the vampire cat. Because it hadn't woken as they motored in and came ashore, he thought it must be dead. Just as he reached out to turn it over, it sprang at him screaming and scratching, chasing him back to the boat, where he used an oar to fend it off. "It was black with long hair, and with long fangs and wild round eyes," he said, as he showed me the raking claw marks clearly visible on his arm.

The north wind was growing wilder by the minute. The two fishermen were keen to go. So doubts about the tide aside, I didn't waste their time, but quickly consented to unload the kayak and all the gear on the precarious little sandy beach. I could move myself around the bay later if necessary. I had much less than when I first arrived on the island.

Opening one of the hatches on the boat to check for more of my gear, I saw it was full of big lobster. Even though mightily conflicted about their poaching antics, I really appreciated what these fishermen had done for me; they had no reason to come here, and all they could do now was run back to their camp as fast as possible. I gave them $50, some foody treats and, as an afterthought, my best fishing pole. They seemed pleased and said they'd stop to check on me in about 3 days on their way back to the mainland and drop off any water they had left. Music to my ears, as even with the five gallons they just gave me I had a total of only nine gallons—a big difference from the fifty some gallons I had initially ferried over.

After handshakes and expressions of good luck, they hurried out of the bay and turned north back up the coast, anxious to return to the camaraderie of my old campsite. I was anxious for them. It would be a rough ride.

I was alone. I had got what I wanted. But I was amazed because what looked like the most protected cove on the island was being raked by a furious wind; and some strange effect was making the wind seem worse INSIDE Este Ton compared to outside in the open sea. The racing gust marks in the center of the bay ran fast and feline, like a giant wildcat springing on its victim. I was unable to put up my tent or do anything much to enhance my campsite. Sand was blowing all over my gear and into every less than perfectly sealed bag and box.

Looking out of the bay to the cliffs to the south, I recorded, "Certainly a wild and open coastline here… it's hard to imagine how you could get back to Este Ton if you have to beach—maybe on the rocks, but it looks so, so rugged."

Even with the gale, the sun felt surprisingly warm. It probably wasn't the smartest thing I ever did, but I zipped up my lifejacket, grabbed a paddle and dragged the kayak to the water. Never having paddled in conditions like it, I tried to keep close to shore, where six feet of raised beach offered a little wind protection. I daren't land and leave the kayak because it could have easily been rolled or somersaulted from the shore and swept away.

The inevitable happened—I strayed a little too far out and it felt like a giant paw had grabbed my paddle and was trying to wrestle me down. All I could do was lay it flat against the kayak and lower myself till the gust subsided. When I was able to sit up and paddle again, I was half way out the bay, pulling for my life against being swept out along that rocky, surf-lashed coast. It felt as if some furious spirit was desperate to get me out of there.

After barely making it back beneath the relative shelter of the steep pebble beach, I stepped into foot-deep water and walked the kayak half way around the bay till I had to jump aboard again to paddle past a last, deeper, bouldery stretch keeping me from the sandy beach with my possessions.

I was shocked when I looked at a large foam pad that I had bungeed to one of my heavier boxes. In my absence, something unseen had set about it, leaving dozens of deep slits that looked ominously like claw marks.

But no feral cat could have made such incisions; the beast would have to be the size of a tiger. I looked again at the running wind gusts. A new paranoia was taking shape.

Surveying the steep, sun baked

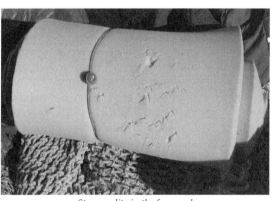

Strange slits in the foam pad

slopes all around, I began to wonder about those long-fanged feral cats. There was no water anywhere. How could they survive, indeed thrive, on the island if coyotes couldn't? Perhaps they did live by sucking the blood and body fluids of their victims.

I found my machete and, wanting it close-at-hand, drove its heavy blade vertically deep into the warm, receiving sand. Love your enemies… but carry a big stick! I had some way to go on the path. Fear makes faith weak.

Peering along the shore to what looked like a small mesquite tree, I noticed a pair of smug-looking ravens keeping a low profile, gazing down at all my gear and supplies, apparently just waiting for me to go walkies. That gave me another, somewhat less disturbing, perspective on the foam pad. The slits were triangular or chevron-shaped. Obviously the work of vandalizing beaks. I should have known that ravens were somehow involved. I walked over and drove them off with a shout and a few animated gestures.

In spite of the magnificence of the backdrop, and my enthusiasm for the move, I couldn't help looking back with a little fondness on my days under Turtle Head. I had exchanged my familiar world and the safety of my fishermen friends for a place that so far promised discomfort and problems, and seemed to ooze threat from almost every bush and rock.

The usual morale battle ensued. I tried to tell myself that it wasn't all black—just ravens, vampire cats, and coming dark nights swarming with drug runners. Otherwise, what was there? Just dying of thirst, cooking in the sun, the kayak being ripped from the beach and blown out to sea, a malicious boat-smashing coastline, the tent being submerged at high tide, "fishermen" coming to join me, especially late at night, with the beach at high tide only yards wide, and all of us camping practically on top of each other. And then I had the coming warmer-weather creatures to think about—noseeums, scorpions, jellyfish, rattlesnakes. And I didn't want to address how I was ever going to get off the island.

But one thing put all that in perspective. I fortunately had something to fret about apart from my own miserable hide. I thought of the panga fishermen returning north in the gale, and felt responsible and a little sick at the thought of anything happening to them or their boat because of their desire to help me. To allay my guilt, I helped myself to a large 16-ounce midday can of Tecate beer—an almost unheard of luxury for me on the island. Looking through my binoculars at a cross on top of a steep craggy hill on the west side of the entrance to the bay, I offered a silent prayer that they were safely back laughing and smoking with their companions.

Thinking and drinking were getting me nowhere. It was time for action. The beach area was at the mouth of a narrow gully, which formed the only sensible pathway inland. I wandered up the gully, small shovel in hand. As I expected, with its bushes and spreading cardóns it had clearly been the bathroom with a view. Old tissue and turds were liberally strewn about. I buried the most egregious piles that were nearest the campsite.

There was a "kitchen" area at the base of the more sheltered north slope, where the gully ran onto the sandy beach. Its table, chairs, and shelves were different levels of boulders. And in between, there was a sorry mess of broken glass, open jagged cans, eggshells, bits of plastic and fishing line, plastic bags (some still partially filled with salt), and heaps of ashes. I gathered up most of the easily accessible trash; I was not inclined to go blindly poking between the rocks with my hands. An old rusting 55-gallon barrel was the centerpiece of the kitchen. It was open on top and filled with more trash, mostly sharp edged cans, partially buried by ashes. I cleared out the rusty cans, and laid a heavy plywood board on top to make a high, stable table.

A few yards away on the opposite side of the gully was a smaller plastic barrel (maybe 15-gallon capacity) with the top cut away; I half filled it from the trash lying on the sand. Then I made my way over the stones and boulders along the shore, fifty yards in each direction, grabbing whatever old batteries and waterlogged or flapping plastic bags were evident. The trash bin was now packed full. I covered it with another board. A project for the next day would be to take all the trash I'd collected up the gully to find a place to bury, or at least conceal it.

In an hour, I'd made a huge improvement, and partially restored what has to be one of the loveliest locations on the island (perhaps in the entire Sea of Cortez) to something like its pristine former glory. Given a couple more days I'd have the place looking like no one had ever been there.

I carried on around the bay to check out the other beaches and possibilities for a campsite. All offered just gravel and stone, and all were even less sheltered in this norther. It was a blessing that I came there on such a day so I didn't inadvertently camp where the wind funneled through.

It looked like the only obviously "safe" way to hike out of the bay was to head north up a long, cardón-dotted valley paralleling the coast. And that's where most of the wind was coming from. The valley ended on a steep ridge. What was on the other side was unknown to me. It might be a sheer drop or it might be a relatively safe trail to the north. I'd have to find out. Otherwise, every other "escape" from my beachhead looked challenging and perhaps not even possible without ropes and climbing gear.

I walked point to point around the entirety of Este Ton, taking note of the absence of driftwood in the bay, no doubt because fishermen and other visitors were burning it faster than it was being deposited. And maybe because the entrance was south-facing, so not much flotsam driven by the prevailing north winds would make it inside.

Later in the afternoon with the wind moderating, I took the opportunity to erect the tent on a slightly elevated patch of sand just to the south side of the gully entrance. Before doing so, I shook, brushed and swept out all the sand and grit so it was wonderfully clean inside. I hoped that it was "high" enough to avoid the danger of a flash flood roaring down the canyon, as it surely had countless times before... or it might at least give me a little extra time to get out of the tent and out of the way. Because of the uncertainty with the tide, I placed a colorful "necklace" of hard plastic floats around a large rock embedded in the sand a yard from the tent door. If seawater started surging around the rock I imagined it would make quite a noise in the night. Again, it might buy me precious seconds to rescue what I could. The wind fell away to a calm peaceful evening. I dragged the kayak up beside the tent, right into the gully.

An ominous "full" moon rose behind me over the island. It looked to have "risen" just before sun down, suggesting that it was a little short of real opposition, and I was still a day or two away from the peak tides.

Just before I retired to the tent, the wind started picking up again, initially from the north and then more from the west, across the bay. I only permitted myself a single, small beaker of beer. My mini-keg was beginning to feel disturbingly light; but, in truth, I didn't have much appetite for any food or drink. All I really wanted was a good night's sleep.

With most everything safe inside the tent, or seemingly weighed down and secure in crates or beneath all the rope and netting, I stretched out on my sleeping bag and began a half-hearted attempt to write up the day's events in my journal. The wind started gusting stronger, tugging the tent and sending fine dry sand blowing before and into my already reddened eyes. I busied myself putting anything loose or susceptible to the insidious sand in bags and boxes, smiling at how short a time my tent and gear had stayed clean.

It was a wild, windy, gritty night. But it remained a warm wind. The temperature hovered around 68°F. I only managed to sleep for short spells. Shortly after midnight I woke to see that the high tide was just three or four yards from the tent and rising, and the wind was now blasting straight into the bay from the southwest, further driving the water up the beach. My rain fly was lifting up, teasing me with the moonlit scene outside before snapping shut like I'd just been swallowed by a whale.

Later that night, the wind shifted to the east, roaring straight down the valley, threatening to strip the wildly flapping tent from me and blow it into the bay. Reluctant to emerge, I could hear the worst gusts moaning down from the mountains moments before they struck. Full gallon water containers were blown over and were rolling around. A folded chair was rattling against the rocks. I was praying that the kayak or some weighty part of the camp wasn't about to fly through the air and brain me. The tent pegs had all ripped out of the sand. I was tempted to pull down the poles and wrap the tent around me till conditions improved, but so much sand was moving I feared I'd end up buried alive! However, when the partially filled kettle blew off a plank and dropped between two boulders, I had to emerge—losing water was not an option.

So out I went at 1:30 A.M. to wedge and weigh down what I could. The high tide hadn't retreated. The sea was still lapping just a few feet from the tent, close to the ring of fishing floats; and outside the bay, the wild moon-silvered sea was booming and roaring, almost drowning out the moaning of the wind.

It wasn't till around 3 A.M. that I was certain that the tide had turned... the water was a paddle length down from the high tide mark. Even so, I got little sleep. A couple of hours later I noticed the inland canyons were deep in shadow. The moon was sinking. The sun would soon be up.

Chapter 31

The Inevitable Dragon

Woe unto you, when all men shall speak well of you.

Jesus [Luke 6:26]

Dawn! The wind had eased from violent to just loud and aggressive. There were passable imitations of sand dunes around my sleeping bag. I was exhausted. But my campsite seemed to have more or less survived the night. I was about to emerge when I heard the caw of ravens. I could see them through the side mesh as the tent rainfly lifted, perched on boulders just twenty yards away. I shouted. They took off, mixing their indignant cries with the wind.

Kayaking would be too dangerous, so I opted to explore inland, setting off up the valley from the beach, taking just the usual items in my daypack, and my emergency gallon of water to hide somewhere.

I described what happened then in a message which was eventually posted on the Nomad discussion board.

> Next morning with the wind moderating, and better able to appreciate the stunning beauty all around, I set off for an exploratory hike. Before I had gone fifty yards I slid to an urgent stop, my leading foot was inches from a five-foot-long pinkish rattlesnake. As it was

Crotalus Mitchellii

so close to my camp I had no choice, I had to kill it. A single rock throw smashed its neck immediately behind its head.

And that started quite a discussion:

This is just plain wrong. How can Graham have such little respect for wildlife? He claims to have had no choice, but he had plenty of choices that would not have involved killing the rattlesnake. The first was to leave the rattlesnake alone. The second was to use a long stick and move it well away from his camp. He has a better chance of being stung by a scorpion than to be bitten by a rattlesnake. His paranoid attitude toward rattlesnakes has been apparent in all his writings. I would think that someone with so much experience in the desert would have a better understanding and "respect" for desert animals.

From the description, the rattlesnake sounds like it was a Crotalus ruber, a Red Diamond Rattlesnake. Isla Angel de la Guarda is part of the Islas del Golfo de California Biosphere Reserve, an ecologically unique and important group of islands. Populations of animals on islands are more susceptible to extinction for many reasons: Limited resources, competition for resources, changing abundance of prey populations, and of course, stochastic events like people killing every snake they see.
It seems to me that, while what Graham is doing is very interesting, in the long run his attitude is having a negative effect on the island and its animals.

Have to agree… It is illegal to kill the wildlife on the islands according to the reserve's own rules, he is likely violating his permit, if he obtained one like he is supposed to.

I agree 100%—it is absolutely wrong and propagates further destruction and ignorance

What a freakin harebrained thing to do .Murdering a snake to make a buck with another two bit story is what it comes down to.
He's got nothing better to do than wander around a rock in the middle of the SOC for a month and he couldn't find the time to relocate the snake?
That's pretty lame - but I'm sure one of the self righteous Baja aficionados will spew more in defense of his apparently senseless actions. Hell, someone hurry up and get the GPS waypoint linked so all the tourist can find their way to where the deed was done.
The way it's going though, in 10 more years the whole of Baja will look like Rosarito and all the attitudes to go with it will already be in place.
—and I am sure that all you folks that have passed judgement on Graham's

actions routinely let termites and blackwidows run around your house?
We all have different perspectives—it is called "tolerance" when we
recognize that.

Graham is not at home he is on an ecological protected island.
The red diamond rattler is one of the least aggressive snakes I have ever
come across. I came across one once while hiking at the upper end of
canyon cajon. He was sunning himself on a rock I needed to use to bypass
a waterfall. I used my hiking stick to toss him about 10 feet down slope.
Upon landing he coiled up and rattled for about 3 seconds, then he
stretched out and went back to sunning himself.
Yes, I have also killed a red diamond that was in my yard at El Dorado.
Relocating him would only have moved him to someone else's yard.
It's not so much that he killed a snake but where he did it.

I would not have killed the snake, either, but I know that Graham is terrified of
rattle snakes. Does this excuse it?? NO. but I believe that we should at least
understand where Graham is coming from, and not be so quick to judge him.
By the way, (and most don't know this) snakes bruise very easily, and "throwing" a
snake almost always does mortal damage to any snake, the way I understand it.
I personally have been "hit" twice by rattlers, both times on my boot, so was not
damaged. But it is rather unsettling to be struck by a rattler, and the self defense
urge comes into play instantly. In my case, neither of the snakes were killed, but I
came very, very close. Both times were in knee high grass, and I never saw the
snakes until it was too late.
Your point about the "wildlife preserve" is well taken, and the most disturbing
thing about Graham's actions, but I still don't think that we have to "attack"
Graham for his instinctual reactions. He does need to reconsider his "fears", and
get a handle on them, I agree. And he does have to take seriously where he is—and
the restrictions on human impact.
Actually, I am surprised that he even mentioned the snake episode. He must have
known the uproar it would cause.

I'll have more respect... for some of these peoples opinions when they go live
on a deserted island for months at a time with very little supplies...then when
they send in a report about encountering a rattlesnake close to camp and just
letting it be or relocating I will gladly applaud them

One of the disturbing aspects of this is that it was Graham that did this. It
wasn't some city dwelling tourist that seldom leaves a paved sidewalk
and comes across unexpectedly upon this creature. This comes from a
man lauded for his treks across the wild landscape of the Baja desert. A
man in tune with all aspects of the wilderness. A man who has built a
reputation of understanding and appreciating all of Baja's primitive
aspects. So he comes across one of it's 'dangerous' inhabitants and bangs
it over the head. Strange.

Dear Nomads,

I am really happy to see that you all are reading Graham's letters here and that it sparks conversation... However, Graham's writing (about personal interaction with nature) does a great service to promote the awareness of the natural beauty of Baja.

He DOES eat rattlesnake, and I would bet that the one that could have bitten him made a delicious meal for the man that WALKS all over Baja (and camps without generators or other pollution causing devices)!

I do worry when people put a poisonous snake in a higher position than a human being on the natural order. I am sure it was so close to being a danger to Graham's life, that there was not another choice.

Let me ask you this... those noisy pangueros that forced Graham to move to the new spot: Do you have any doubt that they would kill any or all rattlers that they found in their camp? Let's not jump to conclusions and hear what Graham has to say about this, as it surely will be described in greater detail in book #4.

Gracias amigos! D

I'm curious why you would make him out to be some kind of responsible naturalist who is opening the eyes of the world to the natural beauty of Baja. I'd say his behavior with the snake refutes that completely. I've probably had 15-20 encounters with rattlers and the common thread is their desire to get the hell outta Dodge, ASAP. A walking stick as a deterrent (not as a bludgeon) is really all that one needs. Zip your tent at night and you're safe. Remember, these things will let YOU know when you're too close.

Did he really kill and eat rattlers in his treks across the peninsula? There are many ways of getting from point A to B on the peninsula. I can't fathom that he had more than one situation where the snake HAD TO BE KILLED in a "him or me" scenario.

I'd venture to say he's begun to use the snakes for dramatic effect in the books.....or he feels it's something like Alfred Hitchcock's cameo appearances. After all, it's a little difficult to create a man vs. nature drama where there are few dangers......and a panga with supplies or a rescue is just a radio call away.

I still think this whole thing is falling a bit short of an adventure. Then again, maybe all we're being fed is "the tease." Really, what Graham has going for him is a non-traditional work schedule (damn, those Mackintosh boys have good gigs!) and an extremely lenient wife. I'm envious, but that's about it, for me.

Maybe, more than anything, I'm having trouble with the motivation here. The book seems to be wagging the adventure, instead of the other way around. I feel like I'm witnessing the creation of a book, rather than an adventure. You decide to walk the peninsula with a burro, that's one thing....

Why, even I'VE managed to predict the plot points.......remember my post on page four of this thread?

C'mon, now, he MUST have earned "immunity" in a competition with that member of the KAYAK tribe he encountered, no? Or did members of the PANGA tribe come to his aid?

Predicted next episode of Survivor: La Guardia...........SNAKES!!!

Allright, so I hadn't counted on members of the Uncouth Tribe of Pangueros coming along. But they aided him and they willingly moved him. Seems I was spot on with the snake. I'm thinking that this now qualifies me for co-writing credits.

I might as well take a crack at the next couple of episodes. Residuals add up, ya know.

Handlining for Yellowtail: Snakeskin Amulet Works With NGK Sparkplug!

Chuckwalla: It's Not Just for Breakfast Anymore.

Eating Crow: Early Nemesis Gets His Due......But It Tastes NOTHING Like Chicken

Close Encounters of the Shark Kind: Foodchain Reality Bites....Almost!

Dances with Dolphins: Yo! Us Mammalia Gotta Stick Together...

Yeah, I'm a sarcastic sod. Commercials have always had that effect on me. But keep 'em coming. It's becoming more entertaining than I expected.

I don't feel the need to question... what Graham did, after reading 2 of his books that are both stories of him wandering around Baja its easy to tell that the guy isnt prone to going around killing unneccesarily...in fact the impression of him I got is that he has quite a unique relationship with animals ...again I feel this way after reading his books which gives me some background on Graham, after all the criticism he has received on this thread it seems obvious that most of the critics have not read any of his books......maybe its like the guy stated above that some are envious or maybe because its just so easy to be a critic on an internet forum, whatever the reason I think some folks are missing the point of what Graham is doing

Leaving your comfy living room? Then take note: Civilization stops at the shoreline....after that we enter the food chain.

What a hoot! I am smiling my way to the fridge for some rattlesnake leftovers.

My response is just in place of one Graham cannot give due to his location.
As I told another Nomad who emailed me, comments about Graham's actions are fine (this is a discussion forum after all)... But don't get all worked up if I (or others) respond with the other side in Graham's defense.

A rattlesnake bite can be deadly and should get medical treatment... that is not possible where Graham is. I do believe Graham felt he had no choice, and on the spur of the moment, it is better to go with the choice that insures you will live.

I do think you guys need to appreciate that Graham is even telling us this stuff and not be ragging on him for doing so. That is my opinion...

I think that the kill/don't kill opinions are great and do apply in a debate.

But, unless you are there, how can you judge the actions of an individual protecting himself?

I've never killed an animal in any situation, but, I probably would defend myself if I thought that was needed.

I'm sad to see the judgmental crowd again jumped on some minor details and sullied the man. This is what is wrong with many of these boards. It's not enough to enjoy the stories and sharing. We have to be judgmental, although most of us have never been in the same situation, or have the same experience/expertise to make the call. I don't care if you have seen 20 rattlesnakes. When it comes to dealing with the elements in Baja, Graham is one of the world's experts. I've never met the man but I've read his books, and my opinion has not changed.

He's human, with flaws and fears and instincts of self-preservation. Something he does will not be to everyone's likings. Deal with it. It's called being tolerant. You are not in his shoes, being days away from the nearest hospital, or see his situation through his eyes on a remote island.

Reading his adventures enriches my days, and it'll be a tragedy if guys like him quit sharing or water down their adventures so much that their stories begin to read like a Disney movie of the week.

I've driven all over Baja for years and I biked, flown over, boated, kayaked, camped and fish along most of its eastern shore. But seeing other posters regularly bashed by armchair self-righteous experts, I and quite a few others I know quit sharing. Now, we just go out and enjoy ourselves and keep things private to ourselves and a few select friends.

Kudos to the Grahams ... (and others) of the world. They have the stomach for it. If you have been around these boards long enough, you notice guys who come and post some good adventure stories, get bashed for some minor details that offend someone's sensibilities, and you never hear from them again. It's no fun when the joy of sharing is drowned out by the noise of whining. Oh yes, this is my first post and probably only post. I'm going to put on my shoes, probably made by some child laborer in China, go out and start my car to put a bigger hole in the ozone layer, and drive the family to Red Lobster for that shrimp dish that my kids love but that have been caught together with 10lbs of discarded bycatch...but heck, I didn't kill no rattlesnakes this month so I MUST be superior to Graham.

I have to read through a lot of unrelated stuff to get to the heart of this thread. While I was disappointed in Grahams act with the snake, it wasn't the end of the world.

I think most people agree that killing the snake was not required and whether or not he has a fear of snakes does not justify his action either. As to the proximity stuff, he said 50 yards didn't he? Hell, for you folks in the suburbs that like 3 houses away. It is not like he opened his tent door and it was coiled on his boots.

So he was wrong for killing it but it is now done. Unless it was one of the last of it species then we should be O.K. In all fairness though I have killed about 7 rattlers in my life and 3 of those were eaten. I have also captured another 6 or so and released them unharmed. Therefore, I am not one to say "Don't kill it!".

There was one in a patch of weeds in Bear River that I almost stepped on while fishing that river for bass one summer. It was about 3 feet long and as big around as a soda can... and me and my brother caught it, walked the mile home with it, got yelled at by our parents and set it free.

So every now and then I will catch a king, garter (yuck) or other snake near our home to show our children before releasing them on our property. I have yet to see anyone bitten by a rattler or snake so the danger factor is way overblown. Yes, people do get bit, by dogs, by horses, by spiders and by snakes but it is very rare.

Macintosh should be off the island, and explaining the killing of that snake in a Mexican court, not in a new "adventure" book. Some people think he shouldn't be "ragged on" on a message board? Hey, we'll take what little justice we can get; he should get worse.

The islands are supposed to be ecological reserves, not locations for some guy to set up his next for-profit venture. ANYONE who thinks that a snake found near a campsite on these islands can or should be killed should vacation elsewhere. Like Cabo San Lucas.

Macintosh could spend a month in "Cabo" and write about it. It might be more interesting than his planned and canned adventures.

So, would you rather not read of what it is like camping on an island off Baja than to hear the whole story, including the death of one rattlesnake? Graham is not hiding the snake kill from us, yet because he did tell us, those of you who put the poison viper above humans are having quite a field day here! When F killed the red diamondback that came into our busy camp area (dogs, people) in April, 2003, you snake-lovers also had a fit. Sorry folks but in my opinion man IS a natural part of this planet and man can kill the lower beasts for survival (food, safety, etc.). Graham has a permit to be there, as stated in the earlier mails from him... Maybe he will turn himself in? Jail would be a quiet place to write his next book, after all!

OK. now hold up a minute. It was Graham OR the snake? The Snake WAS NOT ATTACKING a helpless creature! You need to be more realistic here and don't try to defend Graham.
So which one was Graham's reason for killing the snake?
Safety? He was in no danger, there are probably several snakes, not to mention scorpions within 50 yards of his camp.
Food? Having been there, done that, I would not consider it a meal. Was he starving to death?
Etc.? This must be it. Since there is no reason to kill something except eat it, keep it from eating you or to prevent it from eating your food. Any other reason is just killing for the sake of killing.
Killing the snake was just him being afraid of snakes which does NOT make it RIGHT. It just goes to show how ignorant we humans are. I am not holding it against him and want to hear more of his adventure. Just do not make it some big deal, he killed it, he shouldn't have, time to move on.
Oops, gotta go, some birds just landed on my property and I feel the need to kill something, not to eat, just kill...

The argument that killing the snake was necessary self defense is absurd. Killing the snake put him in more danger than just walking away from it. He should restrict his camping to places with no snakes, or places where he can legally kill and eat them, or learn to leave them alone. And yes, Graham has a permit to be there. And I suspect he violated that permit. And I do think he should turn himself in.

I'd still like to hear his updates, even if the guy is a big baby around snakes. "Ohh, I'm skeeeeered of the snake 50 yards from my camp, I have to kill it!" Maybe he'll use my quote in his book and cite me. The work required to kill it was far more dangerous than simply walking around it. Ask any herpetologist. I suggest that Graham, and you D go to http://www.tongs.com/ and buy the Gentle Giant Snake Tong to make removal of snakes completely safe and easy. Or you can use the tong to hold him while you kill him, whatever floats your boat.
Nobody is putting human lives above snakes... If he or anyone else is truly in danger, then hell yeah, kill it, but Graham was not in danger. If he really does like to kill things that present danger, he should have killed all the fisherman that moved into his camp and smoked dope. They were a lot more of a threat than the silly snake!

*By the way [the] correct common name [is] the red diamond rattlesnake,
not red diamondback.*
*Bottom line, if he or anyone else is going to visit another country, at least
follow their rules and customs. If the islands are protected along with the
critters, then follow the rules or write your book from someplace else.*

Gringo Policia... these snake defenders are a real hoot, next time I
encounter one i'll be sure to let it know not to worry for the defenders of
the snake are numerous and are ready to do battle with anyone who harms
the beautiful creature
geez,lighten up... i've camped in Baja many times and have killed a few
innocent creatures like scorpions and other spiders not to mention fish and
who knows what else...the Mexicans who live locally do the same...it seems
to be a matter of personal choice, so why question the choice of a person
who obviously has a permit to be there and made a choice to kill an animal
known to be deadly that was in close proximity to his camp.......even if it
was a mistake, why sit around and harp on it endlessly when it is such a
trivial part of the larger picture of what Graham is doing on the island....does
it give some of you nay-sayers such great pleasure to point out this
apparent flaw in Graham's character that you cant just let it go

*Those of you snake-huggers who somehow think that I also kill vipers because I post
Graham's letters here and am standing in to defend him as he cannot... Well, for
your information, I have not killed any snakes in Baja but have seen several....
rattlers always in APRIL.*
*My daughter's photo with a red diamond rattler appeared in the Discover Baja
magazine article I wrote (about Inky the dog, found on our way into Santa
Maria)... We easily could have killed it, but didn't as we had no need to. Another
red diamond (diamondback to some) I nearly stepped on in Parral canyon... took its
photo and left it alone. A Baja Ca rattlesnake was on the road near Montevideo
petro site... again, took its picture and let it go... So, stop ragging on me...*
*Also, since Graham IS an expert Baja camper, backpacker and adventurer, not some
complaining tourist, I will believe HIM: that he felt the need to kill the snake...*
Get over it... for Pete's sake D

At the end of the trip I had the chance to reply to some of the points being
made on the Nomad board.

From Graham Mackintosh

Well, as for killing that rattlesnake, it was probably the toughest
decision of the trip. My wife, an avid snake lover, strongly disagreed
with what I did.
If I had encountered it away from my camp—up in the mountains or
on some remote beach—I would have taken some photographs,

wished it well and carried on.

However, I had just arrived at Este Ton and was taking my first hike inland, up a little, steep-sided, brush-covered gulley. Without scrambling up slopes or over the large boulders on the shore, it offered the most obvious trail off my little sandy beach.

The gulley was littered with blowing bathroom tissue, unburied caca, and assorted trash left behind presumably by fishermen who often choose the sheltered bay as a campsite. I remember thinking I am going to have to clean this up... and as I stepped over rocks and felt the brush scrape against my legs, the only other thought I had time for was—I had better watch myself here, it's a warm day following a warm night and this place is prime rattlesnake country.

I was an easy stone's throw from my campsite, right in the gulley that leads to it, and I encounter one of the largest rattlesnakes I've ever seen! It was perfectly camouflaged beneath some sticks and reeds. I almost trod on it. It did not rattle. I only noticed it because it moved. Up until that moment, during my first month on the island, I hadn't seen a sign of a snake.

Retreating a yard or two, I slipped off my backpack, took some pictures and then spent several minutes looking at it, looking down to my tent, and debating what to do. In spite of numerous encounters I hadn't killed a rattlesnake in maybe a dozen years. But I had a serious problem here.

I couldn't just bypass it and forget it. The snake was maybe just a two minute slither from my tent and camping gear, from the place that I would be calling home for almost the next month.

I was alone on that island with very uncertain communications. [There at Este Ton, although I could often hear radio traffic from LA Bay, especially if I climbed a bit, I tried unsuccessfully several times to contact anyone on my handheld marine radio.]

The sea was rough after a wild night. The wind could come blasting up at any moment. The tides were running at their fullest and the currents were intimidating. I would not give a lot for my chances if I were bitten by a rattlesnake and had to try kayaking fifteen miles back to Bahía de los Angeles on my stable but slow Cobra Tandem "sit-on-top."

I thought about returning to my camp and grabbing some kind of bag or container in which to put the snake... or using my machete, walking stick, or some other object to carry it away out of the gulley. But such was the size of the snake, and picturing the difficulties of pulling it into the open, picking it up and carrying it far enough up that canyon to safely release it, it just seemed like an accident waiting to happen.

Besides, the snake was getting increasingly lively and I thought there was a good chance if I left the scene it would disappear and I might not see it again till I did tread on it.

Weighing all the circumstances, I reluctantly decided to kill the rattlesnake. A single rock was sufficient. It wasn't something I took any pride or pleasure in. In fact, I felt guilty and sick about it.

I didn't eat it, but I did examine its stomach contents to see what it had been eating.

It wasn't a red diamondback. It was a speckled rattlesnake. Although red diamondbacks—*Crotalus ruber*—are fairly large snakes on the Baja peninsula, there on Isla Angel de la Guarda they tend to be much smaller. The reverse is true for the speckled rattlesnake— *Crotalus mitchellii*—the island version of which has evolved into a very large formidable snake. Most authorities think this is because it arrived on the island first and adapted to the ready supply of large endemic chuckwallas (*Sauromalus hispidus*) leaving the red diamondback latecomers to find another niche. Indeed, I saw several chuckwallas on the slope above where I killed the snake, including the one seen here. I suspect they were the preferred prey.

Sauromalus hispidus—the spiny chuckwalla

Anyway, it was a life and death decision that I wished I did not have to make. Whatever I did, there were going to be consequences. I didn't act because I hate or am terrified of rattlesnakes as some posters rather ungenerously suggest, or indifferent to the responsibilities of being in a protected reserve. However, in the circumstances and in the time I had to make my decision, I felt a greater responsibility to myself, my family… and to not endangering the lives of anyone who might have tried to get out there to get me to medical assistance.

I know many people think I was wrong and will have no sympathy with my action and will not be impressed by my pointing out that I subsequently walked by that spot at least fifty times... or my pointing out that by all accounts there are high population densities of both *Crotalus ruber* and *Crotalus mitchellii* on the forty-two mile long island... and part of me agrees with them... but alone in such circumstances caution is a virtue that has served me well over the years and I just saw things a little differently.

My thanks to those who tried to put themselves in my boots and withhold judgment till they at least heard my side of things.

Graham Mackintosh

After I posted that, the Nomad debate went off in this direction.

In all honesty Graham, although I frown on unwarranted killing, I must admit that I may have possibly reacted the same way. Believe me snakebites are horrible and although no one ever sees someone that's been bitten it is not a pretty sight. My reason(s) are very deeply seeded however. I would be remiss later as you are and regret what I had done. Thanks for owning up to your awkward position and decision, and expressing them here.

Awesome report! Thanks! And I too have encountered some bad to the bone snakes that the hair on the back of my neck spiked up like a dog ready to fight. I was lucky to run away from the scene but if I had to I would have killed that varmont snake.

Please pass along to Graham a thank you for going into detail and defending himself. Like I've said here and in the 2003 thread referenced, if someone really feels in danger, then by all means kill the snake. Even though Graham is a naturalist, he still felt somehow in danger, so killing it was his only option. I hope Graham takes a few trips with some herpetologists or maybe volunteers on some projects so the next time he'll be more comfortable and he'll know just how many snakes were probably closer to his tent than just this one he stumbled upon.

I'm glad Senior Mackintosh survived his trip and had a good time and I hope he continues to enjoy Baja like the rest of us do.

Soooo....OJ WAS innocent
It was a great story....."where's the BOOK?"

I got all three of your book's Graham. Done with the first one and liked it very much. Going to start on the second one this week. Keep up the good work.

To Graham Mackintosh—Graham—as one of the posters who expounded on your "fear" of rattlesnakes, even going as far as saying "I know" that you are afraid of rattlesnakes, I apologize. Of course I did not "know", and I should not have said that.

I based that assumption on what I thought I read in your original book, tho that was many years ago. I obviously was wrong.

Your explanation of the "snake kill" incident makes perfectly good sense to me, and I have no problems with your explanation.

I applaud your adventures, hope you continue them, and hope that you are able to tell us about them in future books.

AS one who has been bitten. Not Fun (28 days In intensive care) I never felt it nessessery to kill the snake… that caused my time in hospital. I hiked in their land, and invaded their space. Note to self: if you enjoy the outdoors, and you come across a snake. Stand still, Watch, Marvel, Walk Away. Nothing dies.

Where on the body were you bitten? I was in the hospital three weeks. It felt like I had a stiff broken ankle afterward. My dad said my head was as big as a basketball and my child size toes the size and look of a ripe purple plums. It took months to loosen up the ankle and recover completely. The snake that got me was only 18" long and full of venom.

I was bitten on the left wrist. I was on Spring Break 1967, and the snake most likely had just come out of hibernation. He was shedding and could not see me until I was right on him. I heard him, looked down, and he was right between my legs. My arms were bare so I placed them behind my back and did a backwards broadjump that would have brought me gold at the world games. I didn't even feel the bite. When I stood up I noticed blood running from my wrist to my elbow. When I wiped the blood I felt the swelling.

I was alone, two miles hike from camp, and about 2000 feet higher than camp. (BAD) It was a long walk out. When I got to the river a fisherman cut my wrist, sucked the wound, (BAD IDEA) and also had to be rushed to the hospital, because venom attacked his mouth and gums.

Wrist 18" Biceps 29" Blood transfusions X 2

Corrective surgery to make my left hand function X 2

Number of times I should of had my head examined X 1000

I've run into rattlesnakes from Baja to Colorado, sometimes alone, on horseback, or with other people. Even stepped over one, realized it, then stepped back away from it only to step on another one! I was lucky and not bitten, but it made me realize how much I had not been paying attention.

The times I've been alone and ran into rattlesnakes are the times I've felt most afraid, but that didn't make me decide to kill one.

The following photos are rattlesnakes I've run into. OK, the one in the water is a sidewinder from my last Baja sea kayaking trip.

That one was alive and well, being blown back to shore. Who know how it got into the water in the first place—maybe foraging near the shoreline when a wave took it to sea?

Anyhow, I think this whole discussion is an important one because it highlights the different perspectives we all have when it comes to caring for the environment. We all draw the line somewhere because of our education, experience, or even judgment.

From my trips to Baja, alone and with other people, I can say that I respect what Graham does. It may seem romantic to have these kinds of experiences, but they are also difficult in many ways. However, I will also say that once you take something away, it's gone. Be it a rattlesnake, a cactus, a mangrove forest, or a whale calving lagoon, and its going will have ripple effects within its given ecosystem. Each of these things becomes even more important given today's population increases and development pressures...

Business end of a Guardian Angel Mitchellii—chuckwalla beware

Chapter 32

The Amount of Venom to Be Counteracted

...cure the disease and kill the patient

Francis Bacon

Mitchell's rattlesnake was named after Silas Weir Mitchell (1829-1914)—"The father of neurology."

Mitchell was born in Philadelphia to a family of Scottish origin. He was a graduate of the University of Pennsylvania, and in 1851 received his MD from Jefferson Medical College.

Before the Civil War, Mitchell published papers on a variety of physiological and neurological topics including, "On the production of cataracts in frogs by the administration of sugar" in the American Journal of the Medical Sciences.

He held a lifelong interest in the toxic effects of snake venom, particularly rattlesnake venom. In 1860 he co-wrote *Researches on the Venom of the Rattlesnake*, with Edward Reichert. Mitchell and Reichert showed that snake venom was protein in nature, and demonstrated the presence of toxic albumins.

In 1861, famed Philadelphia naturalist and paleontologist, Edward Drinker Cope, who has been credited with naming more than 1200 vertebrate species and publishing 1400 papers, named a new Southwestern and Mexican species of rattlesnake in Mitchell's honor—*Crotalus mitchellii* or *mitchelli*, commonly called the speckled rattlesnake.

In the same year, Mitchell was appointed acting assistant surgeon in the Union Army. He was placed in charge of an army hospital in Philadelphia, which brought him to the forefront in the understanding of nerve wounds and nervous disorders.

He was sent to Gettysburg to assist with the care and transportation of the wounded after the battle. He made and collected detailed case studies of nerve injuries in soldiers and wrote or co-wrote the results in numerous articles and books, including *Gunshot Wounds and Other Injuries of Nerves* (1864) and *Reflex Paralysis, the result of gunshot wounds, and other injuries of nerves, founded chiefly upon cases observed in the United States General Hospital,*

Christian Street, Philadelphia (1864) in which the first reference is made to "causalgia," a baffling often excruciatingly painful condition in which there is no obvious connection between sensation and tissue damage. Mitchell coined the term "phantom limb" to help account for it.

He also gained a name for his advocacy of the "rest cure," which became the standard method of treatment for patients, especially women, who suffered from hysteria. Mitchell had a reputation for eccentricity. When asked to visit a woman thought to be dying, he sent all the attendants from the room, and a little later emerged looking upbeat. When asked if she had any chance of recovery, Mitchell confidently replied, "Yes, she will be coming out in a few minutes. I have set her sheets on fire. A clear-cut case of hysteria!"

Silas Weir Mitchell was founder of the American Neurological Society, president of the Association of American Physicians and Surgeons, and the College of Physicians of Philadelphia. He was elected to the American Academy of Arts and Sciences and the National Academy of Science, and received numerous honorary degrees and distinctions from around the world.

As well as writing scores of neurological, pharmacological, and physiological books and papers, Mitchell also achieved considerable fame in his later years as a poet, short story writer, and novelist.

His novel Westways relies heavily on his recollections of the horrors of the battle of Gettysburg; and Mitchell's Civil War experiences were the basis for *The Case of George Deadlow* (1866), a realistic, psychologically perceptive account of the experiences of a quadruple amputee.

On April 18, 1895, Michigan's *Ann Arbor Register* credited Mitchell with finding a "sure antidote" for snake bite.

Strychnine Believed to Be the Most Effective Antidote—Poisons Kill Each Other.

"A sure antidote for the snake poison has been found. The discovery will mark an epoch in the history of medicine…The remedy so long looked for has been found at last in strychnine. The deadly fluid secreted by certain species of snakes was made a subject of study from a very early date, but the old-time investigators knew not how to solve the intricate problems of organic chemistry. All that they accomplished was to create a prodigious number of antidotes, so-called, most of which in their turn were declared infallible. Not one of them was worth a penny. The most notable work in this line has been performed by Dr. Weir Mitchell of Philadelphia who, for the sake of obtaining sufficient quantities of the poison has sometimes kept as many as 100 serpents in his laboratory. His method of securing the venom for examination was to seize the snake by the neck with tongs, forcing a saucer between the jaws. The enraged reptile would then bite into the saucer, on which the poison emitted was left. The substance thus obtained is a yellowish, transparent, sticky fluid, without smell or taste, easily dissolved in water. When dried it will retain its toxic properties for any length of time apparently, looking like a gum or varnish, and it has been preserved for twenty-two years without altering in the least. On this ground it is advisable to handle with caution even the dried fangs of snakes long dead. Boiling, unless continued for a long time, does not render the fluid harmless.

Alcohol has long held the first place in popular esteem as an antidote for snake poison. In truth, it is not such at all, though useful to sustain the vitality of the person bitten against the attack made upon it by the toxic agent. It stimulates the nerve centers and the action of the heart, if taken in small doses. But the mistake ordinarily made is to pour into the patient large quantities of whisky, the effect of which is exactly the opposite of that required. In such great doses alcohol depresses instead of stimulating the vital functions. Intoxication, far from helping the cure, aids the poison. And, by the way, people have often died from snake bite who were bitten when dead drunk.

With the newly discovered antidote the case is exactly the opposite. Danger is far more likely to result from hesitation in using it liberally than from an overdose. Strychnine—itself a poison scarcely less terrible than snake venom—acts directly upon the nerves, stimulating and turning on their batteries, which the snake poison seeks to depress and turn off. Acting with the unerring certainty of a chemical test, it neutralizes the effects of the serpent venom. But it must be administered in extraordinary quantities, even to the point of producing spasmodic twitching of the muscles.

In fact, the ordinary doses must be greatly exceeded, and the administration of the strychnine must be continued, even if the total quantity injected within an hour or two amounts to what in the absence of snake poison would be a dangerous if not fatal dose. The few failures among the numerous successes with the drug thus far recorded have nearly all been traceable to an insufficiency of the antidote… The action of the drug when applied as an antidote is not cumulative. The tendency to relapses is always great where much venom has been absorbed. Apparently yielding to the strychnine for the time, the insidious poison, after an interval during which it seems to have been conquered, all at once reasserts its presence and has to be met by fresh injections, regardless of the quantity previously administered. With children the amount of the remedy to be given must not be judged by the age of the child, but by the amount of venom to be counteracted…"

Guardian Angel Island is a hotbed of species research. There are moves afoot to rename the island variant of Mitchell's rattlesnake. The suggestion being that it has evolved far enough from its *mitchellii* cousins to warrant the new designation *Crotalus angelensis*—the Guardian Angel Island Speckled Rattlesnake. It is unique to Isla Angel de la Guarda.

Whatever name it carries, the island variant of Mitchell's rattlesnake can grow to over 7 feet long. It has a comparatively heavy body with distinct, speckled dorsal cross bands, and a narrow neck. The head is triangular and wide. Its coloration is extremely variable; as well as pinkish, it can be predominantly gray and black, yellowish gray, or orange.

Chapter 33

Tip of the Isoberg

How extremely stupid not to have thought of that.

Thomas Huxley
(After reading the chapter on natural selection in the Origin of Species)

After leaving the snake carcass in camp, I carried my last-resort gallon of water up the arroyo and hid it under a bush on top of a hill.

Looking down to the beach, I noticed a pair of ravens had entered my camp and were poking around. Once more I had to shout to make them back off, then I carefully made my way down to drive them away. I put the snake in the open plastic "trash bin," covered it with a wooden board, and put a heavy rock on top till I decided what to do with it.

Then after making another quick reconnoiter around the bay, I hiked north up the valley paralleling the coast. All the time I was watching my step, concentrating, looking for another snake. On my left as I went up there were three dark and distinct cone-shaped hills with probable paths to the shore between them.

I reached the head of the valley, peered over, and was glad to see a steep but very doable descent into a wide wash. There would be no problem beaching my kayak and walking back this inland way. The broad pebble and shingle shore where the wash met the sea also looked like a great place for beachcombing and collecting wood.

I lingered awhile on top, savoring the view across the channel to LA Bay. With a new angle on the town, I could make out buildings and structures with my binoculars— Smith Island was no longer blocking the view. I called for a radio check… only silence responded.

Backtracking down to Este Ton, I walked along a stony causeway to the hill

Down the other side—looking northwest

dominating the west side of the cove entrance. It was a steep challenging climb, but I pulled myself up, and in the dying wind and warming sun sat by the cross, which was just two sections of agave stalk tied together with string.

In every direction the view was breathtaking—a panorama of blue sea, rolling waves, delightful bay, rugged coastline, magnificent colorful mountains, soul-touching emptiness. Looking across the cove to my little tent, I could easily believe that no one else existed.

On a hill across the bay stood an old rustic cross

I had wanted to be alone again, to find peace, to sense the sacredness about me, and to experience it with a happy grateful heart. And when I thought how close I came to being nailed by that snake, I knew I had much to be grateful for.

The cross was so simple, so sincere, so perfect. How strange that simple folks, like fishermen, can so often grasp what scholars, scribes, and the erudite outpourings of a hundred bible schools can totally miss. The tortuous towers of twisted dogma and ideology, with their layers of intricacy and ludicrous complication at best say nothing, at worst erect a barrier. As if God was like a jargon-juggling scientist, lawyer, or doctor needing to mystify and obfuscate to set themselves apart and above to protect the sacred knowledge from the ignorant.

As with any over-elaborate system of knowledge—revolution is inevitable, allowing us to see things anew, and like Huxley proclaim, "How extremely stupid not to have thought of that." The truth, the revelation: compellingly simple like the theory of natural selection, or like the parable of the Good Samaritan... or like that cross of sticks, lashed together by weather-beaten, reverent hands.

I headed back to further clean and organize the camp. Some of the trash I took up "Rattlesnake Gulch" and added it to a heap of bottles and rusting cans that was already there. Then I dug an exploratory hole in the soft, light-colored volcanic soil and toyed with the notion of burying some or all of it. But it was difficult to know what to do. Leaving it all exposed and stacked on the surface would at least make it easy for someone to run over in a boat and pick it up. But then what? Spew it onto one of the dumps around LA Bay? I left the hole ready while I thought it through.

I could think of worse things than dropping the glass bottles and metal cans into the depths of the Ballenas channel. The cans would soon rust into oblivion. The glass bottles and jars wouldn't pollute, wouldn't be an eyesore, and might possibly offer homes and protection to whatever creatures lurk at 4000 feet.

Later, I took the snake carcass 75 yards from camp and began dissecting and cleaning it in the sea. I examined its stomach contents. There was nothing recognizable inside—just a thin yellowish liquid. It had probably just woken from a long "hibernation," and was waiting for its first meal.

As I was removing the skin with the head and tail attached, a cloud of quarter-inch-long, almost-colorless isopods came out of nowhere to make their contribution to the cleaning.

I was reminded of something that John Steinbeck had written in the Log from the Sea of Cortez:

> Tiny found the shell of a fine big lobster, newly cleaned by isopods. The isopods…in their millions do a beautiful job. It is common to let them clean skeletons designed for study… in a very short time the skeleton is clean of every particle of flesh, and yet is articulated and perfect.

We're all familiar with isopods in the form of those cute little roly-poly sow bugs or pill bugs that infest leaf litter and other damp places. Isopods are crustaceans, relatives of shrimps, lobsters and crabs. And of the 10,000 described species about 6,000 are found in aquatic habitats. And those 6,000 species are probably just the tip of the isoberg. Many more are being discovered and named every day. Some of the marine forms are the stuff of nightmares—ugly parasites (tongue-biters, beach lice, whale lice) or voracious predators that are the terrors of the deep, actually more often of the shallows, and heaven help the creatures that can't escape their predatory clutches. Their fate—to be eaten alive and slowly reduced to a skeleton.

Most marine isopods are less than half-an-inch long and usually emerge at night to feed. What predacious isopods lack in size, they make up for in numbers. Nineteenth-century North Atlantic fishing charts marked whole areas of sea bottom as "lousy ground." Any netted fish would likely fall victim to these isopods before it could be recovered. Even the mighty shark is not safe. At least twice—in Florida in the 1970s and South Australia in the 1930s—commercial shark fishing has been shut down by isopods so infesting the captured sharks, that the catch was unfit for consumption. And fishing activities can have an exacerbating effect. There is evidence that isopods swarm in areas of high habitat disturbance such as bottom raking and trawling.

Attacks on humans are usually more annoying than injurious because most bathers have the ability to quickly escape. But, for example, several divers were attacked while cleaning a jetty in Sydney Harbour. Before they could get out of the water, much of the exposed skin between their masks and wetsuit hoods had been eaten away.

The term isopod means *like feet* (iso = like or alike, podus = foot) because they all share the characteristic of having a body composed of seven thoracic segments each bearing a pair of similar legs.

While I was cleaning the snake, the isopods certainly liked my feet. And distracted by what I assumed were annoying little "bites"—actually they were probably just preparing to dine by grabbing on to my flesh with their fourteen viciously hooked claws—I carelessly pricked a finger on one of the sharp needle-like teeth in the lower jaw of the snake. Seeing blood I forced as much out as possible to flush out any traces of venom or agents of infection.

Apart from a small white lump that formed, I had no ill effects. It might have been a different story if the teeth hadn't been exposed to the sun and air for much of the day and immersed in sea water for thirty minutes. That was enough for me—I laid the skin out to dry on a rock and threw the skeleton and innards into a quiet corner of the bay for the hungry "likefoots" to finish the job.

The sun was burning through the cloud. It was time to think about shade. Someone had left two long agave stalks sunk into the sand about six or seven feet apart, just above the highest tide mark. I decided to requisition those, find another pair of poles of similar size and a bunch of cross ties, and make a rigid box structure that I could cover with layers of netting, and maybe insert a small rolled-up tarp for even better sun protection. If the wind allowed I could unfurl it… and then quickly roll it back up if necessary. I had a blue seven-foot by seven-foot tarp that should work.

Leg protection

I would need to drive the two new corner poles into the sand, so they would have to be long—ten feet or more, and I'd require cross ties of almost the same length. There were no dead agaves near camp. So, wearing canvas leggings from knee to ankle—I'd had enough bites on my leg for a while—and carefully watching my step, I walked into the steep hills carrying a small utility shovel, which could also serve as hammer, ax, and saw. After spending a little while considering if the "ribs" from fallen cardóns would work—the ones I found were too short and flimsy—I ranged further afield till I spied what I needed.

The desert agave, or century plant, forms a rosette or cluster of spine-tipped basal leaves. For maybe 30 years it grows slowly without flowering, then finally a stalk shoots up from the center of the rosette, growing one or

Agave stalks

two inches a day till it stands maybe fifteen-feet-high. On top, a magnificent array of flowers scents the desert air for just a few weeks before producing tens of thousands of seeds—a vital source of food for desert animals. And then the "exhausted" plant dies shortly afterwards; the stalks drying out woody, like sturdy bamboo.

It's easy to twist them and break them off at the base, like a stick of rhubarb. I stripped the stalks of the bayonet-shaped leaves with the small shovel. Each leaf has a very obvious sharp terminal point; but smaller undeveloped leaves run up the stem with the upward pointing, hard as needle, spines resting tight and inconspicuous against the stalks. As I was slicing down I managed to poke one of those spines deep into my right index finger. I pulled out the half-inch-long black tip but a piece of the point broke off and stayed dark inside.

After returning to camp and poking around with a pin to dig it out, I was slice-by-slice chopping away the bulbous base at the end of one stalk when I heard a loud insistent buzzing coming from inside. Another chop revealed a cavity from which a large, dull-colored bee emerged, fell to the ground, and wandered around looking disgruntled and disoriented.

It was a female carpenter bee, genus *Xylocopa*. Carpenter bees resemble bumble bees, but have no yellow banding. Most are hairy, black or blue, often with a metallic sheen and may be up to an inch long and proportionately wide. Females sting, but are usually not aggressive. This lady had every right to sting me into next week.

As many as a thousand species of bees (order Hymenoptera) occur throughout the Sonoran desert, of which Baja California and its islands are a part. Most live solitary lives (as opposed to the social honey bee) and either dig underground tunnels in which to lay their eggs or, like the carpenter bee, dig tunnels in wood.

Some species utilize dead tree limbs while others prefer agave and yucca stalks. Throughout the night the female bee chews through the wood to enlarge a tunnel sufficient for her comely girth, often leaving a little tell-tale pile of sawdust on the ground outside. Carpenter bee tunnels typically include multiple sealed chambers, each filled with one egg and enough "bee bread" to feed the hatched larva until it metamorphoses into an adult bee. During the day the females roam in search of flowers from which to gather the nectar and pollen to make her "loaf."

Male carpenter bees patrol around agave stems where females are building nests. Hovering there all day, the diligent males closely scrutinize every female bee coming and going. Only those with which he has mated are permitted to enter the stalk. So either way she's screwed!

Other males will attempt to drive their male counterparts away through sometimes wild air-to-air combat, bumping, colliding and biting one another until one gives up and flies off. It is not unusual to see three, four, or more males engaged in this combat. They never stop to feed or rest. And following their script, the exhausted stingless males soon fall to the ground and expire; their little packets of sperm left in the care of the mated females.

The females often spend the night sleeping in the tunnels, guarding the entrance and keeping watch on their offspring. Eventually, the life cycle runs its course; the young bees chew through the walls of their safe haven and may spend weeks in the tunnel till ready to emerge.

In building my home I had inadvertently destroyed its home, and possibly doomed its offspring. As I drove the sharpened ends of the stalk into the beach, I hoped the bee would recover and have enough energy left to make a new home and family.

Later that afternoon, I tried fishing from the kayak inside the bay, but with the wind I was always drifting too fast for it to be practical. A mass of pelicans well-fed and satisfied stood on the rocky point and reef at the mouth of the bay looking at my pitiful attempt to hook something.

Initially, at least, pelicans had seemed relatively scarce on the island, but week by week they were much more in evidence, and there at Este Ton they were clearly abundant. Yet, I still hadn't seen a single turkey vulture! I made a more determined effort to look, checking out every

Pelicans at the entrance to Este Ton

large soaring bird, and every one perched on top of a cactus. Where were the vultures?

Next day, before breakfast, a cool, cloudy morning, I ventured out of the bay on the kayak and paddled south a half mile. I felt oddly

Pelicans and cliffs

uncomfortable and wary beneath the cliffs. I was not sure about the currents and wind patterns, where the dangerous rocks were, where I could land, and if I could walk back. It was similar to how I felt when I first arrived at Humbug Bay—vaguely threatened, and perhaps ready to latch on to any fear that seemed to account for the feeling. There it had been the ghost pangas, here I hadn't put a "face" to my fear. Sure, I was now wary of waking rattlesnakes, but snakes I could handle. I had years of experience dealing with them. My chief comfort—knowing the paranoia will pass.

Back in my camp, I had just shaved, washed my hair and made myself gorgeous, when I heard a panga... coming from the north. Suddenly, two pangas, with pangueros dressed in heavy jackets and bright, foul-weather gear appeared at the mouth of the bay. I thought they were going by at first, but they were clearing the dangerous outer reef before turning sharply back into the entrance. It had to be my amigos running back to the mainland? Sure enough, they waved and called to me, and gently planted their bows on the sandy beach.

Fishermen bringing me water

They had come to drop off their extra water—two relatively clean gallons in one container, and a gallon or two inside a cracked and open plastic barrel which was full of suspended impurities, including two soggy dead spiders. *No problema.* I could cloth filter and boil the water, or run it through the small hand-pump water filtration device I'd brought. What counted was I had water for maybe three more days... three more days of freedom.

The fishermen seemed very jolly about heading back to Kino. The guys who had taken me to Este Ton told of their adventures beating back to the north; a slow business but they had made it safely. After the tension of the previous days it was good to laugh, take photos, and know you're in the company of friends—friends who are definitely not moving in! I told them about the snake and showed them the skin. The older one of the group wrote his name and address on a matchbox and invited me to visit him and his family on the mainland.

The man who I thought had looked the fiercest, picked up a large oyster half-shell attached to a weighty rock. The coarsely ribbed and spiky exterior of the shell betrayed nothing of the beautiful, amethyst-and-white mother of pearl interior. The meat of the oyster had long since been shucked, and the shell had been cast on the ground, close to the "kitchen." Beyond recognizing it as an oyster of the genus *spondylus*, I hadn't really paid much heed to it until that poor and humble man presented it to me, rock and all, as a gift. He was not going to leave without giving me something. The object once cast aside and ignored, now heavy with meaning and newly appreciated beauty, occupied a central place in my new home. Wedged between rocks, it served as a good solid shelf, and as a reminder that you can't judge the inside of a shell by a rough, dull exterior... or a man by his appearance.

Amigos leaving for the mainland

Later, after they'd gone, two more pangas raced past the entrance heading south—their companions likewise returning to Kino I guessed. They looked over and waved but didn't come in. Now, as far as I knew, I had the island to myself.

I was hoping my friend Bob and his companion would be coming over as scheduled about February 22, and definitely before I was completely out of water.

Chapter 34

Valentine's Day

Him that I love, I wish to be free—even from me.

Anne Morrow Lindbergh

The sun had set. The light was fading fast. While I was waiting for the moon to appear behind me above the island, a bat swooped down and fluttered against the back of my chair, sending me leaping to my feet. At the same moment, across the bay, there was an explosion of what I presumed to be mostly pelicans from the point—scores of them taking briefly to the air and then flowing *en masse* into the sea. It's hard to convey the racket a hundred or more pelicans and their squawking avian consorts can make with broad fluttering wings and splashing webbed feet on such a still evening. I looked through my binoculars, but couldn't tell if they'd been spooked or simply pounced together on a moon-revealed school of fish. I had to wonder if one of the "vampire" cats was over there shiftily looking around, self-congratulatory about this good beginning to its night's work, drinking the warm, quenching blood of its victim as the great lunar orb finally separated itself from the horizon and hung brilliant, as full and round as a feline paw print in the night sky.

I woke at 5 A.M. It was 57°F and partly cloudy. The moon was now hanging out in the west. And speaking of warm blood, I had occasion to think of my wife: "By my reckoning it's Happy Valentine's Day Bonni. I'll be thinking about you the whole day."

The go-dependency was working like a charm. I was exploding with empathy, gorged with gratitude, turgid with tenderness… and my libido was rising up like a submarine-launched cruise missile, punching through the surface, locked on target. Love was in the air.

By 6 A.M., with the sea flat and the sky clearing, I loaded the kayak with boots, sunscreen, snacks, water and the usual survival items, and then paddled out of the bay.

The water was draining fast from the Sea of Cortez, the current running river-like, north to south. Initially, heading south under the cliffs would have been the easier option, but more mindful of my return than my departure, I battled the stream with lusty strokes, knowing a north wind would speed me home. And I'd already found a way to walk back from that direction if necessary.

Osprey nest on arch

By paddling out from shore occasionally, I could see miles of the cliff-lined coastline, perhaps as far as the southern tip of the island, and would almost certainly spot any approaching pangas.

I wanted to go ashore and examine an incredible rock arch, pulpit-crowned with an osprey nest, that I had first seen with Cal and then again as I approached Este Ton with the fishermen. And there it was majestic, astride a stony beach, just above the high tide line. Now alone, expectant, barely aware that I was paddling, I moved towards it as if on a stream speeding towards a cataract. Oracle, crystal ball, great maw, sacred portal? Its majesty increased.

I could see Bonni reaching for me

One moment, a vast rock-hewn raven, another, a mammoth, doomed, stuck fast in tar. And the wide mouth, through dark quivering lips, plainly wished to speak to me of ages past and eons yet to come, and purposes unfulfilled. But with imagination outstripping courage, and fearing to walk beneath the stabbing beak or heaving belly, I broke the spell, excused myself from setting foot on such holy ground, and took timid refuge in the mundane.

The current grew feeble. Beachcombing yielded

another sturdy plastic crate, and more netting, poles, planks, and firewood. My sit-on-top made a good stack-on-top. I was seriously overloaded going home. Sitting at the back of the kayak with all the stuff piled in front of me, I conjured up Bonni's smiling face and warm hand reaching, but I could hardly see where I was going. As the water was now so calm and clear, and I was cruising so slowly, I had no concerns about striking an unknown rock or reef. And by keeping just fifty yards offshore, there was typically at least fifty to a hundred feet of water beneath me. I was in no hurry to return. Making amends, I couldn't resist landing on every tiny, cliff-backed "virgin" beach to pick over the more interesting debris that had been cast ashore.

As soon as I felt the first hint of the tide's return, I started back. It was a wise decision as a surprise southerly breeze conspired with the inflowing current to get my Valentine heart pumping a little faster. The wind whistled through the high stack in front of me. The kayak began to pitch and roll. I prepared myself to dump most of it on the shore. While I was moving closer to check out the landing beaches, the capricious wind again fell to nothing. The sea calmed and so did my heart.

I paddled further out into the channel. I was sitting 500 yards offshore, looking at the island's colorful red mountains, wondering how to approach and maybe cross them. The water was full of shiny scales, like snow flakes, drifting and sparkling in the descending shafts of sunlight, measuring the blue-black deep. A long line of pelicans snaked above. I heard the whoosh of a whale. It sounded close, but I couldn't see it.

Jellyfish   *Eared grebe*

I paddled back reluctantly, prompted by the very sensible wish not to waste an opportunity for an easy return. Close to the safety of the bay's entrance, I dallied again, floating gently along, indulging in the glory of Guardian Angel's splendid coastline. The tide was rising. I gauged my motion in the current; there was nothing alarming. I felt in complete control.

Fearing that a line of dark agitation way to the south might herald a front of blasting wind, I positioned myself close to and a little south of the entrance to the bay, but nothing more than a few gusts came passing over. Then all fell breathless, flat calm again.

Just inside the bay, I maneuvered to take a photo of a large pulsing jellyfish. A minute later I found an eared grebe, floating dead on the surface. I held it up, took a picture, and wondered how it had died.

Then I felt foolish touching it with bird flu such a concern. After soaking the offending fingers a few moments in the sea, I paddled over thousands of sardine-like baitfish imparting their "rain drops" effect all over the surface of the bay. Other smaller fish hung around closer to the shore—all with impunity. There were no splashes from yellowtail or other large predator fish. Several lines of pelicans flew overhead—not one bird attempted a dive.

Drifting slowly by the reefs at the mouth of the bay, unhurried, safe, two minutes from my camp, I was surprised by a sudden loud noise, like the agitation of an enormous washing machine. Tsunami? A boat? I was baffled. It was certainly no earthly boat. Looking up, I saw 30-40 dolphins in a line, heading south, frantically leaping—some right out of the water—diving, and splashing. Feeding or frolicking? I wasn't sure which. But I suspected that at any moment I was only seeing a fraction of the dolphins that were there.

It was a remarkable picture—fish beneath the water, dolphins on the surface, a line of pelicans above—life seemed to be stacked up like the layers in the cliffs.

I headed to my beach to unload and noticed that the ravens had paid a visit. Cans, glass, and plastic bags had been beaked from the trash and re-scattered all about; one of my saucepans had been cast to the sand, and my solar shower bag had been punctured. Oddly, I was more amused by their vandalism than concerned. On such a day I could love even a raven.

It remained calm. So I grabbed my fishing gear and paddled back over to the reef at the outer entrance to the bay, and there I provoked a similar mass take-off of pelicans, cormorants, and gulls to the one I had heard the previous night. I tried jigging close in among the rocks that emerged at low tide. A few bolder pelicans refused to be distracted from their preening, scratching and stretching a wing or a neck as I drifted by.

The gentle southerly breeze tempted me to paddle along the rugged shoreline to the south to assess the potential for walking back that way. It looked likely at low tide, but at high tide I'd need to do some wading, maybe even a little swimming. I stepped ashore on a lovely pebble beach with huge pink and pistachio-green rocks. These house-tall boulders offered shade for the asking. If the beach had been sandy I might have considered moving over there.

Back on my beach, I kept adding to and improving my shade house. I enjoyed watching it evolve, putting on more pieces of net, more cross ties and supports. It was a humble enough dwelling, but lounging feet up beneath, I felt like a king surveying his peaceful kingdom… and for a while at least regally enjoying a pleasantly cool beer. But the latter was not essential!

As the sun, long down behind the peninsula, left its final rays like a feeble frantic voice calling in the sky, the moon was sending forth its first subtle, heralding beams, almost as if it were reaching out, too late, to rescue its sinking love—sun and moon beams, like fingers desperately sliding past each other. Tomorrow the moon would come forth into a night as black as a raven's beak.

It had been a Valentine's Day glowing with warmth and color… a glorious reminder of the delicious sadness of separation and of the depth of the sacrifice a man must sometimes make to follow his calling!

For dinner I had cooked tomatoes, onions, beef jerky, noodles and flour tortillas. I allowed myself a large can of Tecate and that little bottle of Appenzeller Schnapps, followed by making a big dent in a small box of See's candies that Bonni had given me to take to the island. And after indulging in a KitKat and a mug of hot chocolate, I was feeling even more extraordinarily sweet and loving.

Suddenly, a wind came wafting down the valley, tugging at the tent and flapping a loose tarp. Before I sprang into action to secure my campsite, the wind moderated into a warm caressing breeze. I stood there awhile, gazing up the canyon, sensing, listening to the sound of the breeze, studying that big old moon, bouncing a few thoughts off it in the direction of San Diego.

Chapter 35

The King

My religion is very simple—my religion is kindness.

Dalai Lama

When I had time, I went through the large, packed emergency bag in my tent and congratulated myself—what a rich haul of treasure it would all have been in a survival situation. Yet, I didn't feel the urgent need to hide it again at Este Ton. Filling with perhaps foolish faith—how the tide turns—I felt more inclined to have it ready to share with anyone in need.

After breakfast, I sat beneath my sunshade, with binoculars and bird field guide close at hand. An unusual bird flew by and landed along the rocky shore, twenty yards to my right. With his big head and beak he looked an odd, clumsy kind of fellow. Able to study it for several minutes, I turned on my tape-recorder and called out:

> Definitely a kingfisher; blue-gray back and wings; white underneath, white throat band, gray chest; long relatively heavy straight grayish beak; tufted shaggy head; shortish gray tail, spotted white; small cute legs.

I turned to the field guide and identified it as a male belted kingfisher. I noted that I had only seen one before, also in Baja, in Bahía San Quintín on the Pacific coast. Although not common, the belted kingfisher is perhaps the most widely distributed bird in North America having been recorded in Mexico, Canada, and all 50 states. From a high perch or a hovering position it dives into the water for small fish. The call is a series of harsh, rattling notes. For some reason I liked this guy and immediately felt a bond with him.

After sun-, wind-, and raven-proofing camp, I laced up my boots, strapped on my leg protectors, pulled on my day pack, and was ready to hike and explore inland. But where? I felt all dressed up with nowhere to go; every direction from the shore looked sheer and intimidating. I chose one of the seemingly easier approaches to the mountains... but after an hour it became so steep I was sliding down as much as climbing up, and the leggings felt so awkward, I'd had enough. I took photos, rested, admired the wild beauty of the island, and then leggings removed, worked my way slowly down to the beach.

Back in camp after a simple lunch, I made further improvements to my casa. I scrambled up the low cliffs thereabouts to take pictures of the structure from every angle and found a dead black cat on a flat area beneath a small bush. There was no smell. The process of decay was long past. It was frisbee-like and mummified. Empty eye sockets stared at me. There seemed to be hardly any skeleton beneath its long black coat, as if it had been flattened by an enormous force, a victim of some cosmic catastrophe. I kicked it a few inches and it scuffed over the dusty stones as effortlessly as a hunk of stiff dry leather; a few small black beetles were exposed and quickly scurried out of sight. I left

My home in Este Ton

the cat carcass there to survey its former home… and maybe keep an eye on me.

A hummingbird had appeared several times in the gully just above my tent and I wanted to identify it. So I took my bird book, binoculars, camera, tape recorder, and a quart of water, intending to walk no more than a hundred yards to find a comfortable rock and make a note of all the birds that I could identify.

I didn't get very far on my birdwatching. There's one of the big chuckwallas on the rocks there. Boy, he looks huge through the binoculars; its tail looks like you could use it as a mace. Heavy, spiny… that's a beautiful, beautiful animal; he's licking his right, rear leg; it looks almost human it's so big. And there's another one. They are up on this slope behind me here. One of them looks close to 18-inches long, the other 9-10 inches.

Mummified feral cat

Wondering how far it would let me come, I pulled out my camera and climbed slowly towards the large chuckwalla sunning itself on the slope. I managed to capture about ten pictures and get within four feet before it slid into a slit in the rock.

In his den

The spiny chuckwalla—*Sauromalus hispidus*—is native to Isla Angel de la Guarda and a few adjacent smaller islands. As the name suggests, it is distinguished by its spiny body, particularly its legs and tail. All other chuckwallas have smoother skin. It commonly grows more than a foot long; the largest individuals may reach close to 20-inches and weigh over 3-pounds.

These lizards warm up in the morning sun before seeking food. Their optimum body temperature is about 100°F. Although strictly vegetarian—eating fruit, buds, flowers, and leaves—a large chuckwalla can deliver a crushing bite; adult males often bite off each other's toes. When threatened it is able to inflate its body and wedge itself tightly in crevices.

Another Sea of Cortez chuckwalla, *Sauromalus varius,* native to Isla San Esteban, is even more massive and is the largest of all chuckwallas. Studies have shown that these two island "gigantics" have grown larger compared to their ancestors, whereas their peninsula and mainland cousins have diminished in size.

After hiking or kayaking it was always good to be back early to have plenty of time to get organized and prepare for the night, especially checking that there were no chuckwalla-hunting rattlesnakes around the kayak or the boulder pile making up my kitchen.

It was a pleasant evening. And I was pleased with how cooperative the large chuckwalla had been. At times he looked like he was posing for me. The wind dropped. It was cooler. I heard there was rain in Southern California. It seemed like a good time to treat myself to a warming glass of French brandy—courtesy of pilot Mike Essary.

My set up was such that I could cook dinner and eat while admiring the beauty of the sunset. With a little help from a few clouds, it was a constant source of delight to ponder and watch the warm, fruity, pastel transitions, and see the gradual infusions of gold, pearl, and jet. What a poor representation was anything that could be rendered on even the largest computer or television screen. The colors before my eyes were so vast and cosmic I could almost hear, touch, and taste them. They invaded my mind and illumined my heart. And even as they faded, a new world of gilded shadows and silhouettes held brief impressive sway.

I peered through my binoculars at two ospreys, black before the sunset, one perched on a cardón, the other sitting on a nest across the bay. And there was "my" pelican diving into the shallows in front of me, startling me with his sudden explosive impact on the water. I called him my pelican because he was so often there alone, at the last light, on the same rock close to my camp. He knew me and I knew him.

There was a great blue heron on the point opposite, perched by the cross, and as it grew dark, in silhouette, it seemed more real and more magnificent. Finally like some Jurassic bird dinosaur it rose with a resounding primeval squawk and slowly beat its way north over the coastal hills, dropping out of the bay and out of sight.

And when night fell at Este Ton, the sandy area about my campsite came alive with the kind of pea-sized black beetles I'd seen beneath the mummified remains of the cat. There was typically one or two on every square foot of beach above the high tide line. Not as dramatic as the birds or the chuckwallas perhaps, but these tenebrionid beetles are clearly a highly successful group. In some desert and desert island settings their biomass easily outweighs that of the combined biomass of birds, mammals, and reptiles in the same area. The Baja peninsula and its islands support over 382 known species of tenebrionids, 25 of which are endemic to the islands of the Gulf. And most of them are highly adapted ground dwellers which in their need to conserve water have resorted to a nocturnal lifestyle, forsaken the use of defensive secretions, and given up the ability to fly.

Beneath fused elytra or wing cases, many of these beetles still retain vestigial, non-functional wings. And that observation posed a question to a young naturalist that helped revolutionize the way man looks at the world.

From an early age Charles Darwin was fascinated with beetles. Even while ostensibly studying theology at Cambridge University, Darwin confessed in his autobiography:

> But no pursuit at Cambridge was followed with nearly so much eagerness or gave me so much pleasure as collecting beetles. It was the mere passion for collecting; for I did not dissect them, and rarely compared their external characters with published descriptions, but got them named anyhow. I will give a proof of my zeal: one day, on tearing off some old bark, I saw two rare beetles, and seized one in

each hand; then I saw a third and new kind, which I could not bear to lose, so that I popped the one which I held in my right hand into my mouth. Alas! it ejected some intensely acrid fluid, which burnt my tongue so that I was forced to spit the beetle out, which was lost, as was the third one.

In Darwin's notebooks of 1837-38, written over twenty years before *The Origin of Species* was published, he mused: "…useless wings under elytra of beetles—born from beetles with wings, and modified—if simple creation merely, would have been born without them."

As his ideas came to fruition, he wrote: "…we may conclude that the existence of organs in a rudimentary, imperfect, and useless condition, or quite aborted, far from presenting a strange difficulty, as they assuredly do on the ordinary doctrine of creation, might even have been anticipated, and can be accounted for by the laws of inheritance. [and Natural Selection.]"

When discussing vestigial organs Darwin more than once made reference to such an organ as being as "useless… as the shrivelled wings under the soldered elytra of many insular beetles."

One study of islands in the LA Bay area strongly correlates high tenebrionid beetle population density with the absence of rodents. Rodents being nocturnal, find most of the tenebrionids easy prey. Given the numbers of those beetles there at Este Ton, I thought it likely that rodents were largely absent. And, again, one has to suspect that feral cats were the likely culprits.

I stayed up reading and listening to the radio, waiting for the moonlight to reveal the clouds. A rushing gust of wind came across the bay, another from down the canyon behind me.

With pages flying and sand blowing, there was too much wind to read outside, so I threw the book inside the tent and simply sat out, pondered, stargazed, and allowed my thoughts to be carried along as if in a new moon tide.

Drifting in the current, spinning in the whirlpools, reverential, irreverent, religious, profane, questing, questioning, it was easy to lapse into a different, perhaps more primitive, consciousness. If you want to know God… take yourself, alone, into a desert place and rest awhile, still your heart and listen. Don't go the same way, go the sane way.

I thought, what greater happiness can a human being experience than to be devoid of fear or anger, a heartbeat away from laughter, at peace inside and out, tuned into simplicity… mind healthy, hopeful, knowing that his God is a God of love and compassion, and knowing that he has the time to seek and serve her?

Again, the largest screen couldn't do justice to the depth and breadth of a cosmos that was so all encompassing, stirring, and liberating of the senses and the soul. Stars and constellations were starting points waiting to be infused with meaning. Headlands, boulders, and arches might tell and prophesy, but nothing was written in stone. No party, no ossified faith, no fossilized philosophy had all the answers.

The only thing I knew for certain was that I had been given a mind and a heart and God expected me to use both… not to mindlessly or heartlessly yield to any authority, be it Bible or Koran, pope or mullah, premier or fuehrer. I could not believe in anything that didn't satisfy both mind and heart. Spiritual truth, like science, should be open-ended, expansive, always subject to test, especially the check of a compassionate heart.

Considering the state of the world, I reflected on the great commandment. What does it mean to love thy God with all your heart and soul and mind? To love your enemies? And to forgive, seventy times seven? I thought about the implications.

When in that awesome moment we finally approach and stand before our God, what ought we to say, to pray? "Forgive us our trespasses AS we forgive those who trespass against us." Wow! That couldn't be much clearer. Not just forgive me God as I'm a miserable selfish bastard of a sinner that fundamentally only cares about my own glory and salvation… and to hell with the rest of them. But forgive me AS I have forgiven. How provocative, how perfect? How many of us can feel comfortable bringing down such judgment on ourselves?

And Jesus makes it clear that the kingdom, the Promised Land, is not of this earth. Yet we so readily accept that the God that Jesus revealed to us, supposedly directed "his people" to liberate the promised land by slaughtering every man, woman, and child who happened to be in their way. And in our mindless sickness we sing songs about Joshua and the walls of Jericho, and teach our children to sing of this edifying episode, this merciless slaughter of all within the walls, except Rahab the prostitute who selfishly sold out the city to ensure her own and her family's escape. And we attribute the ensuing carnage, if we think about it at all, to a loving God? No wonder our children, so many children, grow up so ready to think that violence is the answer. Kill, no need for conscience or compassion. Never mind what Jesus said, we'll find some other Biblical notion to justify the need to kill. In God's name kill and clear the promised land for the chosen people. Destroy the "sinners." Wreak God's vengeance. And after the slaughter, live happily ever after. Generations will extol your courage and sing your praises!

And down through history your glorious example—it must be glorious don't we teach our children to sing about it?—will be destined to inspire fanatics of every denomination and persuasion.

And a thousand years from now, if history had taken a different course, good German children would no doubt have been singing tales of Adolf and Auschwitz, and how he was divinely inspired to heroically liberate Eurasia and create *lebensraum* for the chosen race.

How can we all be so blind? So delusional? So bereft of compassion?

We should compel everyone who sings or preaches about the walls of

Jericho to watch a long graphic movie of what it means when a heartless nationalistic or religious fanatic goes about a campaign of slaughter. The dying fathers begging for mercy for their huddled and terrified families, the screaming mothers vainly trying to protect their infants with their own bloodied hands and bodies, the little children clutching their soft toys running, and run through with spears, hacked apart with swords, and bludgeoned with rocks and sticks. The survivors dragged from their hiding places pierced and slashed, dying in terror and agony in pools of their own blood, while the victors mock them and shout praises to their God. Jesus, it sounds awfully modern, doesn't it?

Perhaps one day such a movie will be made by a great and courageous director, and our Judeo-Christian worldview will be changed forever.

Is there a single record of Jesus ever justifying Jericho or lauding Joshua's actions? More likely you can see just about everything he taught as a condemnation of what transpired there. Do not kill. Love your enemies. Turn the other cheek. You have seen it written but I say unto you.

If God gifts us the Promised Land, then fighting and killing and bringing hell on earth to hold on to and expand its borders is not what he expects. He commands us to do something much more difficult and heroic. He expects us, the peacemakers, to generously share our God-given gifts… to share them, and to have faith sufficient to relinquish them if necessary. To know and have faith that through sacrifice and example, as Jesus sacrificed himself on the cross, men's hearts can be changed, the truth can be known. Yes, he brings us a sword… but not for us to yield, rather for us to fall victim to, if necessary. All for the purpose of expanding the borders of the Kingdom of Heaven. To those with little faith, it's a hard, incomprehensible message. No wonder it went down like a rocket to hell and was quickly ignored and understated and revised by most Christians. We simply do not like our God getting in the way of our cruel, prideful, selfish, and self-righteous ways.

Back to earth, I looked about to see that all was well. And with the moon casting its silvery glow of approval on my new structure I confess to struggling with an absurd vanity. I doubt that the designers and builders of the Seven Wonders of the World, or the famed walls of Jericho, felt much greater pride than I did as I wrestled with a goodly hunk of the Seven Deadly Sins. Perhaps I was entirely free of only envy and anger.

At 8:30 P.M. as I entered my tent, the moon revealed the clouds were moving west to east. Yet at ground level the wind was gusting down the canyon, from the east… it was an odd reversal, an inexplicable bucking of the trend.

Chapter 36

Rain and Other Gifts

The animals were very beautiful. Here was life from
which we borrowed life and excitement.

John Steinbeck. The Log from the Sea of Cortez

February 17—A cloudy morning. Snug inside my sleeping bag listening to the last fading surges of AM radio reception, I gradually became aware of an incipient sound beyond my headphones. Rain!

I had to say it aloud, "It really is raining." Just scattered spots at first, then it fell widespread and steady, with little wind to complicate matters. Quickly dressing, I went outside to take the steps I'd more than once rehearsed in my mind to keep my tent and gear dry while I collected as much water as I could.

I unfurled the blue tarp in my shade palapa, [the local word for such a rustic beach structure] poked a small hole in the center and placed a bowl beneath. I attached another tarp to the outside of the frame and angled it down to create a chute to collect the runoff. Then I laid out my largest tarp over a natural depression in the sand so the water would pool there. The morning was warm. I was wet. It felt wonderful as I positioned whatever bowls, pots, and containers I could lay out to catch the precious drops. My lifejacket, kayak backrest, and paddling clothes were all white rimmed with salt, so I laid them out on the kayak to be rinsed clean.

The rain came in two waves and was over by midmorning. I had a small sponge for gathering condensation, so I looked to see what surfaces might be

Collecting rain

Rinsing gear on the kayak

profitably wiped. The tent rainfly offered almost half a cup. The entire effort yielded an extra gallon-and-a-half of water. Some was a little muddy, salty, or plastic tasting, but to me all of it was a gift from heaven.

After the rain, now feeling damp and chilled beneath the sunless gray, I pushed the newly rinsed kayak into the bay and sat on top ready for some vigorous trolling. Before I was three paddle strokes from shore, a raven descended on my camp. I headed back in, shouting and gesticulating to drive it off. The raven took to the air and before it could take three wing beats was "jumped" by an osprey. A wild low-level "dogfight" ensued with the raven twisting and turning and using all its acrobatic skills to defend itself; it finally landed on a cactus a hundred yards away. The osprey swooped at it a couple more times to drive home its point. I walked the length of my beach, made one final bellow loud enough to bring down the walls of Jericho and, even though the raven was out of range, I picked up a large stone and slung it to make my point.

I smiled at the departing osprey, and marveled at the seemingly coordinated attack that we had made. When alone, it's easier to sense the miracle that everywhere surrounds us, and to better appreciate how our fellow creatures can surprise and delight with the most exalted companionship. What a world of spirit works through this familiar living world. What channels are waiting for us to explore. If we had but eyes to see and ears to hear, we would know that we are never really alone.

I pushed the kayak back into the bay. This time it took about ten paddle strokes before the obviously very unrattled raven landed in my camp and went leisurely about its beaking business. I felt conflicted—half-filled with begrudging admiration for its arrogant persistence and half-gleefully indulging my imagination with murderous fantasies. Love your enemies, I reminded myself. Turn the other beak.

I headed for a fish boil three hundred yards out, and trolled close to the location for forty minutes with no more result than warming myself up a bit. I wondered if I was somehow sabotaging my own fishing efforts because I really didn't really want to catch anything.

Certainly I didn't want to catch pneumonia—my wet bare feet began to feel corpse cold, so I hurried back in to chase off the raven, which mercifully had contented itself inflicting mischief rather than mayhem. Then with the sun trying to poke through the clouds and the day brightening, I got into my tent to warm up.

Later, I was under my palapa, appreciating a little shade, quietly reading, when a small bird came hopping along and stopped two feet from my two feet, looking at me like he had something to say. Then it flew up onto one of the sticks of the palapa and stayed there while I sat underneath and flipped though my bird book. This was my kind of in-your-face birdwatching. I identified it as an orange-crowned warbler. And it was a very bold little fellow; maybe he thought I was another orange-crowned warbler.

The male belted kingfisher flew back into the bay. It seemed if he stopped flying he would drop like a stone. He returned to the same rock 20-25 yards away, where I'd seen him before, and perched there undisturbed by my presence, looking a little ponderously unbalanced with his big head, but he was friendly and trusting. He seemed happy alone, going about his business, inoffensive, chattering away.

I identified with and felt protective of both of these birds. They were part of my growing family. I had my family and my mansion. God, how little we really need to be happy.

My other home and family came to mind. Rich, warm memories. I thought of the time Bonni lovingly watched me gazing out the window, beer in hand, deep in thought, and then whispered apologetically to a concerned friend, "Graham is a product of the welfare state. Free health care, free education through college, totally ruined him; now he's only fit for sitting on his ass on some island somewhere talking to himself."

Chapter 37

The Undead

*She is older than the rocks among which she sits; like the vampire, she has
been dead many times, and learned the secrets of the grave…*

Walter Pater

For several days the weather was perfect—warm, with just a little wind to
keep any flying bugs away. And there at Este Ton, every day brought a
week's worth of fun and fascination. Hiking, kayaking, fishing, even staying
in camp, I reveled in the delicious sense of not knowing what was going to
happen next… or even what thoughts were going to invade my soul and
shake up my complacency.

A question occurred to me. If we discovered that the devil created beer and
all the rest of the material world, would we be obliged to worship and revere
her as the creator?

Disturbed, I hiked around the bay, beyond the cross, to the headland that

Dead or Alive?

ends in the bay's outer reef,
where the pelicans liked to
congregate. The rocks there
were largely granitic with
fascinating colorful sills and
dykes infused with what
looked like rose quartz and
amethyst.

There at the base of a
massively veined rock wall,
curled up in a shallow
crevice, I spotted what
appeared to be a benign
and cuddly sleeping black
cat. Mindful of the young
fisherman's warning, I
approached it cautiously,
calling louder and louder. I
threw a small stone which
hit its rump. No reaction.

Finally, I picked up a heavy, rounded piece of driftwood suitable for knocking out all of its benign lives if necessary and slowly turned the beast over.

It was a shock to see its wide-open greenish eyes staring back hypnotically, and the long sharp fangs poking from its mouth. The cat looked like a vampire reposed in its coffin, one of the undead—slowly, siren-like, beckoning me closer, a strange mix of cute and creepy, like one or two of the weirder women I've known. Finally, I understood the true meaning of the Mackintosh coat-of-arms with its Scottish wild cat above the warning motto: *Touch Not the Cat without a Glove.*

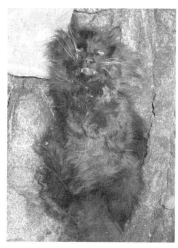

The vampire cat

I now had a different perspective on the cross. If I were a fisherman camped at the bay and I'd seen a couple of these kitties prowling around at night I'd probably be sharpening stakes and erecting crosses all over the place.

"In all the time I've been here," I reminded myself, "I don't think I've seen one mouse or rat or ground squirrel... not a single rodent, dead or alive!" I was more than ever convinced that the cat invasion was partly if not entirely responsible.

Dead cat number three

Another wreck to ponder

Closer to camp, I found the stiff and mummifying carcass of another cat—this one white with black blotches—in a crevice at the base of the low cliffs enclosing the north end of my beach. I tried to lever and force the thing into the open, but it was as firmly wedged as a cornered chuckwalla; and the more I pulled at it, the more the heavy sickly smell of death was released. Even though it was just forty yards from my tent, I decided to leave it where

Humboldt squid

it was for now before I ended up with half a fetid feline in my hands.

Walking the stony, rocky beaches outside the bay, it was impossible to walk fifty feet without finding s o m e t h i n g fascinating, be it a fishing gaff, a piece of wreckage, or a pair of five-foot-long Humboldt squid washed up together.

When Steinbeck and Ricketts entered the Sea of Cortez on the *Western Flyer* in 1940 they traveled extensively from Cabo San Lucas to the north end of Guardian Angel, from the peninsula to the mainland. Day and night they collected close to shore and observed and sampled the creatures of the open waters, comprehensively documenting their findings. In 2004, a group of biologists was able to retrace their journey "sailing with the spirits of John Steinbeck and Ed Ricketts" in a similar vessel to highlight the changes that had occurred in the Sea of Cortez over the intervening 64 years. As one of the scientists reported,

Suckers and "teeth"

"We went everywhere they did. We saw squid every night, but Steinbeck never reported squid."

William Gilly, a biology professor at Stanford University's *Hopkins Marine Station* in Pacific Grove, California, is arguably the preeminent authority on Humboldt squid (*Dosidicus gigas*).

And much of what little we know of their mysterious lives comes from the tagging work of Gilly's laboratory, which has attached special tags recording both temperature and depth to Humboldt squid captured and released in Monterey Bay, California and the Sea of Cortez. Eventually, the tags pop off and float to the surface where they send a portion of their data to a satellite. If the tags are recovered from the sea, even more data can be accessed.

The Humboldt squid lives just one or two years, but even the most conservative estimates accept they can grow to six-feet-long and can weigh over 100 pounds. To fuel this phenomenal rate of growth, squid are fearsome predators, equipped to dine on just about anything big enough to get their attention or vulnerable enough to take a bite out of. They can outmaneuver virtually any fish and are capable of incredible bursts of speed over short distances by ejecting water from their body through a jet-like siphon.

They have two "feeding" tentacles covered in powerful toothed suckers that shoot out at arrow-like speed to seize their outmatched prey. When those tentacles retract, they pull their victims into the writhing grip of eight other tentacles similarly covered with suckers, all lined with sharp, shark-like teeth, perfectly designed for gripping and rasping flesh. Finally these powerful arms then draw the prey to the squid's razor-edged beak just waiting to bite out fist-sized chunks of flesh.

Although they swim and hunt in groups of hundreds or more, there isn't any great bond of affection between them. Any squid caught on a line or otherwise impaired is likely to be quickly swarmed and devoured. One study looked at the stomach contents of 533 Humboldt squid caught off Mexico and found a quarter of them had been dining on other squid. The larger squid, especially the females, were much more likely to be cannibalistic.

During the day, Humboldt squid are thought to descend to the oxygen deficient waters around 1,000 feet to 2,500 feet, perhaps to enter an optimal zone between oxygen starvation and staying out of reach of large predator fish, seals and whales that can only dive there for short bursts. Professor Gilly also points out that this "oxygen minimum layer" is replete with biolumi-nescent lanternfish, which the squid with their huge eyes are particularly adept at feeding upon. At night, they move much closer to the surface to feed.

Common in the Humboldt Current off the coast of South America, Humboldt squid have been dramatically extending their range in recent years. Gilly has been studying them for a quarter century, and knows of no reliable reports of Humboldt squid in the Sea of Cortez prior to the 1950s. Indeed, it was only in the 1970s that they began to appear with any kind of regularity. Today, they seem to have established themselves throughout the Sea of Cortez, all along the coast of California, and into the Pacific Northwest. A few specimens have been taken in Alaskan waters.

Global warming and elevated sea temperatures may be partly responsible, but Gilly and other researchers think it likely the Humboldt squid may be moving into niches left vacant by overfishing, and thriving there because of the pressure on populations of species that would normally feed on them.

Certainly in the Sea of Cortez, populations of sharks, marlin, tuna, swordfish, wahoo, snappers, groupers, and other large predator fish have been drastically reduced by commercial and sport fishing.

Since the late 1990s squid have become an important fishery in Baja California, with over 100,000 tons landed in a good year. Much of it caught on hand lines and processed near Santa Rosalía, then exported to China, Korea, and other Asian markets.

Finding Humboldt squid washed up, often alive and flashing their remarkable maroon and ivory color changes is an increasingly common sight along the shores of the Cortez. Baja author Gene Kira recalls:

> The first Humboldt squid I ever saw had washed ashore near Bahía de los Angeles' Punta la Gringa camping area, and it was still alive. As I struggled to pull it up on the gravel, I noticed that I was leaving yellow hand prints on its reddish-brown skin. As it flopped about in its death throes, I discovered that I could write my name on its body with the tip of my finger, and the letters would remain there, flashing different colors, for several minutes.

Because of the presence of the squid as a food resource, more sperm whales are being seen in the Sea of Cortez than ever before.

Researching Humboldt squid one encounters two names over and over. One is Professor Gilly. The other is Scott Cassell. He offers a different expertise and a somewhat different perspective on these amazing animals. Following a Special Forces military career, Scott Cassell has been a commercial diver and underwater film maker for over 20 years. He has made hundreds of dives filming Humboldt squid and other dangerous marine creatures. His film credits include stock footage for numerous television programs and specials with such enticing names as "Shark Week" and "Dangerous Waters."

Cassell first heard about the squid in 1995, while filming gray whales for a German television station in Laguna San Ignacio. Intrigued, he headed over to the Sea of Cortez to dive under the pangas of the squid fishermen in the southern Sea of Cortez. After a brutal and punishing first encounter he has been diving with and filming the "red devils" ever since.

On one dive, at about 200 feet, Cassell was attacked by a perhaps 200-300-pound monster squid which he caught on film for a documentary titled Red Intelligence. In his underwater work with Humboldts he says he has been either "tested or full out attacked about 80 percent of the time."

He has developed equipment and techniques to deal with such attacks. "These precautions included: anti-squid armor suits; armor plating for the vulnerable parts of my mixed-gas rebreather; anti-squid cage; and back-to-back diving techniques." And to "prevent being pulled down by a pack of squid" he advocates the use of steel cables to connect divers to their boats at all times.

Cassell can probably claim more close-up encounters with these squid than anyone else. He said, "Humboldt squid have approximately 1,200 sucker discs, each one lined with 20 to 26 needle-sharp teeth. This allows the Humboldt to attack its prey with more than 24,000 teeth at once. And nestled in its bed of eight muscular arms and two feeding tentacles is a disproportionately large, knife-edged beak similar to a parrot's. But the Humboldt is much larger than a parrot..."

Cassell tells of some of his experiences.

> When I arrived in Mexico for the dive, several fishermen told tales of how people had experienced violent deaths after falling in the water with these red demons... they would be pulled down and devoured in moments... I decided to perform the first dive alone, tethered to the support boat... I could hear the crew yelling to me: "They are right underneath you, look out!" A surge of excitement and dread filled me as I looked down past my fins. There were more than 20 giant squid right below me. Ranging in length from five to six feet, they hovered nearby just looking at me, studying me... they flashed from white to pink to bright red then back to white, all within a split second. It was beautiful! They looked like animals from another planet, totally unearthly. As I floated there transfixed, a large squid moved to within two feet and flashed again. Mesmerized by the strobe effect, I didn't see that another squid was rushing in from my left. Bam! It hit me with a tentacular strike that felt like being hit with a baseball bat square in the ribs. Shocked by the power of the strike and unable to breathe because of a cramp in my chest, I turned to see what had hit me and saw four more squid headed toward me. The first came in so fast that I could barely track it with the camera, and then Bam! It struck the camera, which in turn struck me in the face. I was starting to feel like I was in a barroom brawl.

> The monstrous squid remains motionless just ten feet away... I trained my camcorder on him and begin to record.... Then, with blinding acceleration, he lurches onto me with a powerful "thud crackle." He slams into my chest. The impact was incredibly powerful, knocking the wind out of me. His huge arms envelope my complete upper body and camera and I can feel my chest plate move as his beak grinds against it. The crackle and scratching of thousands of chitenous ring teeth against my fiberglass/kevlar chest plate is unmistakable.

> [We] are 75 feet deep in the Sea of Cortez waiting for demons to appear. As we search the black water below our camera lights, a green glow begins to move toward us. Bioluminescence is signaling the approach of a shoal of Giant Humboldt squid rising to investigate us... I was there filming "Humboldt: The Man-Eating Squid."

Scott is co-founder of Sea Wolves Unlimited, which offers squid-diving expeditions for those with a penchant for being suckered, shredded, and gnawed upon. But when seeking a "pure" encounter he prefers to dive alone.

Professor Gilly is skeptical of the man-eating label, and in spite of the opinions of Cassell even resists calling Humboldt squid dangerous predators. "They are equipped to do damage, but so is a dog," he said dismissively.

"A lot of people want to make these things out to be mean and vicious and dangerous," Gilly says. "To the best of my knowledge there's no documentation that they've attacked anyone. Yes, there are divers who have let them grab on to them and drag them around. And yes, if there was a bad-ass squid who wanted to do damage, it could. When I snorkeled with them, one did come right up to me like it was going to eat [me], but then it just touched me on the hand with its tentacle."

He adds "Of course there are other guys I've worked with who want to play up the sensationalism aspects and wear chain mail in the water."

Cassell retorts: "Gilly is trying to make them out to be cute little ET's... They are, in my opinion, the most opportunistic animals in the world, feeding on any type of fish they come in contact with and occasionally mammals... I've interviewed many people who have been attacked by these squids. There are also stories of disappearances, always unexplained, around the Humboldt squid. Always fishermen... I've actually seen a Humboldt squid attack a thresher shark twice its size, bite through the very tough skin of the shark and pull out a fist-size chunk of flesh."

Cassell adds, "I've had my eardrum ruptured by getting dragged down from 45 feet to 75 feet; I've had my right arm dislocated by a squid grabbing my camera and yanking it; I've had 25 stitches from a particularly bad bite on my leg; and I've been smashed on the face more times than I can remember because they always seem to go for the camera when I'm looking through it."

"I respect Gilly's work in the lab," he adds, "but he's like a guy who has been on safari once and saw only lion cubs instead of big lions... I'd love to take him diving and hover about ten feet away while he gets binged by some big ones. E.T., eh? Cute, eh?" Cassell says it's one thing to be "in with the babies... You really need to see the big guys."

One man who would probably not question Cassell's characterization is Alex Kerstitch. On a night dive in the Sea of Cortez in 1990, Kerstitch, a National Geographic photographer and biologist at the University of Arizona, was with three other members of a film team attempting to document the squids' behavior. Squid heads were dangling in the water off the side of their boat and someone on board was hooked up to and attempting to bring to the surface a 14-foot shark. Alex Kerstitch was the sole still photographer; the others were shooting video footage and using more powerful lights which seemed to deter the approach of the squid. The divers were aware of the exhausted shark being lifted towards the boat as they kept an eye on the dozens of Humboldts rapidly flashing red and white beneath them. Suddenly one of the larger squid raced at the shark and snapped out an "orange-sized chunk from its head."

Kerstitch was 30 feet below the surface when he suddenly had the sensation of his feet being locked together and pulled violently down. While he looked at the tentacles wrapped around his legs and the pulsing bursts of the large squid attempting to drag him into the black depths another large squid latched on to his head and neck, and began rasping and snapping at the only part of his body not covered with neoprene. He was down about seventy feet before he was able to fight his way free and kick for the surface trailing blood from neck wounds.

"They took his camera, his necklace, his dive computer and gave him some nice bites around the back of his neck," Cassell said. "He knew he was a lucky man who had escaped death. Every time he told that story you could see the fear."

Others who have extensive knowledge of Humboldt squid tend to take a more middle of the road view about the dangers of being in the water with them. Louis Zeidberg, a postdoctoral researcher studying Humboldt squid in the laboratory of William Gilly said, "I think I'm somewhere between what the armor guy feels and what Gilly feels… I think the primary difference is, when people go down and hang heads of squid off the side of the boat, then jig other squids and start a feeding frenzy, you're going to have problems. These are cannibalistic animals. Like sharks, they go bonkers with blood and chum in the water."

"We know so little about them," explains Professor Gilly, "because [they quickly die in captivity] and spend 95 percent of their lives at depths well beyond those safely observed with scuba… We don't know where they spawn, and their eggs have never been found in the wild."

But like most predators they can be tempted to where the food is and there have been several recorded sightings of schools of squid feeding on the surface, day and night. Those who fish for them are very familiar with the sight of squid following what's left of their hooked colleagues right up to the boats.

In spite of turning up north and south of their more normal relatively warm water range off Peru and Ecuador, all indications are that Humboldt squid have so far confined themselves to the west coast of the Americas. From Chile to Alaska, they have now spread into waters with temperatures ranging from 40 to 90° F.

No one knows why they have not yet moved further into the Pacific or around the tip of South America into the Atlantic. Perhaps the life cycle of the Humboldt squid is somehow associated with the great depths found where plates collide, subduct and spread. It seems like a fascinating subject for research.

Indeed, there is a spreading concern among US scientists and fishermen that the Humboldt squid firmly entrenching themselves along the west coast of North America are certain to dramatically impact a number of fisheries. A near twenty year study conducted by the *Monterey Bay Aquarium Research Institute* (MBARI) recently lent credence to the claim.

And the same dramatic range extension is causing disquiet in the Southern Hemisphere. In October 2007, Chile's *Santiago Times* reported the concerns of Federico Silva, president of Sonapesca (Chile's National Fishing Society), that increasing squid numbers will have grave consequences for Chile's fishermen. He refers to them as a "plague," adding that, "The fishing industry in Chile has suffered a grade eight earthquake." According to statistics from Chile's *Institute for Fishing Promotion*, the estimated biomass of the commercially important hake species around her coasts was 1.5 million tons in 2002, but by 2004 the figure had been reduced to 272,000 tons.

However we characterize them and whatever their environmental impact, it seems that Humboldt squid are in the Sea of Cortez to stay, at least for the foreseeable future.

As I studied the pair on the beach before me and gazed at their tooth-filled suckers and formidable beaks, I had to feel that there might be a lot more unexplained disappearances of swimmers and kayakers in the future. [For further advice on this, see Chapter 42, "The Nuts and Humboldts of Safe Baja Kayaking"] What should our response be? Certainly, it can't hurt if we all develop a taste for calamari.

Now, if I were a just and loving God and I wanted to punish unpeaceable publicans and sinners and heartless zealots who would happily visit hell on anyone who happens to disagree with them, then I would definitely populate the old eternal lake of fire with ravens slowly ripping out livers, crazed feral cats siphoning out fang loads of boiling blood, and untold numbers of marine isopods hooking their victims with their fearsome little "like feet" and forever nibbling away at every tiny scrap of seared flesh... but the true kings and demons would be the voracious red devil Humboldt squid. A few of those guys fighting over your testicles and you'd definitely wish you'd behaved yourself.

But just to make sure, and being a deity diligent for justice and equality, I'd fix it that all new arrivals, men and women, would find themselves generously endowed with clumps of testicles and simultaneously be permanently afflicted with PMS and particularly painful menstrual cramps.

When I snapped out of my reverie, I realized that the ravens were searching for breakfast in the hills above the shore. Two of them buzzed one of the osprey nests, croaking and rattling away. The osprey pair replied with their panicky shrill calls. One partner stayed on the nest; the other tried to chase them away.

This time the ravens backed down and retreated, but it must be just constant vigilance defending their chicks and eggs from the powerful marauding beaks. The paired ospreys with their talons and sharp beaks can usually put up an effective defense, but some of the other nesting birds must suffer serious losses.

I still hadn't seen a single vulture on the island. It was possible that the ravens had driven them off by simultaneously raiding their nests and taking over their niche, but ravens and vultures have been coexisting for ages on the peninsula, so it seemed much more likely that it was again the presence of the feral cats that had upset the equilibrium. Among turkey vultures one of the main tactics for nest defense has been vomiting on intruders, an approach that maybe doesn't work too well with cats. Whereas one can imagine ospreys, ravens, and even gulls mounting a very effective "mobbing" defense against any climbing cats.

A bird flicking its tail up and down on a large boulder ten yards offshore caught my attention. It made a distinctive "weet, weet" call, and its bill was fleshy pink with a darker tip.

My *Golden Guide* suggested it was a spotted sandpiper in its winter coat. "It bobs the tail up and down almost continuously …no breast spots in winter… call is a shrill two or three note piping."

Female spotted sandpipers have really got it made when it comes to mating. After courting a male, she will lay a clutch of eggs, leaving them for him to incubate and raise, then fly off to court another male. As many as five males have been observed caring for the offspring of a single female.

On the way back to my camp, I climbed off the beach up one of the gullies between the dark conical hills north of Este Ton and there identified three more birds: a verdin, a Costa's hummingbird, and a black-throated sparrow.

Passing through to a relatively flat open area, I took four or five really deep breaths and was spinning around looking up at the sky and mountains, praising the creator, saying "Oh thank you, the air is so clean." As I uttered the word "clean" I put my foot down awkwardly and twisted my ankle. Unfortunately, my boot wasn't laced tightly enough. The ankle was painful and weakened. I was hoping it wasn't seriously damaged. Anything restricting my walking ability was a big concern.

It had come to me late in life—I was born to be outdoors, in motion. Not flying along on some noisy machine, but walking, paddling, plodding steadily, unhurried, relating to all around, getting there eventually. Experiencing a different kind of exhilaration.

The flying was going on between my ears—mind racing, strange thoughts, outrageous heresies, daring myself to trust and go further. All the while thinking, thinking, thinking. The equivalent of walking an island beach. Among the trash, endless fascinating finds. Throw the junk back. Keep in motion, keep exploring, keep seeking. Earn the right to sit and relax and enjoy that beer.

Chapter 38

Feast or Famine

*A man can be himself only so long as he is alone, and if he does not love solitude,
he will not love freedom, for it is only when he is alone that he is really free.*
Arthur Schopenhauer

Back in camp, certain my ankle was fine, I was relaxing, getting my mind in
gear, sitting in the shade, stringing out my last beer. The air was warm. It was
a sunny evening, at least on the island, but there were clouds over the
peninsula.

I was just watching a pelican, a bunch of pelicans diving right in
front of my campsite. I could see activity in the water, beyond the
birds, I was rushing down with my fishing pole when this big sea
lion, a bull sea lion, stuck its head up with a fish in its mouth… and
everything is coming to my little beach including some cormorants.
There are at least two sea lions out there, so I lost interest in casting
from the beach with them around. I don't think a sea lion will be
tempted by a flashing lure, but I don't want to find out the hard way.

Next day, I hiked to the north, inland, where there seemed to be a faint
animal trail trending south around the back of the coastal mountains. I
wondered if I followed it far enough, could I outflank the cliffs and descend
to the coast?

The trail led me up and along a series of ridges, and across an area of basalt
-type rocks studded with quartz crystals. Eventually I was able to peek over
a high ridge to a valley dropping steeply, apparently straight down to the
coast. I didn't attempt the descent, but it at least offered the possibility of an
inland return to my camp from the south.

Expecting Bob Vinton and his friend to arrive soon and stay about a week,
I was hoping that they would bring plenty of water. But I couldn't take that
for granted.

I jumped on my kayak and paddled north and south on mirror-like seas,
gliding over ever increasing numbers of rays, sand sharks and tentacle
waving jellyfish, stopping at the longest beaches, gathering the ample
driftwood. There wasn't a sandy beach anywhere. The best landing I could
hope for was on smooth pebbles.

A mile south of Este Ton, I peered up the canyon that seemed to offer that inland hiking route back, and confirmed from sea level that although it might be a long slog, it didn't look impossible.

The kayak was typically stacked high. It didn't matter. I was always ready to jettison it all into a sudden unmanageable sea. The supply of driftwood was inexhaustible, and I had all the time in the world. On my beach, I soon had way more wood than I would need in a month, and rather suspected I was gathering just for the sheer purpose and joy of it. And there was no one there telling me I was being foolish.

February 22—the day my friends should be arriving. It was 54°F at 5:30 A.M. In that photographer's golden hour with the sun rising over the horizon, the glowing peninsula was lit as if from within while most of Este Ton was in shadow. The sky was about 30% cloudy. There was a strong gusting north to northeast wind. As I started to secure everything, the possibility gradually sank in that no one would be coming, certainly not today.

From my final gallon of good water, I used a quart to make oatmeal and a mug of coffee. Then I hiked north taking a quart with me, which meant I'd have just half-a-gallon of ready drinking water when I returned, plus the rain water as back up.

A mile or so offshore, a Cessna was flying low, heading north. I rushed to turn the radio on in case there was a message for me. Not a peep. The plane disappeared and never returned.

I kept looking out to sea hoping to see a panga beating out from L.A. Bay. There were practically no waves close to shore, but out from the shelter of the cliffs, white caps stretched across the channel. It would be a rough, possibly a dangerous crossing.

Then came the realization, I had taken it to the limit; there was no room now for dangerous assumptions or naïve hopes. Bob could have changed his mind as easily as the wind could be blasting for days. It was time to be heading back, dealing with the water crisis, unequivocally switching into full survival mode, mentally preparing myself for whatever lay ahead. And, oddly enough, I was feeling really excited by the challenge.

Back in camp, I filtered the best half-gallon of rain water. It tasted OK, a little brackish, with undertones of plastic, and it made me cough a little. Some went into dinner, along with the juice from a can of sliced carrots. Now I had just one can left to look forward to—a can of Spam. Carrots, instant mashed potato, with some reconstituted jerky made a surprisingly good dinner. The next day I'd be making water in earnest.

There was much to think about that evening, especially after seeing my first live scorpion on the island. I spotted it by firelight, peering out from under a large boulder by my kitchen rock pile. It was yellow, almost 3 inches long, and was not the normal *alacrán*—the ubiquitous wiry Baja scorpion. I certainly didn't feel comfortable with it so close to my feet, my chair and all my cooking utensils. Unfortunately, as I approached with a twig to try to hook it out, it quickly scrambled out of sight.

I sat patiently by the rock, but the scorpion refused to emerge again. Knowing he was there, and suspecting that his buddies were waking up, I wore gloves for the first time to pick up firewood.

Even though it was a mild 58°F at 9 P.M., I was keen to get inside my sleeping bag, where I deleted 220 pictures from my camera memory cards, which allowed me to relive the whole island experience so far, as if my life were flashing before me.

February 23—I woke early at 5 A.M., before dawn. It was 50°F and flat calm. I stared at the constellation Scorpio, high in the southern sky, which brought the scorpion back to mind.

It remained calm, a perfect crossing morning. I was convinced that if Bob didn't come that day, he would not be coming at all. While I washed myself knee deep in the bay, keeping an eye open for both jellyfish and stingrays, I noticed a red rash on my inner thighs, probably the result of using the same old salt-encrusted shorts for kayaking. I rubbed on Vaseline and changed my clothes.

> I have a few aches and pains…If I bend over washing dishes in the sea, or stay in one position too long, then I can hardly stand up. I have to move and I can walk it off real easy. As long as I'm active I'm fine… but in one position too long, my back tends to freeze. There's no pain to it normally, but it's indicative of old age creeping up on the old boy.

Leave well alone can be sound advice, especially under survival conditions. I rather foolishly tried to clean the oily black soot from the outside of the kettle by scraping it in the wet gravel on the beach. The kettle came up well scrubbed and partially shiny, but unfortunately the next time I rigged it up as a still, a pin-prick jet of scalding water as long as an agave stalk shot out from the side. I removed the cork, allowed the kettle to simmer for a while and then left it to cool, and somehow it plugged itself—maybe through a mixture of smoke and salt deposition on the outside and salt and calcium deposition within. The kettle was back to being as black as ever, but at least it was working fine.

The rest of the day was spent trying to make drinking water from salt water. The first batch was brackish—a little salt water must have boiled over from the kettle. I used it for cooking and reconstituting jerky. After that, I made about 1¼ gallons of good water, almost half of which I immediately used for cooking and hot drinks. I looked at my last two pieces of fresh food—a shriveled hunk of jicama and a single small brown lemon. After that, I'd have just the Spam and some dry food left.

By way of experiment, I ate a little red seaweed, which was not unpleasant, then I nibbled on an ear-like green variety, also fine. That was followed by a few ocotillo flowers. I also knew from my many peninsula hikes that I could resort to eating pieces of different cacti—especially prickly pear, barrel cactus, and cholla.

For dessert I sampled some scarlet mammalaria cactus fruits, which were actually rather good and refreshing, and probably loaded with vitamin C and other nutrients. But the fruits, being just peanut sized, weren't going to contribute much to acquiring my daily minimum of a gallon of drinking water, especially if the warm weather continued.

Flowers of the ocotillo

Mammalaria fruits

Padina concrescens (brown algae)

A captured scorpion

That night, after a protracted firelight wait beneath an explosion of stars, I caught the scorpion. When it showed itself in the same spot, I snuck up from the side and vigorously scraped the sand from under it with a stick. In spite of it trying desperately to run back beneath the rock, it kind of tumbled out.

I shepherded the scorpion into an empty aluminum saucepan, where it was swinging its tail wildly and scrambling to crawl out. I didn't want to kill it, but I didn't want to lose it either. So, I dropped it into another saucepan filled with seawater. It sank and ran around under water. I reached in with a pair of pliers, grabbed it gently by the long tail, fished it out, and then put it in a plastic container and closed the lid.

Friday, February 24—Day 49. Temperature at dawn 49°F. Clear. Calm.

I listened to the news before emerging. It seemed the world, at least George Bush's world, was falling apart... his proffered vision seemed to be for perpetual war or for some far off promised implausible victory over... over who?... How precious few were the years of relatively painless glory from Gulf War One. And how little did we receive of that "peace dividend" when the Berlin Wall fell!

Following a photo session with the scorpion, I kayaked off to bring back more wood. Ignoring the high stack already on my beach, I told myself that acquiring yet more was vitally important to my survival. It was definitely an addiction—a conscience-salving, self-deceiving excuse to be out there on a glassy sea, full of life, rather than doing my duty by the bubbling still.

Then after returning to camp and unloading, I threw a couple of snacky items on the kayak and went out fishing. It was too beautiful and peaceful not to be on the water watching the wing tips of the passing pelicans almost imperceptibly touching the sea. And I was still at peace with the fish. The few I caught were gently unhooked and slid back into the depths. Of course, that would change when I was fishing in earnest.

Back in camp, I found I'd been "ravened"—the lid had been thrown from my trash barrel and all the contents had been scattered in the mouth of the gully. Nevertheless, I continued warming to my constant companions. How many of us, I thought, need the lids lifted from our heads and all the trash thrown out.

Restless on the beach, and with hardly a cracker and a slice of jerky in my stomach, I headed out yet again. A higher duty called. Hungry, but not for food. Paddling slowly, I drifted to the rhythm of the blades gently slapping water. Fascinated by the sight and sound of the churning eddies. Deeply invested in the moment, I was as absorbed as if I were creating new worlds and galaxies. Taking it in, taking my time, simply experiencing, talking to myself, glorying in the absence of hurry, feeling really, really good:

> So glad that I, Graham Mackintosh, am here, alive, two hundred yards offshore from Guardian Angel Island, experiencing this moment of February 24, 2006. This precious and unrepeatable moment—this day, this year, this lifetime.

No longer sitting between sea and sky, suspended on a piece of floating blue plastic, I was floating high above, looking down at a tiny speck, at someone else, from the perspective of another time, another place... parameters and constraints dissolved, insignificant.

I had no regrets about the past, no anxiety for the future, no fear of man nor beast. I was truly free. Not the kind of freedom that grasping politicos glibly spout, or the kind of license that borders on egocentric insanity, but freed from all the dogma, hypocrisy, rudeness, anger, greed, and deception of this world. For a few precious moments I felt free of it all. Refreshed by tears, cradled by a beautiful presence, I felt able to cope with anything, even death itself.

And suddenly, I'm down to earth. There's a motor. A very, very real, worldly, grumbling, intrusive motor. A boat heading my way.

Chapter 39

Double Surprise

To weight loss, to triumph over adversity, to
personal enlightenment… and to beer!
Martin Lipp, M.D. *The I-Like-My-Beer Diet*

The boat was coming down from the north. It was definitely not a panga. As it moved past the low causeway leading to the high point across the bay, I could see there was a cabin with fishing rods lined up alongside. It was a sport fishing boat.

I was delighted to see Roger from Villa Bahía, along with his skipper Alfredo, and Alfredo's teenage grandson. When I saw there was no one else aboard I guessed that Bob and his friend were not coming and Roger had motored over to take me off the island. However, he said that Bonni had been concerned and had asked him to check on me and bring me out some water and other necessities. They had gone first to Humbug Bay, and finding my old campsite abandoned had motored down to Este Ton.

Roger added that my friends Chuck and Evelyn, adventurous retirees from the Upper Peninsula of Michigan and Ontario would be out in a week or so to camp with me. Then he'd pick us all up after a few more days. He had a letter from Bonni explaining all. Alfredo had been out to the island many times in his long fishing career, but it was Roger's first visit and he was blown away by its beauty, especially there at Este Ton with the red mountains reflected by a perfectly flat blue sea. I directed them to my beach and kayaked in behind them.

The tide was sufficiently high to allow Alfredo to nudge the bow of the boat half way up the beach to facilitate the unloading of a dozen gallons of

Roger and Alfredo with the
Villa Bahía launch

water, 30 cans of beer, an abundance of fresh fruit and vegetables, a cooler full of iced sodas, a gallon jug of wine—I got a hangover just looking at it—bags of pastries and cookies, two pillow-sized bags of Costco tortilla chips, and a similar jumbo-size bag of salted peanuts in their shells. I was stunned by this sudden abundance and hoped it wouldn't reverse my steady wholesome weight loss or destroy the spirituality of my final days.

In spite of my misgivings, I enjoyed an ice-cold beer and a banana on the beach. Then they hopped back on the boat and went outside the bay to fish while I put everything away under tarps and netting to keep it out of the direct sun. I had to laugh as I looked at all the booze Roger had brought. My liver would be flapping like a stranded fish if I finished even half of it.

To any landlubber, three heavy four-gallon containers of water must seem like extravagant overkill. Spending so long making the precious liquid gave me a very different perspective. I was amazed that Roger hadn't brought just a little more. And I thought back to all the beer and goodies Mike and Lennart had brought over in Igor's spacious boat; and they had just six or seven gallons of water. In both cases I was tingling with gratitude; but it did show how different a man marooned might view the world. I would gladly have turned that gallon of wine into water.

With everything secured I picked up my fishing rod, jumped back on the kayak and paddled out to the boat which was drifting less than 100 yards from the bay's entrance. All three aboard were pulling up two or three bass and lingcod at a time.

When I expressed my admiration for their prowess, Alfredo motioned for me to give him my rod. He removed the lure and attached a lead weight with three hooks loaded with cut fish bait. In seconds I was hauling aboard a three

pound lingcod. My fishing session was over. Dinner would be fresh fish and vegetables.

I was surprised to see a panga heading up from the south, close to shore, very likely intending to run into Este Ton. I paddled over to intercept them. It was five of my fishermen friends from Bahía Kino. They asked nervously about the people in

Pulling up two and three fish at a time

the other boat. They seem satisfied with my account, and said they would be basing themselves in Este Ton for a few days. Some amigos on a second panga had broken down and were waiting on another island to be picked up and towed back to Kino. I paddled back out to Roger to explain the situation, said goodbye, and said I'd better head in.

My friends had all settled on my beach, close to the palapa. They helped carry up my kayak, and the fierce looking one presented me with three cupcake-size hunks of shellfish meat—the large adductor muscles that a mollusk uses to pull tight its shell or pull it down onto a rock. They asked me if I had a small grill they could use to cover their fire and a spare empty water container. No problem. I also gave them a bag of tortilla chips, a packet of mini donuts, and five ice cold beers. I cleaned my fish and cooked it with rice, tomatoes, onions and spices… and added the shellfish.

While I enjoyed my wholesome meal, my neighbors were all drifting away to find a shady place to smoke and siesta. I invited them to use my palapa, crates, and chair, and left them while I went out kayaking again.

It remained hot and flat calm. I wanted to try more of this productive fishing with cut bait. Out, deeper than usual, the bites came fast. In minutes I was pulling up a lingcod. I removed the hook and gently dropped it back into dark, deep water, but it was in trouble, floating upside down, getting weaker and weaker. So I pulled it back on the kayak to keep it for bait. I caught and released a three pound bass. After a moment's hesitation he power dived to the bottom.

When I returned to the beach at 4:30 P.M., the five fishermen were sleeping all over. One in the shade of the palapa, another two in a makeshift tent on the beach, and two more in the shade under the cliffs. I pulled the kayak up the sand and prepared for the night. I re-heated my fish and shellfish lunch, then doled out some pastries to the emerging fishermen, and invited them to use any of the firewood I'd collected.

They headed out about 7:30 P.M. leaving me to enjoy the evening's tranquility, comforted by their presence and protection. Beer in hand I listened to the sound of crickets, and the usual noises echoing around the bay. It was a glorious clear night, black, with stars perfectly reflecting in the water.

My only concern was the tide. Another new moon was due in just a day or two. As the sea crept up, I moved some of the fishermen's blankets and clothes, which had been casually strewn all around and were likely to be washed away. I was amazed they weren't more attentive to such things. Mota, no doubt! The water almost reached the first poles of the palapa. Convinced the tide was falling around midnight, I was finally able to think about sleep.

They returned shortly before dawn, and quickly wrapped up their activities and retired. Wide awake again, I listened to my radio till it was light enough to emerge from the tent. Then with them all asleep I gathered a few breakfast items, soap, and a toothbrush, and dragged the kayak down to the water. It was still breathless, and there was no indication that it wouldn't stay that way. I headed south and paddled several miles… bold because I had company.

I passed a brown, rocky islet surrounded by preening pelicans and crowned with guano. It looked like a huge dollop of chocolate ice cream with frosting and an osprey nest on top.

On the way back I landed at a beach with a high, colorfully layered canyon

Osprey nest on islet

as a backdrop. Walking inland I happened upon a concrete mining claim marker with the very appropriate name *El Arco Iris* painted upon it—The Rainbow.

After exploring several beaches and paddling some way back I pulled the kayak up onto a beach to have breakfast, wash myself in the sea, and cover my exposed skin with sunscreen.

While I was standing knee deep pushing my kayak back out, a bee was buzzing me up and down and seemed determined to land on me. I tried gently wafting it away, but it was persistent. A more vigorous sweep knocked it into the sea—not what I intended. I fished it out with my paddle and watched it fly away.

Rainbow canyon

With just the occasional passing whiff of wind to get my attention, I eased my way slowly north in no great hurry to be back in camp. When I finally paddled into Este Ton, there was considerable activity on the beach with the fishermen processing their night's catch. One of them was breaking apart lobsters, manually twisting and separating the heads from the meaty tails. There were two different species—slipper and spiny lobsters. I took photographs of both types of heads thrown onto the beach. The gulls were happy.

One of the fishermen kindly helped me carry up the firewood I'd brought back. Then with minimal ceremony I snatched a few cookies and a soda, my fishing gear and cut bait, and paddled to the north taking advantage of a beautiful warm afternoon. A cormorant emerged before me with a fish that he soon swallowed, then he dived again. Passing the arch, I saw two sea lions, both with fish in their mouths.

I moved into new territory and excitedly explored the virgin beaches, but I walked slowly as conditions seemed ripe for a snake encounter. They would be hard to spot amongst the confusion of gray and reddish stones, driftwood and colorful debris. What I did spot was an inflated plastic soccer ball that had floated ashore. I thought one of the fishermen might appreciate that for his family.

Slipper and spiny lobster

Drifting back to Este Ton, I was fascinated by the reflections of the island in the sea. The silence was broken by whales breathing, breaching and booming in mid-channel. Schools of herring or anchovies abounded. Several sea lions poked their heads up to look at me.

I caught a cabrilla, which I released, then another unfortunate lingcod, which came to the surface with its innards swollen and protruding through both ends of its alimentary canal. I moved into shallower water hoping not to catch another, and soon hooked and released three bass and a sculpin.

I floated along cherishing my time alone, a mile from camp, totally absorbed, surrounded by astounding beauty, investigating anything that caught my eye, confident all was well.

Suddenly I heard a panga, approaching from the south, close in to the cliffs. I paddled back a little more directly. The panga raced into Este Ton. Fishermen? I was curious, who were these newcomers? My old friends or others from the mainland? In my haste to find out, I paddled

Easy paddle home

through the reef at the west entrance to the bay rather than around it.

I arrived to find a fire burning under the palapa, and a mass of bodies on blankets, on my chair, puffing mota, lodged between the three pillars of my campsite: kitchen, covered stores, and tent.

One of the familiar Mexicans introduced me to some "good amigos" from Bahía Kino. In spite of my beaming smile I was already longing for my

Another beach to explore

peaceful place back again. I had to go with the flow and make the best of it. And when I walked down to the water to clean my fish, the fierce looking man who gave me the clams, and the large shell attached to the rock, followed me down, smilingly took my knife and cutting board, and expertly fileted the lingcod for me.

While I was frying the filets, four of the fishermen started kicking around the soccer ball I'd found. I tactfully declared that 2006 will be the year for Mexico to win the World Cup. That really energized them. I spread all my kayak gear—seat, lifejacket, shorts, to dry in the last warm rays—then washed down the fried fish with a beer and banana. A couple of the newcomers were studying the rattler skin I'd left out to dry. When I later put the skin back on a rock I noticed the rattle was missing!

I was glad when the strangers headed to another beach in the bay, just around the little point to my north, to set up their camp. A little while later I offered "my guys" each a donut and a beer.

By sunset everyone seemed to be asleep. In an attempt to keep my campsite reasonably clean and offer the subtlest of hints, I discreetly placed their discarded burnables in my plastic trash drum and took the rest of the trash up the valley and out of sight.

Only a gentle breeze ruffled the water. The bay had quite a gathering of gulls squabbling over the fishcamp cast offs. Even the ravens busied themselves usefully with the carcasses, perhaps temporarily sparing a few of the chicks and eggs of the other birds on the island.

Just before dark, the fishermen around my camp struggled from their slumbers and prepared to head out, a little grumpily it seemed. The issue was too subtle for me to comprehend, but judging by the mutterings and raised voices something was causing dissension. As soon as they were gone, I checked that all their clothes, blankets, and other gear was high enough; amazingly quite a deal of it still didn't seem to be safely above the probable high tide line. When they returned there wouldn't be much beach left with the extreme tide; they'd all be crammed around my tent, certainly high and hopefully dry.

I sat and read after dark. The newcomers around the corner on the other beach were apparently not going out. There were a few wild yells, then as I was walking around with a light, some loud comments seemed to be directed to me. I couldn't make it out. Thinking it wise to communicate something, anything, I shouted back, *"buena suerte."* Good Luck! I hoped it wasn't too inappropriate. Rather wishing they'd forget about me, I switched off my light and sat in the dark listening to my radio.

An hour later, beneath countless stars, a panga entered the bay and headed to the occupied beach. I assumed it was my guys, but after much shifting and banging and unloading, the panga disappeared back into the night leaving the strangers still calling and clattering. I kept silent. My imagination conjured up all kinds of scenarios, about which the least I know, and the less everyone thought about me, the better.

After preparing the kayak for a quick and quiet morning get away, I slipped into my sleeping bag about 10 P.M. Shortly after, a panga came into the bay, first to the other camp then they headed over to me. The fishermen had returned… for the night? Sure enough, I sensed them all wrapping themselves in blankets and settling cozily close around me with much rustling of tarps, coughing, farting and snoring.

I'm not sure if it was the peppermint schnapps I drank to help me sleep, but I woke around dawn with a headache. Maybe it was the strain of feeling like a stranger in my own camp? I took two ibuprofen. I didn't go kayaking, but resolved to spend a day studying and practicing Spanish.

We were all up by 7 A.M. There was a surprising air of purpose about the fishermen's activities. After breakfast, one of them came over and gave me back my grill. He mentioned that the fishing and diving wasn't productive enough so they'd be leaving soon. Concerned that my friends might leave and the strangers stay behind, I tried to ask as tactfully as I could if they will all be going. When he suggested yes, and said they wouldn't be back again this "season," I had to refrain from going into a celebratory dance.

I cut up a cantaloupe, an apple and a banana and walked around with a jolly bounce in my step offering the fruit on a plate to all takers. When my buddies began clambering into their boat, I gladly gave them the remains of a pack of honey roasted peanuts. We waved goodbye, and they were gone. In my delight I forgot to ask for any surplus water. Then ten long minutes later the other panga left the bay too. Yes, yes!!! Alone again. Time for more meditations.

Maybe not. From just beyond the bay I heard the panga motor going into idle and then shutting down. I scrambled up a slope and raised my head enough to see that the boat had pulled on to a tiny pebble beach beneath some cliffs just two hundred yards down the coast. Thirty minutes later, they come roaring back into Este Ton. I waved to them. No one noticed or deigned to respond.

While they were idling aimlessly in the middle of the bay looking like they were debating some debatable task, I called out, "Do you need anything?" One of them pointed back along the boat and said something about mota or the motor. I guessed they had a problem but they didn't seem to be doing much about it, just lounging back and waiting. The motor had sounded a little harsh and was putting out a fair amount of smoke, as were the crew. I prayed to the great Yamaha god for all the healing he could speed to them. Finally, with a little tinkering the engine growled once more into life and they headed out again.

As I followed the fading roar all the way down the island, I stoked the smoldering fire left forty yards from my camp, added a little driftwood, and gathered up all the trash I could burn.

Then I kayaked out to be sure they'd gone. Looking down I saw the clean waters of the bay littered with offal and old batteries, most of it too deep for me to easily retrieve. And instead of drifting over jellyfish, I was saddened to see a number of plastic bags on and in the water.

Discouraged by this casual indifference to the magnificence of the cove, and sensing the pollution in the water, I paddled from the bay with soap, a large towel and a small bottle of shampoo, and landed on a quiet beach just outside to bathe in the open sea.

Back in Este Ton I visited the other camp and was amazed at how much five people could trash a beach in one night. Paper, plastic, cans, polystyrene cups and plates were flung everywhere. Bathroom tissue and unburied caca littered the back of more than one bush. There had been no attempt to hide, burn, or bury anything.

I buried the caca, filled a couple of large plastic bags with all the trash and then glided back to my camp to consign most of it to the flames. I'm afraid global warming took a backseat to my desire to restore the bay to its pristine state. I wandered up Rattlesnake Gulch to deal with any obvious caca there. Then I spent an hour or so pacing my beach, picking up used foil food packets and ketchup packets, many of which I had given them.

With my friends Chuck and Ev possibly coming in a few days I didn't want any more such visitations. I was conflicted though, and I wondered how much of the cavalier indifference of these fishermen was due to the mota, and how they might be induced to treat the treasure that the Lord had granted to Mexico with a little more respect.

Chapter 40

Halcyon Days

Who sees with equal eye, as God of all,
A hero perish, or a sparrow fall…

Alexander Pope

I settled down to a peaceful late afternoon reclaiming my space, pulling out and taking stock of all my supplies, unloading my coolers and letting their contents cool in the air. Then I sat on the beach alone, determined to make the most of whatever hand I was dealt, be it company or solitude, scarcity or abundance. Above all, I wanted to coax my mind back into its more receptive "wilderness" mode.

It was close to the new moon! I estimated that the high tide would be at its most extreme that night—probably between 1 A.M. and 2 A.M.

At first I wasn't particularly bothered as I seemed to have the measure of the tide, but listening to various radio stations, I heard rain, lightning, and flood warnings from California to Arizona. A Los Angeles news radio station, KNX 1070, was reporting 3-4 inches of rain in coastal areas of the city and over 5 inches in the mountains. A San Diego station reported flooding along beach areas and told of hurricane force winds in the San Francisco Bay area.

High tide mark. Running out of beach

It all brought to mind the potential for a "perfect storm" of high tide, strong southerly or southwesterly winds, and torrential rain. After wrapping my "early warning" floats around the rock, I got inside the tent to put all my important items away for a quick grab in case a mini tsunami came washing up the beach, or a flash flood came scouring down the valley.

It was shaping up to be a sleepless night, one that might well find me seeking sanctuary in the rocks, wedged between a couple of dripping chuckwallas.

I peeked out from the tent several times to check on the tide. The water flooded under the palapa, and began lifting and floating off the cold charcoal buried beneath the sand. The tent and the high point of the beach were just a yard or two higher.

But as the night wore on, I grew increasingly optimistic. My bay was a world apart from what was happening north of the border. It was calm and peaceful. There were some clouds to the west, but otherwise stars shone all about. The temperature was still 62°F. By 2 A.M., the tide had definitely started to recede. I was jubilant.

Standing down from the tension, I gazed on a night of astounding beauty, a night for humility, a night to offer thanks to God, a night made doubly magical by the presence of the most wonderful bioluminescence. In the gently agitated glow zone where tiny waves chaffed the shore, countless speckles of light flashed briefly like fireflies or shooting stars. The inevitable unseen sea lion, betrayed by sudden eruptions and vortices of lime green, was cruising and surfacing and exhaling twenty or thirty yards from shore.

I peed in the water, and peered admiringly at the ghostly swirling core spinning out luminous waves and ripples that overtook and inundated the fleeting points of light and mixed with the reflection of the stars. I was struck by how much it looked like one of those Hubble telescope images of a distant galaxy with its hundreds of billions of suns spinning like a top around a dense cluster of ethereal light.

I pondered and speculated and connected. What worlds, what eons of evolution, what life forms, what histories I might be creating—we all might be creating as we stir and spin through our ordinary unsuspecting lives, sadly fearful of our own insignificance. And yet, just maybe, in some unbelievably miniscule span of time, some unknown race of conscious beings, some strange civilization, might have come and gone, worshipping the supreme sea lion creator that their wise men had divined… or the great red-headed lord of the rains, captain of the flood, the law giver, the one whose name was too holy to speak who had showered them with blessings.

And what laws I would give them, what commandments, what calls for justice and compassion. What parables, what psalms of universal love and wisdom. How simple and straightforward would be the message. No ethereal games; no cryptic puzzles; no toying with salvation. It would be a message even a child could comprehend—a message of light and clarity, a call to universal brotherhood and sisterhood satisfying to both heart and mind. How easy the burden. How impossible to misunderstand. No popes or bishops or bible schools required.

What a divine responsibility we might bear. Whole races may have passed hanging on our every word, yearning to know our will, and maybe getting the message hopelessly blurred—never quite grasping that the power, the glory, and the kingdom are cosmic. We're not talking real estate here... rather, very unreal estate. Peace and compassion, and their necessary companions: faith, courage, and vision. Not earthly conquest and genocide in the name of the one true God... no self-serving trumpeting of the elect, the chosen, the master race. Not my genocide is right and yours is wrong. But ALL genocide is wrong. Period. Amen.

Few words. A one page holy book. Maybe two. That would be my "trickle down" economics. To know the rest, get out there alone—along the shore, on an island, up in the mountains, beneath the stars. And rest there until your tears flow. Guided by compassion and the faith to stand alone, seek and know your God. And know the treachery of heartless theology.

I recalled an article I'd read in the *San Diego Union-Tribune*. It mentioned an example of a soldier sacrificing his life for his fellow soldiers. And the writer held it up as an example of THE greatest love man could show—a man laying down his life for his friends.

Such heroism and sacrifice rightly astounds and inspires us, and moves us to tears. But THE greatest love? The assertion went unchallenged. An even greater, rarer, more mind-shattering example exists. A man sacrificing himself not for his friends, but for those seeking to humiliate and destroy him. A man laying down his life for his enemies. Now that's enough to bring God to tears. The moral force of such an act is truly staggering and almost beyond our limited human understanding. Almost, but not quite. Such a man would be a man for the ages, a man whose heart and mind were merged with the divine. Jesus understood. "For if ye love them which loves you, what reward have ye? do not even the publicans the same? And if ye salute your brethren only, what do ye more than others? Do not even the publicans so?" Until we understand, how can we be Christians? We are not born again. We are in danger of simply being boring.

With the sky clearing fast, I allowed myself to fall into a deep sleep. I was awake again at 5 A.M. glad to see the kettle-shaped constellation Sagittarius "steaming" away, and Scorpio crawling across the velvety blackness...and two bright morning stars, which I assumed to be Venus and Jupiter, looking down like kindly eyes in the sky.

February 28—I kayaked south, but didn't go too far because of a rising wind and a vague sense of possessiveness about the bay that I had ordered and cared for. I landed at a narrow cliff-fringed beach a few hundred yards from my camp, and there in a little canyon slicing up into the cliffs, I was sad to find a recently dead orange-crowned warbler, probably the same one that had been visiting me. I took several close-up pictures and used them to make a positive identification back in camp. But identification was irrelevant. Species, genus, race, class, whatever sins it bore—it didn't matter a farthing. I felt like I'd lost a precious, cheerful friend, one of my family. That bird did not pass unsaluted or unmourned.

"...without your father's love not one of them can fall to the ground"

After stepping off the kayak back on my beach in Este Ton, I heard the rattling chatter of the belted kingfisher and looked up to see him flying across the bay towards me—five or six rapid strokes and then gliding on half-closed wings. It was my other buddy coming to share my sadness, I thought. Suddenly, what looked like a peregrine falcon—it was too far away for me to identify—came swooping in a power dive, claws extended.

The ponderous kingfisher seemed caught in the open, in the middle of the bay, helpless, doomed. I expected to see an explosion of feathers as the bird was struck and stunned. At the last second, the kingfisher dropped into the bay with a splash, and emerged to fly off in a different direction. The falcon was as surprised as I was... but just momentarily.

It turned and closed again. I willed the kingfisher to head to the shore, to the rocks, to come to me... but it continued to hover, a yard or two above the water in the middle of the bay, seemingly inviting its own destruction. The falcon powered in again, claws opening. And the same thing happened— down went the kingfisher into the water, splash, and out it shot in another direction with the baffled raptor trying to line up for another try. The kingfisher fended off attack after attack with the same maneuver. Even so, it seemed just a matter of time. The heavy-beaked kingfisher had to be tiring.

However, amazingly, it was the much larger falcon that disengaged and flew over to the shore to recover. And the belted kingfisher, which would live to fish another day, flew to the opposite side of the bay and took his well-deserved rest. I had the feeling I had been watching some ancient, scripted performance. My admiration for the gutsy little bird rose dramatically, and I was so happy that I hadn't lost a second friend so soon after the first.

The belted kingfisher's scientific name, *Ceryle alcyon*, has its origins in Greek mythology. Alcyon, was daughter of Aeolus, God of the Wind. In grief and despair after her husband drowned, she threw herself into the sea, and both were transformed into kingfishers.

It was said that kingfishers made floating nests on the sea. To honor his daughter, Aeolus commanded the winds to stay calm during the time of the kingfishers' nesting, which was thought to be the two week period around the winter solstice.

The expression "halcyon days," which has come to us to mean carefree, joyful, peaceful days, originally referred to that fortnight, which, in the Mediterranean, often brings calm weather. Mariners in the ancient world held kingfishers to be sacred birds, and many carried feathers or even entire kingfisher bodies to induce Aeolus to charm the seas.

My remaining time on the island resolved itself into a whirl of activity. I made a direct easterly hike up one of the steep canyons behind the beach, watching carefully for snakes. As expected, it soon became too steep to continue.

I knew there was an endemic penstemon on the island, so it was really exciting to come across a beautiful red flowering example which I correctly assumed to be the rare *Penstemon angelicus*. Not far away, I took photographs of bees inside the showy white petals of a prickly poppy, which was likely another island endemic. Back in camp, after cleaning sand from the tent, I kayaked north to "current comb." I paddled enthusiastically from object to object to see what was drifting by.

A porcupine puffer floating dead

Island reflections

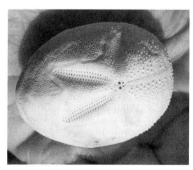

A heart urchin

Bullseye pufferfish

Rocks. Speak to me!

Brothers and sea stars. Speak!

I wandered around filling up my camera memory cards with shots of coastal views, interesting plants and animals, rocks, shells, driftwood, self-timer shots of myself walking naked by the bay, reflections of the same in the sea. Everything I cast my eyes on seemed doubly precious and larger than life, worthy of note and admiration. It turned into a torrid afternoon. I immersed myself in the bay for a cooling swim. I knew my spiritual aspirations were on target when a tiny bullseye puffer swam right on to the beach as if it were trying to break free of its appointed realm and speak to me. In my heightened awareness it was easy to believe I had found another friend.

Stepping from the sea, I watched a raven hopping over the boulders, poking his head into the rocks, trying to get at the decaying carcass of the black and white cat. I gave him my blessing on that one.

Dusk brought a picture of desert pastel peace. A stormy night seemed inconceivable. Seeing the sliver of a "new moon" planted the same smiling image on my face. The peak high tide had passed. Halcyon days indeed.

Chapter 41

Survival of the Fittest

I know this sounds totally like wishful thinking
and guess what?—that's exactly what it is.

Spirituality for Dummies

I made a final trash-collecting run around the bay before my friends Chuck
and Ev arrived. They should have flown out from Michigan to San Diego a
few days previously, and I was expecting them to arrive on the island
Sunday, March 5. Bonni wrote me that she would offer them our truck to
drive down to LA Bay, so after they'd camped with me we could all return
north together. Anyway, that was the plan.

And then I, almost ceremoniously, opened my last remaining food can—
Spam! An instance of "survival of the unfittest." Perhaps thinking about what
dried delights now lay before me, it made for a surprisingly tasty dinner with
tomatoes, herbs, and dried mashed potatoes—with plenty to look forward to
the following day.

It was an odd sensation not knowing if I'd be stringing out my remaining
food for unknown weeks, or whether I'd be camping in good company with
cup and plate overflowing... or even, out of the blue, leaving the island with
someone sent to get me.

Saturday, March 4—While washing some clothes in the sea, I spotted two
gulls dragging a large, remarkably passive fish by its fins through the rocky
shallows to the
beach. It was a
scorpion fish, definitely
alive, and perhaps
overconfident within
its array of venomous
spines. I doubted
that those spines on
its fins and gill
covers would have
helped it much out
of the sea. Warty,
chunky, big-mouthed,

Spot the scorpion fish

reddish, speckled, and camouflaged—it was easy for me to identify with it; so ugly, it was kind of beautiful. I chased the gulls away and just had time for a picture before the fish swam back into deeper water, apparently unharmed.

I washed myself in the bay and poured a gallon of sun-warmed seawater over my head. My drinking water was almost gone, so I washed down a simple lunch with a diet soda and a beer. I had no desire to touch the gallon of wine.

It was fairly windy and a little on the cool side. It felt more comfortable out of the wind, in the valley just inland, where I enjoyed sitting on a couple of large rocks, bird and bug and chuckwalla watching. Occasionally I'd glance out to sea looking for Roger's boat.

I had just identified a black-chinned hummingbird and an ash-throated flycatcher, when I heard the chattering of the kingfisher. I stood up to greet the conquering hero, hoping he was coming over to spend time with me on the rocks. As soon as I picked him out I realized that he was again being attacked by a falcon; and while I helplessly looked on, a second falcon appeared. The two were making a concerted attack in the middle of the bay, over and over driving the poor kingfisher into the water. Surely, this time the gallant little guy would be worn down and exhausted, torn apart before my eyes. Not even Aeolus could save him. I rushed down to the shore thinking about kayaking out and intervening, but before I could get on the water, the kingfisher had done enough to send the two tired raptors to the shore while he made his escape and caught his breath on the opposite side of the bay.

There are numerous examples in articles and blogs which describe belted kingfishers in similar interactions.

> Flying over one of the… ponds was a belted kingfisher being pursued by a northern harrier. The kingfisher would fly along zigging and zagging. When the harrier got very close, the kingfisher would drop into the water, and fly out in the opposite direction, escaping the attack. The kingfisher stayed over the water at all times, and this must be what prevented the kill.

> A… goshawk gave chase as the kingfisher flew within 20 meters. When the hawk closed to within 1 meter after a few wingbeats and thrust its legs forward, the kingfisher dove into the water from a height of approximately 3 meters. The kingfisher emerged immediately, rattled, and rapidly flew away. The goshawk turned quickly when it had flown past the splash made by the diving bird and was within striking distance before the kingfisher had flown more than 50 meters downstream. The kingfisher dove again, emerged at right angles to its previous course and flew directly to a dead snag after which the goshawk returned to a branch. Although quiet after landing in the dead tree, the kingfisher began calling when the goshawk landed. It then flew within 1 meter of the hawk, again initiating a chase sequence.

In a 1977 article, biologists Ronald Kirby and Mark Fuller reported a wide range of such interactions from brief typical predator-prey chases to instances where the kingfisher definitely appears to have initiated the interaction:

> ...an adult male kingfisher was observed fishing... an immature Cooper's hawk landed quietly in a dead tree approximately 50 meters from the kingfisher's perch. The kingfisher immediately began a loud rattling call and shortly flew directly at the hawk. When the kingfisher flew closely over its head, the hawk left its perch and began pursuit. The kingfisher dodged rapidly and landed after the hawk had given up the chase.

They argue that encounters where the kingfisher initiates an attack by its persistent approaches toward a raptor "may be explained as mobbing behavior, since the kingfisher's actions result in a thwarting of predatory activities." They suggest...

> ...that the purpose of this behavior is similar to that espoused for mobbing in general, an increase in fitness for either the mobbing bird, its mate, or kin. Benefits thus accrue to a bird if the mobbing behavior subsequently allows uninterrupted feeding behavior on a feeding territory, a result that was in fact observed. Mobbing behavior makes information regarding the presence and nature of a predator available by informing other potential prey of the raptor's presence and location, the hawk's probability of capturing any prey within the kingfisher's territory would be reduced; therefore it would be more efficient for the hawk to leave the area and search elsewhere for more vulnerable prey.

It remained windy and cool. That evening I was well-wrapped. A waxing 30 per cent moon was gently sinking to the west. While the moon was hovering above the peninsula, I was convinced I could hear a crashing panga. It was very real and sounded like distant fireworks or gunfire. Might it be Chuck and Ev coming over, that late, with that much wind?

Chuck Bosley and Evelyn Simon are a remarkable couple from the Sault Ste. Marie area—bold and courageous seniors, still lapping up life and going places that would cause even the hardiest and fittest to hesitate. Africa, the Middle East, the frozen North Woods, Baja—for them, all places to camp and revel in the glory of nature. Este Ton was made for their keen powers of observation and easy laughter. I would have welcomed their company, but the moon sank and the night grew black, and no one appeared.

As Chuck and Ev told me later, they had in fact, tried to come over that Saturday evening, a day early. The following day there was a huge fiesta scheduled up in Mission San Borja, and just about the whole town of Bahía de los Angeles would be wanting to get up there to indulge in the day-long ceremony. And that included Roger's boat skipper, Alfredo and his family. So after loading all their camping gear, food and water on the boat, enough to get us all through three or four days together on the island, they made their attempt, taking along a couple of the younger guests at Villa Bahía for the ride. It was going to be a rough ride, but one never quite knows how rough till one gets out in the open Ballenas Channel, out beyond the protection of the bay. The launch battled for over fifteen minutes beyond the islands, according to Ev "bobbing like a cork, rocking side to side, waves coming over the bow, everyone aboard was getting soaked and turning nervous." She said her heart was in her mouth because she's always had a fear of drowning and thought maybe her time had come.

Chuck, quick with his jolly laugh, saw it a little differently, "I kind of enjoyed it. I hated to turn back. I like that kind of stuff. The waves were coming over the bow. So who cares? We might get a little wet."

Their camping gear was all in plastic bags, but the water was starting to splash over it and wash it along the gangway. According to Ev, "We were out more than half an hour—maybe a third of the way over."

Alfredo said they'd have to decide soon, because when they reached the half-way point there would be no turning back, they'd have to run to the island. Ev said, "We decided you weren't worth risking death for. We decided to turn back. And the skipper was really focusing as we pulled around, trying to avoid getting side slammed by a big wave. It was very nerve-wracking." Everyone on the boat was disappointed, but also mightily relieved.

Back at Villa Bahía, they unloaded and took the stuff back to their room. Roger said there would be no one to take the boat out till at least Monday. And he couldn't guarantee that, as most people returning from the fiesta tend not to be in the best shape after all the partying and drinking. So they decided to go camp and do some botanizing in the Cataviña area and then run down to Guerrero Negro "to pet the whales." Chuck chuckled, "We got wet from the blowholes, as well as our run to the island."

Evelyn and Chuck just south of El Rosario

Sunday, March 5 (Day 58)— It was a calm, breathless morning, so I kayaked south to "Long Beach" to collect extra firewood in case I'd be thrown back to relying on my stills for drinking water. After the sun rose, it was delightfully warm. Every so often, I glanced over my shoulder for any sign of a boat from LA Bay.

I returned with a full stack of firewood. Following a spicy breakfast, I paddled out again, partly thinking this may be my last opportunity, partly to postpone the work and tedium of operating the still, and partly to better scan the channel to see if anyone was coming.

All morning, conditions were perfect, and no one showed. I gradually resigned myself to the fact that like Bob and his friend, Chuck and Ev probably weren't going to be joining me. Otherwise they would surely have taken advantage of the flat calm crossing and already been there. It must have been a very nice day up in San Borja.

By noon, the only thing I was now expecting was to be out of water within twenty-four hours. All images of company, flowing cups, and calorie-crammed cornucopias were banished from my mind. I began boiling seawater in earnest, making a gallon over the remainder of the day.

The wind stayed absolutely calm. Whilst refilling the kettle in the bay I spotted a large colorful jellyfish practically on the beach, and a small erratically swimming fish whose wounded sides suggested it had just escaped hungry jaws or perhaps a bird's beak. The slowly circling fish suddenly made contact with the batteries of stinging cells in the tentacles of the jellyfish, vigorously shuddered and then broke free, but only for a few seconds before it swam into them again. The second brush seemed fatal; the small fish rose to the surface and went belly up. It was soon lying limp and dead on the shore.

Wounded and stung

Large jellyfish

I tried using the dead fish as bait to see if I could catch dinner. I had several bites, but couldn't land anything before it was ripped from the hook. Dinner consisted of dried mashed potatoes, peanuts, and some chocolate cookies... eased down with a refreshing, cold beer.

It was a quiet evening, the breeze gentle, the moon amazingly bright. In spite of any possible ordeal before me, I was a long way from wanting to leave the island. Sleep came easy about ten o'clock.

Monday, March 6—Another perfect morning. I was now convinced I'd have visitors. Either Chuck and Ev coming to join me, or more likely Roger from Villa Bahía to take me back.

I had breakfast, and resisted the urge to kayak away. Optimistically, I delayed working on my stills, and treated every minute and island experience as if it were my last. And I didn't have long to validate my hunch. About 9 A.M. I heard a boat... and there was Roger and Alfredo, and Alfredo's wife—whom in spite of a lifetime in the LA Bay area had never been to the island. There was no Chuck and Ev. So I knew it was over. And what a way to leave… on such a perfect day. Just like the day I arrived.

It took about two hours for me to pack and break camp. Alfredo and Roger spent much of that time fishing productively just out of the bay; hooking up almost every time a hook sank to the bottom. The ease with which they lifted the bass and the lingcod was almost a mockery of my humble efforts the previous two months. But I was glad I didn't take a single extra fish. The ospreys that flew over needed them more than I did.

Saying goodbye to my osprey friends

I left the firewood piled high and the shady palapa standing and intact for others to use and enjoy, at least until a southerly summer storm came crashing into the bay. I didn't take much from the island, just pictures and memories, and whatever trash I could easily grab. My one indulgence, Bonni's special present, which she will no doubt treasure forever, the necklace of fishing floats that I'd used as my early warning device. A smart idea, because when she's wearing it, I'll always know exactly where she is, and whether she's coming with that cold beer. Colorful string of island fishing floats! Look for it soon on eBay.

While loading my boxes and bags on the launch, I nearly took a scorpion stowaway with me. I managed to shake it off on the beach and watched it scurry out of sight under some dried seaweed. Better off there than in my house in San Diego.

Sad goodbyes. Final look back… the boat's wake leaving behind the receding sea-reflected cliffs and sky. Astounding beauty. Another well-deserved cold beer. Mission accomplished.

Home now calling. Warm bed beckoning. Bonni waiting. The go-dependent phase in abeyance. For a while at least, we could look forward to its opposite. Sun and moon united. Newness. After that, there was only uncertainty and human frailty—a beer belly bulging like the East Pacifico Rise, love handles bouncing back like shock waves from the San Andreas, and the vague hope, that in spite of all my glaring limitations as a writer, I might have been able to convey something of the wonders I saw and experienced on the island. And why in spite of all of Baja's changes and problems, I keep going back, keep hearing the voices, keep answering the call.

And the first thing I did when I got home (well, actually, the second) was read the back-and-forth of the Nomad discussion. I made my reply. It ended with my account of the snake encounter included earlier. It began:

March 14, 2006 San Diego
From Graham Mackintosh

Back home in San Diego twelve pounds lighter, I've been able to review the postings about my Guardian Angel Island trip on this message board.

Wow! I thought I used the term "marooned" in quotation marks as a convenient handle to describe my situation. It was meant lightheartedly. So I was a little surprised by all the excitement that caused some people.

As for all the stuff about Survivor, I can't really comment on that; I've never watched the program and have no desire to. I'd much rather be somewhere like Guardian Angel Island—hiking, kayaking, beachcombing, bird watching, exploring, and generally relaxing and meditating beneath the stars.

I do have the equipment, know-how, and common sense to survive alone in such circumstances if necessary—several times I ran out of water and had to make drinking water from the sea—but that was not the intention of my trip. I was not on the island looking for trouble. If I never had a dangerous or unpleasant moment out there I'd be a very happy man.

My goal was to get to know the island, its history, geology, wildlife, ecology, the people who come and go, to photograph it, to experience it and, if the spirit moves me, to write about it and try to distil its essence to my readers. As it has taken me about two years on average to do the research and write each of my three books I have to be sure my heart is in it before I take the plunge.

I'd like to think I'm aging gracefully and the Graham Mackintosh that wrote *Nearer My Dog to Thee* and *Journey with a Baja Burro* is a very different person from the more naive "swashbuckling" author of *Into a Desert Place*. Some people don't like the change; others haven't even noticed it. But certainly there is evolution—backpacking to burro packing to "base camping." The journeys have got shorter, the physical demands easier, the interests different. Shoot, I may just cuddle up to the comfort of my computer screen and sit on my "burro" for the next project and write a novel!

Chapter 42

The Nuts and Humboldts of Safe Baja Kayaking

I don't profess to be an expert kayaker, but for anyone about to dip a paddle in the Sea of Cortez, here are a few things to consider.

1. Know what is in the weather forecast… especially WIND, WIND, WIND. Consult online weather sites before you launch. Look at all available forecasts. There are several "Internet Cafes" in LA Bay.
2. Carry a waterproof Marine VHF radio and extra batteries. Don't be shy about calling for a weather report at any time on VHF channel 16. Many folks monitoring will be aware of the weather forecast. It could save you from a world of misery and could even save your life. Know the VHF channel for any local boaters' weather nets.
3. Always keep an eye on the sea and the sky. Look behind often. Take action if you see any unusual fronts or clouds. And always be prepared to paddle ashore or to shelter to wait out bad weather.
4. Think ahead and keep a little in reserve. Never exhaust yourself needlessly battling wind and current and put yourself at the mercy of the elements. Never put yourself in a position where you have to make a dangerous landing.
5. Know where you are and where the protected bays, sandy beaches, and lee shores are. Carry a compass, a waterproof GPS, good maps, and satellite images, and garner all the local knowledge you can. Don't hesitate to ask the fishermen. While it's always possible that they could plant a machete in your skull especially if you make tactless comments about the need for a triple fence at the border, it's not likely. Whereas if you end up in the water unprepared and ill-equipped during a storm while sensible folks are all in the bar or watching TV then you're probably lined up for a date with the local isopods.
6. Wear a lifejacket. On more hazardous excursions use one with reflective tape and strobe light.
7. Carry flares, whistle, and signal mirror.
8. Carry a kettle, a few corks, and some copper tubing suitable for making

a still. If you can afford it, take a reverse-osmosis pump capable of making fresh water from salt water.

9. Never paddle alone. But if like me you're never going to listen to this, be doubly cautious. Leave a note or tell someone your plans.

10. Give consideration to how bright and reflective are your boat and paddle. Remember, a capsized kayak that is white underneath is difficult to spot in a churning sea. Or if you're alone in a remote location frequented by armed and dangerous drug runners keeping a low profile and staying out of sight can be a consideration.

11. Have a second paddle and tie the one in use to your kayak with a strong line. It could be blown from your hands or kayak, and in the event of a capsize you don't want to be in the water wondering which to swim to first.

12. Check your kayak and gear at every opportunity. You only have a few millimeters of plastic, fiberglass, or whatever, between you and hypothermia and all the creatures of the sea, especially huge sharks, hungry orcas, and merciless Humboldt squid.

13. Be realistic and brutally honest about your limitations. If you've got away with it a dozen times don't assume you will the next time.

14. Carry tide charts. Know the relative position of sun and moon, and how they will affect the tides.

15. Be extra careful if it will soon be dark.

16. Paddling at night, don't assume that the green glow around your kayak is just bioluminescence. You may be about to witness a squid feeding frenzy.

17. If you go alone, unless you're proficient at "Eskimo rolling" and self rescue techniques consider a sit-on-top with plenty of cargo space. Don't think there'll be any easy way to get back on your sit-inside in a howling gale. The sit-on-top makes a great snorkeling platform; you can ordinarily slip off and climb back on at will. You can load it up with driftwood and other beach finds, and use it as a water collector when it rains. You might get a little wetter but that won't matter much in Baja. Hypothermia from prolonged immersion in the sea is the biggest danger. Getting out of the water and getting underway is crucial.

18. Whatever kind of kayak you have, practice getting back on or in. But if you practice in calm conditions and relatively warm water, imagine how it will be in high winds and breaking cold surf, with your hands and feet and brain getting numb, and schools of ravenous Humboldt squid taking apple-sized chunks out of your ass.

19. Wearing shorts might be fine if the wind is down and the sun is shining, but carry extra clothing: jackets, waterproofs, even a wetsuit or drysuit. Visit your local kayaking or boating store to see the latest in waterproof and protective clothing. And put it on early if conditions warrant. If there's any danger you might end up in the water put on socks, shoes,

gloves, hat... cover as much bare skin as possible. Not just to combat hypothermia, but as protection from jellyfish and the sun... and anything else that might have an affinity for your tender hide.

20. Carry extra food, water, footwear, matches, sunscreen, space blanket, mirror, flashlight, and a good first aid kit which should include sutures, tourniquets, and hemostats enough to curtail massive blood loss and keep you alive and comfortable for several days in the event of a particularly nasty animal attack.

21. Don't panic. Fierce storms and gusts may subside as quickly as they come on. A single rogue squid may eat his fill before causing you mortal injury.

22. If you have a bad feeling—act on it. There's probably a good reason.

23. Carry a waterproof camera, and keep it close at hand. Alternatively, keep your non-waterproof camera in a dry bag or sturdy Ziploc bag or two. Remember the built-in flash as an emergency signal.

24. Carry an umbrella for both sun protection and as a sail.

25. By all means carry fishing gear. Fish and have fun on your kayak. But be careful if you fish for squid. They are capable of turning the tables and making a sucker out of you.

26. Consider carrying bottles of ink to throw into the sea to fool the squid. Unscrew the caps first.

27. Carry lots of good, relaxing, informative reading such as *Jaws, 20,000 Leagues Under the Sea*, and *The Deep*. For those of you planning to camp on the islands, do as I do, pick up some solid medical texts with lots of colorful pictures of the effects of snake bites and graphic accounts of the various stages involved in succumbing to scorpion stings.

28. Before your trip I would urge you to search online and familiarize yourself with all the kayaking disasters and near disasters that have occurred in the area that you will be visiting. Analyze the mistakes made and the conditions behind them so you yourself won't become the subject of a search. And while you're at it, find out what you can about fatal stingray and jellyfish encounters, the unbelievable pain inflicted by scorpion fish and cone shell injuries, Above all, read everything you can about Humboldt squid. They're on the up and up.

29. Be paranoid. Come home safe.

Chapter 43

Juan Coyote

John Weed, 55, (Kayaker John) is a real kayaker and a great story teller. For the past ten years he has been a regular winter resident of LA Bay, and has a unique insight into kayaking the Midriff and into the lives of the Mexican fishermen who visit from Bahía Kino.

I was able to meet him and ask him a few questions at LA Bay immediately after my return from the island, and again months later as he was passing through San Diego on his return to his home near Placerville, in Northern California. All the photographs below in this chapter were taken by him and are used with his permission.

He grew up in a family of distance runners, and started competing in races at about ten years old. In college he was running over two hundred miles a week...

[John] And then I bought a nice racing bicycle that could go real fast, real far and wow what fun. But less than a month later, while going to visit my girl friend, I got into a bit of a right-of-way dispute with a semi tractor trailer rig which squeezed me off into a parked car. I hit and went airborne over the car, and then rolled under the truck's second trailer. The driver slammed on his brakes, and luckily this caused the wheels to bounce, and they sort of were on the up bounce as I watched them go over my pelvis area.

Things were still pretty serious though and the doctors told my family that I would probably be dead within a couple of hours. In addition to a crushed pelvis and broken legs, my femoral artery was partially severed and my urethra was severed completely at my bladder. I was originally hospitalized for three months, and then over the next two years had two sets of surgery and four or five more months in hospital. While in hospital, I watched the 1972 Olympics on TV. That year Germany added whitewater kayaking as an exhibition sport. When I saw those wonderful new fiberglass kayaks, I knew it was time to get one.

It was a year wait to finally get out of my last cast and buy my first kayak. I immediately started doing long paddles on a local lake. A year later I heard about some whitewater races (distance racing through rapid rivers) so I signed up… I took a first and second in the two races I entered. I was hooked and decided that I enjoyed paddling even more than running. I qualified for the US national team in 1983 and 1985, and was winning the majority of races that I entered, which was about fifty events per year.

Now I teach kids kayaking most of the summer, and a lot of introduction to touring and sea kayaking classes for adults on weekends. I started doing that 10 years ago, and spending my winters in Baja.

First time I went to Baja—I had just finished my first season instructing; it was Christmas and my father was living in Mexico, north of San Felipe, married to a Mexican woman, and she died unexpectedly of a heart attack the day after Christmas. I've got five brothers and sisters and we all shot down, got there the next day, talking to him, and he said, "The hardest thing was going to be here in the house without her being here."

I said, "Maybe it's time to go see what Baja is about." So we decided to do a two-week trip… and our two-week trip ended up being three months. LA Bay was one of the first places we went to and I totally fell in love with it. By the time we got to La Paz, it was big city and I said forget it man, I want to go back to that LA Bay place, with all the islands; it has got everything I'm interested in, except I'd like warmer water.

Our first day back there, a man wanted to do a kayak trip across to the mainland. He approached me about taking him, and he had these three women with him… drop dead gorgeous, and as they got to Guillermo's they jumped off their bikes and went running into the water throwing off clothes in the air and jumped in in their panties and bras, and I was like, "Oh my goodness!" The guy comes over and says are you Ed Gillet? Ed had just come in with a group and he was hoping Ed would hook him up with boats and get him across. Ed wasn't interested in it though. So he said, "How about you?"

And I said, "I don't know. Is it okay if I'm gone for a couple of weeks, dad?"

He said, "Yes, I've got a comfortable bed, I'm fine."

So I got suckered into that; but it got me really hooked

*John's LA Bay neighbor and friend amateur botanist
Pete Garcia on Mike's Mountain, overlooking LA Bay*

onto LA Bay and I've been coming back every year since.

[Graham] How long did it take going across from LA Bay to the mainland?

[John] It took us a month. It was the first time any of them had been in kayaks. I took them out and taught them rescues and stuff before we went, but they were still fledglings.

[Graham] That was your first trip across. It must have been eye opening for you.

[John] I didn't understand all the currents and hadn't been exposed to a west wind yet, or things like that... fortunately Ed Gillet, who has done lots of paddling and led lots of trips, took me to the museum, to the big map in there, and showed me step by step how to get across and actually gave me a copy of an article that he had written about doing the crossing. He kind of scared me a little bit as he was comparing

Pete Garcia near Puerto Refugio

the stretch between San Lorenzo Island and San Esteban as being one of the nastiest things this side of Cape Horn when the wind is kicking up. I thought, "Oh jeez what am I getting into." And a fishermen at San Rafael beach was trying to explain to me about the currents out there off San Esteban, and he finally draws me a picture of a whirlpool that's the same size as the island. And the island's five miles across.

As it turned out, when we did our crossing the tide was like flat... and then half way across to San Esteban from San Lorenzo, it's about 12 miles, Lorenzo disappeared behind us in a fog bank. It never caught us. But the same thing happened when we left San Esteban. San Esteban disappeared behind us in the fog. Thick, thick, thick fog. It blew up from the south. It stayed most of the day. And I got a good look at it when we came back, we had a rental boat, a panga, to bring us back, and we couldn't see 50 feet, it was so thick.

[Graham] And now you've done that trip several times?

[John] Yes. This year the currents between those islands, where the upwelling was going on, was loud... I just got on it and basically did a diagonal surf. And it was the fastest crossing I've done between the two islands, on that standing wave. Most people would look at it and think we've got to get away from that, that's ugly... but that's a wave man, surf the sucker. It just shot me; I went like two, three miles really fast. It was about a foot to two feet high.

[Graham] You were on your own that last trip?

[John] Oh yes. Now, I won't bring anybody with me on that crossing.

[Graham] Do you take a wetsuit when you're making these crossings?

[John] Better than a wetsuit is what I use now—a Gore-Tex drysuit. After thirty years of kayaking it's the first one I've ever owned. Before that, I would paddle to the islands in insulated ski pants—because when they get wet I still stay warm, and I can sort of swim in them—and some sort of a fleece top, with a nylon paddling jacket, high collar, tight sleeve to seal me. But I just know I'm performing without a net. If I screw up, I've got thirty minutes and I'm feeding the fish. That's my guess with me, in thirty minutes I'm going to be unconscious. Some people can last a very long time, but I know I don't have time to mess around when I'm in cold water because it's going to nail me real quick. When I'm around Guardian Angel, I'm there in the winter—in the summer it might be 80 degrees—but in the winter the sea is usually around 58-60 degrees because of the upwellings of cold water.

I emphasize when I teach classes to dress for the water temperature rather than the air temperature. You need to dress for submersion. And it's in the spring when the majority of the deaths happen.

Drysuits are great. Worst case scenario, if I end up in the water, I'm still OK because I can even inflate the drysuit and float like a cork out there and have even more insulation. It's going to blow me to the island, no problem. The Gore-Tex can breathe. When you get out of the water and it's cold and icky, walking around in a wetsuit isn't so good but, like last year when I went out to Humbug Bay, I got a late start and got caught in a westy, I was getting blown all over the place, but when I got there to the panga I just flopped over and slept in the drysuit.

And I put a long sleeve white shirt over the top, so that I don't get overheated in it. It's relatively thin; mine is thicker than most; mine is almost a ballistic nylon, it's one that a guy makes for the navy seals. I wanted something drab and stealth-like, rather than the normal bright colors. It has pockets all over it. I keep some things in the pockets: flares, compass, multitool, light. And I keep some survival stuff strapped to the deck.

Some drysuits have a gasket at the ankle, but this one has the feet with it. You have a silicon seal at each wrist and at your neck. If I jump in the water, my hands get wet, my head gets wet; that's it. Everything else dry. This one sells to the military for $900, a non-military version with thinner nylon would be running about $500-700. You can also get a two-piece, or just a dry top, so if you go in, the core stays dry.

[Graham] What's Bahia Kino like?

[John] There's Old Kino and New Kino. Old Kino is fishing village, tarpaper shacks, things like that... New Kino is Malibu, million dollar beach front condos...

My first visit was about six years ago, when a fisherman put my kayak and stuff in his panga and brought me... I met him on Salsipuedes Island... I'd been warned don't ever put your kayak on the beach in Old Kino and walk away from it... So I didn't want to try camping there, and I'd also been told, don't ever go on the beach after dark because the banditos will get you. And this guy's house is right across the street from the beach and he literally drew a line in his street and said, after dark, do not go past this. And he walked me around and pointed out other streets not to go down…

In Kino, I met a guy who had just come back from diving, and he had this big old bag of octopus and one of his arms was crippled up, and I asked him about it and he said it was the bends… He said he was down about 100 feet and the motor conked out on his hooka so he had to come up fast.

I said, "My God, why do you still do this?"

He said, "I have nine children."

Old Kino is like the Wild West, but the last three or four years they've cleaned it up a lot, the whole beach area looks much nicer now… For three seasons, I've stayed in the trailer park in New Kino… and I'll go visit my fishermen friend, but just for the day, his yard is not a place for sleep, it just stinks of fish guts, flies… and the chickens and dogs, all the racket; anyone who wants to advertise something has a speaker on their car going around the neighborhood. But I like Old Kino, it's cool, and all these divers I'd met over the years. "Hey, Juan Coyote, how you doing there?"

[Graham] They call you, Juan Coyote?

Juan Coyote and friends at Bahía Kino

[John] That was a nickname they gave me the first year I met them, when I was out there on Isla Salsipuedes. I got there at night and set up camp. I was pretty beat because I'd paddled from San Francisquito to Salsipuedes, maybe 25 miles or so… Next day the wind was howling, I wasn't going to fish or do anything. And there was this little half cave, up at the point of the island… OK. I'm just going to go sit up there, enjoy the sun, close my eyes and start playing the guitar and harmonica. And I played for half an hour … and as I opened my eyes, here's a semi-circle, at a polite distance, of about seven Mexicans.

Just out of my view in the next inlet were six pangas and twenty-some divers. They were also laid up

Cormorant surveying beach at Bahía Kino

because of the winds… And they hear this music and start yelling, who's got the radio. And they finally figured out it's coming from up there somewhere, so that's when they all came up and I opened my eyes… They all had nicknames, which are only used when they're out there on the island… They wanted me to sing something. I don't like to sing. I'm not comfortable with my voice. So I did Little Red Riding Hood, which has that OWOOOO howl… and when I did that, they said, "Oh it's a coyote," and I introduced myself, my name is John, which is Juan, so they all agreed I had to be Juan Coyote.

Whenever I meet them, I usually take a Polaroid picture and give it to them; they love posing. And when I was in Kino three different people invited me into their homes and proudly showed me that one Polaroid picture stuck up on their wall. And I started feeling bad knowing that picture is going to fade away in about two years. So the first year I paddled across, I brought a whole stack of duplicates of the photos I took with my 35 mm. I left them with my friend's wife to distribute them.

Last year was the first time with a digital camera and I've got a little compact printer so I brought that along with a load of paper, took it all in the kayak and was so glad I did. I took and gave away 78 photos in two days. It's just a real fun gift to be able to give these people. And they'd come back the second day with their church outfits to do family photos.

[Graham] Were they on the island legally, the first time you met the divers?

[John] No. It was illegal to be on Salsipuedes, and it wasn't until the third night that the one who spoke the best English said, "When you see us here, you don't tell them in Bahía."

"Why?"

Well, we're illegal here, and they explained that they're from Sonora and their fishing waters only go out as far as San Esteban Island. Then I got nervous and asked, "What happens if you get caught and I'm here with you?"

"Oh, no problem for you; but for us, we lose our pangas."

That's a heck of a risk they're taking. Which kind of explains why the guys I met have this real cavalier, swashbuckler mentality. They're letting it hang out just by being there, so it kind of takes that kind of person to even risk going out…

Mainly they were diving for sea cucumbers. They bring them up, slit them, gut them, put them into large barrels, usually 50 gallon drums of water, put a torch under it, and boil them for about three or four hours, dump them out, squeeze them, then they put them into a real heavy salt solution and soak them and then dry them, so they look like little dog turds when they're done. And then they sell them to the Asian market. Last year was the first time I ever met any Mexican that has eaten one; most just go, "Ugh." In Korea they think it's an aphrodisiac; and they say they make twice as much a pound for those as they do for lobster.

They also take lobster and scallops, but the *pepinos*, the sea cucumbers, seems to be their biggest crop; these guys will also, when it gets close to time to head back, collect curios, starfish, unusual shells, to bring back and sell. And unfortunately they also take turtles, because it's such a special delicacy even though they risk 20 years in jail if they get busted with them. They know the risks. I've been with them when they're cooking it and I've wanted to take a picture and they go, "Oh, no, no no! We don't want a picture of this going on."

Last year I was camped maybe a mile and a half from where they were camped on La Guarda and they saw me when they were going out diving… and all of a sudden I hear this howl… Hey Juan Coyote! Then those guys hiked from their camp over to my camp and said, "Come on. Bring your guitar. Come back to our camp." And I'm thinking I've got to put everything back away, but they all grabbed bags and started walking back to their camp, and I paddled around and spent about four days with them.

[Graham] Was that Humbug Bay?

Out on the island

[John] No, it was on the other side, down towards the southern end there was a long beach where they used to have a scallop camp… there's a cinder block structure, two rooms, no roof, no windows, but it is a reasonable wind block… it's flat for a long ways out there and the wind gets howling.

[Graham] Have you ever bumped into the military out on the islands?

[John] Yes. I was on San Lorenzo Island, putting off having to make water, I had a desalinater pump and before using it I went for a walk looking at the shells… and this beach was the only one I ever found with the little Nautilus shells. I'm walking the beach and it's a very buggy time I'm there. So I'm all protected from bugs. I had an aluminum pole walking stick, and I'm walking the shore with a daypack on my back, and I hear the distinct rumble of this

Friendly island mouse   *Friendly lizard*

Angel Island black-collared lizard—endemic?

boat... It sounded like nothing else out on the water, a huge diesel engine. So I stop... hoping they wouldn't spot me and they'd just keep on going, so I wouldn't have to deal with them. They got almost by me and then they turned and start coming in... OK, I'd better go down and be friendly. As soon as I start walking down to the water's edge this guy goes out on the nose of the boat and they're coming in slow, and he's got some kind of weapon in his hands, a rifle or something. As they get closer, he turns and a second guy comes out on the nose of the boat with a gun. I go, wow, are they going to arrest me... As they get closer, a third guy comes out, and now all three of them are starting to raise the guns.

Then I glanced down and realize, you idiot! I'm wearing camouflage pants, a black long-sleeve fleece top... I'm carrying what could be seen as a weapon, and I'm waving it in front of my face to keep the bugs out of my eyes, and to cap it off I have a navy blue balaclava over my head (with just a slit opening) to keep the bugs out of my ears and mouth... I just wasn't thinking about what I was wearing. I realized I look like a freaking commando.

So I pulled the balaclava off, and that made them more nervous. I looked like Bin Laden. I've been out months without cutting my hair or shaving.

I swung my pack down and unzipped it and pulled my Polaroid camera out, and they had to hold on as they hit the beach, and as they did that I swung the camera up and snapped a picture... and it literally disarmed them. I smiled and handed them the picture. They were immediately posing with their guns for more pictures that they can bring home for the families.

I said, "I'm glad you saw me, can you maybe spare a little bit of water?" They asked where my boat was, and one poor guy, Joseph, had to walk all the way back to my camp with me to see I actually had a kayak. They couldn't see it as I had it all hidden and it was about half-mile away. Joseph spoke some English and he was able to tell me that the boat was Swedish-made, it was called an *Invader*, and it will cruise at 58 knots, and they work five day cycles out there looking for drug runners, but they do watch for illegal fishing too.

Another time, I was out at La Guarda and when I got back [to LA Bay] some people said, "Did you see the big bust?" They said some divers from

Kino were out there at La Guarda, and they used a helicopter and they swooped down on them… and then apparently this boat came zooming in and they busted them for lobster out of season, and being out of their fishing zone, and they had three turtles with them,

Mexican Navy patrol

… so not only did they lose their boat but they each started their 20 years in prison by the time I got back to shore.

I haven't seen the patrol boats for three years now… This year there were ten pangas and two trawlers out there at La Guarda, and I saw them when I was doing a lap around, and then when I went to Kino two months later and mentioned to my diver buddies that I'd seen some guys out there with the trawlers, they said, yes, those guys got arrested in El Barril… While they were inshore there, the marines came from the water with their boats and the federales came from shore, and they arrested all 30 some guys, confiscated all their boats, everything they had caught, and put them in jail, and they had to pay very hefty fines… Word gets around when that stuff happens, so they're cutting down on getting out there and looking for other forms of income realizing that's a big price to pay when you're busted.

[Graham] Makes you wonder what you get busted for if you have a marijuana shipment on the boat; probably less than for the sea turtles. Have you ever found any marijuana?

Oh yes… I've found it numerous times on the beaches… where it's ended up after drifting around; usually the packages are torn open; some of them look like they've been deliberately sliced in half and tossed over to make them sink.

Chapter 44

The Island's Future

An old poacher makes the best gamekeeper.

14th Century words of wisdom

In 1973 Charles Lindbergh visited Baja California in a chartered flying boat. Shortly afterwards he traveled to Mexico City, met with the cabinet and summoned the Mexican media to a press conference. Naturally they were all expecting a homily on aviation. Instead, Lindbergh lectured them passionately about the Sea of Cortez and the need to preserve its magnificent islands. A few months later Charles Lindbergh died, but his enthusiastic pleas for the Sea of Cortez had not fallen on deaf ears. In 1978, Mexico passed laws granting "Wildlife Refuge" status to the islands that had fired his imagination in the twilight of his life.

The process of appreciation and protection had taken a great leap forward. And in 1995, *Las Islas del Golfo de California* was designated a United Nations Educational, Scientific and Cultural Organization (UNESCO) Biosphere Reserve.

In 2000 the Mexican government re-categorized the islands of the Sea of Cortez as an "Area for the Protection of Wildlife."

Another huge step in raising awareness and putting in place more effective protection was achieved in 2005 when the islands, their surrounding waters and a number of adjacent coastal zones were officially declared a UNESCO World Heritage Site, a site of "outstanding value to humanity." In justifying the designation, the UNESCO report was full of laudatory descriptions:

> "extraordinary importance for the study of marine and coastal processes…" "high marine productivity and biodiversity richness…" "striking natural beauty…" "high cliffs and sandy beaches contrasting with the brilliant reflection from the desert and the surrounding turquoise waters. The diversity of forms and colours is complemented by a wealth of birds and marine life. The diversity and abundance of marine life associated [with] spectacular submarine forms and high water transparency makes the property a diver's paradise…" "The diversity of terrestrial and marine life is extraordinary and constitutes a unique ecoregion of high priority for biodiversity conservation. The number of species of vascular plants

(695) present… is higher than that reported in other marine and insular properties included in the [World Heritage] List. The number of species of fish (891) is also highest when compared to a number of marine and insular properties. In addition the marine endemism is important, with 90 endemic fishes…" "contains 39% of the world's total number of marine mammal's species and a third of the world's total number of marine cetacean's species. In addition the [area] includes a good sample of the Sonora desert ecosystems, considered one of the richest deserts in the world from the desert biodiversity point of view."

And that was followed in June 2007 by President Calderón's administration establishing the Bahía de los Angeles Biosphere Reserve which afforded another dimension of protection to nearly a million acres of marine and island ecosystems, including all of Angel de la Guarda and its surrounding waters.

However, in spite of these accolades and designations, there is no absolute restriction on development and resource exploitation in the region. Indeed the LA Bay area is still under threat from the wildly ambitious and perhaps wildly unrealistic "Nautical Ladder" multi-harbor project proposed under the previous administration of President Vicente Fox. Such has been the opposition, it is hard to conceive that the "Ladder" could get off the ground.

The mood has changed for sure in recent years; proposals for any kind of construction, mining, or reckless tourist developments will meet with a well-funded, well-organized howl of protest, but the pressures to "productively utilize" the region will continue.

Because of a lack of enforcement, and a number of conflicting philosophies about how to preserve or develop the islands, all conservation measures in the Midriff Islands region have had a limited impact. Until recently, whatever protection the islands enjoyed was perhaps more due to their remoteness and inaccessibility and the discouraging amount of drug trafficking through the area than any government action. But that situation is fast changing.

I've been traveling in Baja California for almost 30 years and I've seen a number of changes, mostly related to increasing ease of access and sharply elevated tourist visitation. And I've changed too. I don't pretend to have been an environmental purist through all those years.

The emptiness and majesty of Baja is what attracted me in the first place—the fact that I could camp for a month and never see anybody, or walk a week in the desert and fantasize that I might be the last person in the world. In such circumstances, different attitudes prevail:

"Fearing I'd taken a wrong turn and was wandering into a maze of unknown canyons, my nerves received a temporary respite from—of all things—a rusty beer can. What most people would have regarded as a piece of desecrating rubbish, I saw as an exciting find. I picked it up, studied it, and thought how beautiful it looked, and how much pleasure the contents had given a fellow human being. I wondered who he was and where he was and what he had been doing so far up in the mountains."

Into a Desert Place

It would be harder to imagine reacting like that today. But I'm old school, a work in progress when it comes to the purity of my environmental stewardship. I don't have the perfect record. I've chopped up a few rattlesnakes, buried a few beer cans, and nibbled on a few cacti over the years. So I understand that it must seem incredibly arrogant for me to make any suggestions whatever about protecting an island in another country. But, let me just make a couple of points.

Certainly Isla Angel de la Guarda faces many threats. As Steinbeck feared, "It is one of the golden islands which will one day be toppled by a mining company or a prison camp." Happily, with all the recent publicity about the area's "outstanding value to humanity" we can only hope that the danger has past. But even though just a potential threat, recalling the El Arco Iris mining claim south of Este Ton, I have to wonder what might happen with the discovery of commercially viable ore deposits?

A huge and immediate threat is the damage being done by the kind of illegal fishing and diving activities that I witnessed, and the fishermen's cavalier attitude to depositing their trash on the beaches and throwing it in the water.

There seems to be a more-than-effective regime of enforcement, fines, confiscations, and jail sentences in place. But it makes no sense to have a penalty structure that makes it less risky to be a drug runner than a poacher! We ought to keep in mind that these fishermen and divers are in the main decent folks whose priority will always be to support and feed their families. Policies that lead to excessive jail terms, separation of families, and force these pangueros into the arms of the drug traffickers would seem to be ill-conceived and unconscionable.

I wonder if perhaps the most efficacious and the least draconian deterrent has so far been lacking. And that is the certainty of detection. The fishermen from the mainland have been visiting the island for years, doing multiple trips in a season, camping days at a time with relative impunity. And apart from three "mysterious" helicopter flyovers, I didn't see a single member of the police or the military or a "ranger" or any kind of government represen-tative out there... and not a single boat patrolling the island in two months.

This might be incredibly naïve in the face of the amount of drug movement in the area, but what a minimal expense it would be to keep an official panga patrolling. In good weather a panga could easily loop Guardian Angel in a day. From the money donated by conservation groups and collected from visitor permits, it ought to be possible to employ at least two "rangers" to permanently patrol the islands. These officials would need to work closely with the military for their protection. I suspect their regular presence on Guardian Angel would be enough to curtail virtually all poaching activities.

A growing challenge for the islands will be increased tourist visitation. But what an opportunity. With a little effort and imagination and sensitivity to the needs of the people who live in the region, it ought to be possible to help these fishermen and their families by encouraging their participation in ecotourist ventures. Allied to that, as a gesture of good will, Mexico might consider releasing any fishermen now languishing in jail for their island infractions into a paid program say cleaning up the popular landing areas, and bagging and removing trash from the islands and the surrounding waters. Beyond that, these and other pangueros, might possibly be organized and encouraged to use their knowledge and skills to participate in ecotourist ventures to Guardian Angel and the other islands they worked. Divers could lead trips to show in adventurous day and night dives what they did and how they gathered, and generally share their knowledge. Being out there with groups of tourists they will have to go with the program. Compliance will be a condition of keeping their jobs. It would be a great learning and educational experience for the fishermen as well as the tourists, and a legitimate way for these pangueros to make fast friendships and support their families with dignity. Some could be employed as companions to the "rangers" and be turned into a much appreciated asset out there.

The military likewise needs to show a more continuous presence in the region. There is a Marine base in LA Bay. Perhaps those Marines could be spending more time out there camping and patrolling the islands—even if they have to rent or requisition local pangas to do so.

Protecting the islands will always be a matter of priorities and sensible use of scarce resources. In the face of bigger issues, to expend too much energy at this juncture over-regulating tourists and herding them into fewer localities and constraining them to stick to certain pathways may not be the best use of resources.

Those who have the gumption to get out to the island alone and who wish to simply camp and explore—people like Cal, Kayaker John, and groups under the leadership of Ed Gillet… should not be discouraged. Overall, their impact is probably beneficial in terms of influencing attitudes and building bridges. Areas to enjoy peace and solitude and be truly free are the most endangered places on earth, and they should be available for all who leave a small footprint to enjoy for as long as possible.

If I were doing the island trip again I'd be more thoughtful about say taking any cans out there… I would definitely aspire to pack out everything, and more, than I took in.

Another huge and immediate threat is the feral cat population on Angel de la Guarda. Some tough choices are going to have to be made. If the cats are not removed or eradicated, the character of the islands will be changed forever. It may already be too late for species such as the Angel Island deer mouse.

Chapter 45

Penny from Heaven

Only in the agony of parting do we look into the depths of love.

George Eliot

In Chapter Two of my third book—*Nearer My Dog to Thee*—I wrote:

A tiny, black ragamuffin of a terrier puppy turned up at our San Diego house one day in January 2001… We cleaned her in the kitchen sink, combing out her fleas and pulling off (we counted them, I'm not exaggerating) about three hundred ticks… In spite of her problems, she was a feisty, fearless, friendly little thing, full of herself and full of fun… She was a born comedian. I only had to look at her to want to laugh and sweep her up in my arms… We called her Penny. One day, gazing lovingly into her mischievous brown eyes, and feeling a mysterious rapport, I found myself saying, "Penny, I love you more than I love anything in the whole universe." And the terrible thing was, at that moment, I meant it.

Almost every day Penny was with me when I wrote this book. In San Diego and for two summers in the Upper Peninsula of Michigan, at work, at play, on the road, hiking a beach, kayaking along the shores of Lake Huron, Penny was there keeping me company. Every night of my travels, in all the hotels, she was there, at my feet, under a table, asleep on a chair nearby.

The first sign that she had a problem was Sunday, October 14, 2007. She was following me, staying close, looking at me. At first I didn't realize anything was wrong. But when she settled on her chair, she was unusually withdrawn, breathing fast, heart rate a little elevated. Maybe she'd picked up an infection from a trip to Dog Beach two days earlier?

Then we saw she was limping. She was unsteady on her feet. I examined her paws and legs for cuts, spines, or any sign of injury.

I took her to the vet. X-rays suggested a ruptured disk pressing on her spinal cord. We tried anti-inflammatory medication and severe restriction and rest. Penny was not one to be immobilized. Her condition rapidly degenerated into a total paralysis of her rear legs, followed by urinary incontinence.

I had to go home to England for ten weeks to look after a brother who was facing open-heart surgery. My flight was booked. If we elected surgery for

Penny there would be no one to care for her much of the day while Bonni was at work.

I hardly slept for three nights with her by my bed, tending her and comforting her. The damage seemed to have progressed too far, surgery may not have helped. My wife and I tearfully agreed circumstances were such that Penny would be alone, hurting, scared, dirty, depressed. It would be cruel. We decided to put her to sleep at home surrounded by love and all her friends.

That was scheduled for October 19. The night before, she slept on a sleeping bag covered with towels. I went to bed, miserable and guilty. I recalled that I had left the tailgate down on the pickup and she had jumped out just as we were about to go to Dog Beach. We noticed she was limping as we walked among the dunes; but I found some sharp burs in one of her paws and pulled them out thinking that was the problem. She then ran like crazy, twisting and rolling and instigating all the trouble with her buddies Pedro and Tanner.

That sad night I looked over at her every few minutes. I had no appetite. I felt sick at the thought of losing this wonderful companion, this happy loving dog that never knew a stranger, and greeted all comers, human and canine with her wagging tail. How many times had I heard people saying what an incredibly cute dog! I lay awake tearful, reproachful, wracked with guilt.

Then I felt her presence. In voiceless communication she let me know I had nothing to feel guilty about. I had given her a world of love and the best six-and-a-half years any dog could wish for. The last thing she wanted was for me to feel so bad. I didn't sleep, but didn't cry another tear all night, I just tended my buddy.

If the coyotes sounded too close, I would get up to whisper in her ear. If she peed I'd gently move her and make sure she had a dry towel beneath. I was aware of her every breath and movement.

In the morning, we hugged her and treated her and made her feel special. Bonni had prepared a plateful of little pieces of steak which she loved. In spite of her handicap she showed no sign of being in pain. Her appetite was incredible. Bright-eyed and eager, she took every offered morsel and lapped up all the milk and meat juice we offered.

It was a beautiful sunny day. I took her in my arms and carried her around the yard that was her home, to say goodbye to all the familiar paths, trees, and views. Then Bonni and I sat with her on a blanket in the shade of a pomegranate tree and took a few final pictures and shed the odd tear and watched her enjoy all her treats, especially that steak. In a final glimpse of the Penny we knew, she skillfully snatched at and usually caught any fly that got too close to her face. She was entertained and diverted, clearly enjoying it.

Twenty minutes before the vet was due, we settled her on her sofa, the place we had trained her to go to, when we said "Go home Penny." And she would jump up there as fast as her leggies could carry her, just in case we'd thrown her a cookie. Cookie was the word that meant food and treats to her. She heard it many times that morning.

Penny was a talker. If I looked at her and gently growled, she'd go into play mode, head down, back arched, and growl back, then growl would answer growl till one of us ran with the other in hot pursuit. There would be no chase now, but I growled and she responded, we did it about half a dozen times, till I finally kissed her nose and let her lick my face.

The vet came at 10:30 that morning, right on time, and beautifully and sensitively talked us through it. And with all her doggy and human family around her, expressing their love and thanking her for bringing such fun and joy into our lives, we caressed her and watched her slip gently, peacefully, with a sedative and pain killer for several minutes. Then we gave permission to administer the shot that quickly brought her little life to an end… and sent back our little Penny to heaven.

We left her "sleeping peacefully" on her spot on the sofa for about two hours. Bonni placed a lei of bougainvillea flowers around her neck, then after feeling the cold paws that I had cleaned and cared for for so long, I carried her down to her final resting place, a shady spot at the bottom of the garden, to where we could see her grave from our office and bedroom windows.

Parceled loosely in two paper bags we lowered her gently down and told her again how much we loved her. Then we returned to the house for a few little things to bury with her.

As Bonni and I were going sadly back inside to fetch a 1944 British penny, a picture of her on a kayak in Michigan, and one of her favorite soft squeaky toys, we were about to go up the steps when we were compelled to look above in the tree shading the porch. There was a crazy little bird flying above us—it was grayish black, white and yellow, twisting and turning, swooping down, and chasing and catching flies and almost landing on our heads. We'd never seen a bird doing that in all the many years we'd lived in our house. We both thought the same thing, it was like the spirit of Penny putting on a show to reassure us that she was still around, still catching those pesky flies. We identified the bird as a Townsend's warbler. And what truly amazed me. The only bird that I ever remember Penny killing was a similar warbler, in the San Pedro Mártir:

> There was a small bird on the ground by a fallen log. I assumed it would, like so many others, fly off if the dogs gave chase; but this time it ran and flapped and tried to fly, but it obviously wasn't going to make it. It was probably just a youngster. Penny pounced and ran off with it in her mouth. Sounding like thunder in my heavy rubberized rain gear, I chased her for 100 yards. She eventually dropped it. It was still alive. It felt strong and warm, and there was no blood. I carried it back to camp in my cupped hands. I thought I could secure the guys and give it a chance. But it died in my hands,

a beautiful little black and white bird with a black beak and patches of yellow in front of its eyes.

Nearer My Dog to Thee

Even her slow and dull-witted master got the message. Any time we care to open our eyes and ears and hearts... we can see and hear and feel the love that everywhere surrounds us. Love that has been, love that is, and love that will be. Love that knows no boundaries. Love that peacefully conquers and tears down walls.

Let's teach our children to sing about that.

Goodbye Guardian Angel

Acknowledgments

Thank you, thank you, thank you for all the wonderful ways that you have made this book possible.

Ed Gillet, Roger Silliman, Jean Diaz, Antonio and Bety Reséndiz, Francisco Uribe, Cal and Janice Sherman, Gary Doran, John Weed, Judy Webster, Pete Garcia, Mike and Cindy Essary, Lennart Waje, Tomás Campbell, Igor Galván, David Kier, Doug Means, Chuck Bosley and Evelyn Simon, Andrew Miller, Ellen Goodwin, Raul Espinoza, Mauro Rosini, Antero Diaz, Jr., H. J. Walker, Don Albright, Randy Case.

Bibliography

Into a Desert Place, by Graham Mackintosh. W.W. Norton 1995

Journey With a Baja Burro, by Graham Mackintosh. Sunbelt Publications 2000

Nearer My Dog to Thee, by Graham Mackintosh. Baja Detour Press 2003

A New Island Biogeography of the Sea of Cortés, Edited by Ted J. Case, Martin L. Cody, and Exequiel Ezcurra. Oxford University Press 2002

Unknown Island, by Thomas Bowen. University of New Mexico Press 2000

The Log from the Sea of Cortez, by John Steinbeck

The Baja Catch, by Neil Kelly and Gene Kira. Apples and Oranges, Inc.

Sea Kayaking in Baja, by Andromeda Romano-Lax. Wilderness Press 1993

Miraculous Air, by Catherine Mansfield Mayo. University of Utah Press 2002

Spirituality for Dummies, by Sharon Janis. IDG